"Over the years since 9/11, I've read several books and articles on the war and none of them captured my attention so fully." – Barbara Gilbert

"In a precise and thought provoking review, Charles Edmund Coyote answers several critical questions such as: What really were Bush's motives for the Iraq war? How did Bin Laden evade US capture despite superior intelligence? Did the enormous cost of the war justify the objectives obtained?" – Julian Sanchez, PhD

"Charles Edmund Coyote has been brilliant in gathering information, interpreting it, putting it in context, and in giving the reader an understanding of the bigger picture. It was hard to put the book down." – Ariel Sanders

"It's very apparent that this highly informative, well-written, and thought-provoking book is meticulously researched, very well-referenced, and documented. I highly recommend this book to anyone who wants to know what really happened behind the scenes of the Iraq War! Bravo Charles Edmund Coyote for having the guts to write this book!" – Amy J. Waldow

"This book does a fantastic job of bringing all the pieces of the puzzle together, showing you what they are, holding them to the light, and putting them down so that the entire puzzle is put together beautifully." – Justin Carnahan

"This is an extremely well researched, annotated and well written book at what was behind Washington's motives in Iraq. Some may find their political toes stepped on, but it is a recommended read for anyone interested in understanding why we are, where we are today." – Helen C. Page

"It's hard to believe so much information can be told in a few pages in an interesting and engaging way." – Peggy Maxwell

IRAQ WAR 2003

WHAT REALLY HAPPEND BEHIND THE SCENES

THE STORY OF THE GREATEST BLUNDER IN AMERICAN HISTORY

CHARLES EDMUND COYOTE

The Coyote Report

AVAILABLE ALSO ON KINDLE AND OTHER DEVICES
FOR REFERENCING ACCESS AND RESEARCH

In dedication to the Founding Fathers

Of a Great Nation

49- Cheney let some A.Q. escape
63 - Bush let OBL escape
64 - Rumsfeld was planning IRAQ invasion Now
64-65 military efforts thwarted
77 Bush gave OBL what he wanted by invading IRAQ
78 Bush forgot OBL - eliminated station
82 Bush blunder in attacking IRAQ   1955
85 U.S. allied w Saddam as Qasim turning to Soviets
91 -1982 Reagan helped Saddam against IRAN including
                                                    WMD
95 - GHW Bush visited IRAQ in 1985 to ask IRAQ to
     attack Iran so IRAN would buy more U.S. equip.
97 - US AND BUSH SR. ARMED IRAQ
98 Desert Storm: U.S soldiers exposed to sarin gas when U.S.
     bombs hit iraq plants that had purchased gas from U.S.
101 Conflict - Gove wants to stop chemical warfare, Bush SR
     wanted to punish Shiites / IRAN

111 Glaspie on Iraq - Kuwait disputes 1990
115 1985-9 U.S. loaned IRAQ 5 Bil $ for WMD
116 Did Reagan know - Was he excluded or "protected"?
118-9 U.S. trade laws hurt Iraqi people
121 GEORGE MARSHALL
                    (OVER)

128   GW BUSH ON BOOKS
129   G.H.W BUSH ON NOT INVADING IRAQ
130   BUSH CAMPAIGN PROMISE
★ 215 RICE - CLARKE
217th BUSH ADM RESPONSE TO AQ
    and on
220   BUSH ON VACATION 40% OF 1st 7 MONTHS

From The Author

I love this country, our constitution, and the rule of law under which we were founded, and by which we were guided for more than 200 years. I understand that no nation will remain great without a great middle class. Much of this is being rapidly eroded by misguided militarism, good jobs sent overseas, and a governing class focused more on self-advancement than on their responsibilities to the country and its citizens.

As predicted by economic historians such as Paul Kennedy, the internationalist policies and rampant exporting of America's manufacturing economy are bankrupting the United States, and threatening to impoverish vast numbers of its citizens. It is a pattern great powers have followed since the Roman Republic.

That we can still be a great people was demonstrated in the nation's response immediately following the attacks of September 11. But arrayed against that are powerful currents of greed, conformity, and deficiencies of understanding which are impoverishing our common ability to observe and take effective action.

'Iraq War 2003' illustrates the consequences of leadership that sees the world as they want to see it and not as it is, making policy become ever more extreme and ineffective. This is not what America is about. We are a young nation, and in our short history at times of crises we have generally come to the better path – even if we had first to exhaust, as Winston Churchill once noted, every other possible alternative.

In this time of great, though largely self-imposed, uncertainty, one can only hope that Edmund Burke's affirmation will yet resound: *"The individual is foolish; the multitude, for the moment, is foolish, when they act without deliberation; but the species is wise, and, when time is given to it, as a species it always acts right."* Will we act right or persist in a self-destruction that comes under the guise of strength? Unless we learn from history, we are doomed to repeat it; we will do so as farce and tragedy.

The human story can be told through archetypes, one of which is that of Faust – the devil come bargaining for the soul. That particular story is as old as the temptation of Christ, and as fresh as Charlie Daniels and the rosined bow of a Georgia fiddling contest. It is the story of the unnecessary choice and possibility of losing the prize already bestowed by allowing oneself to be tricked into bargaining for it. It is the story of George W. Bush and the Iraq war of 2003.

Charles Edmund Coyote

TABLE OF CONTENTS

IRAQ WAR 2003

CHAPTER 1
I WILL NOT FORGET

I will not forget this wound to our country or those who inflicted it. I will not yield; I will not rest; I will not relent in waging this struggle for freedom and security for the American people.

George W. Bush, Address to a Joint Session of Congress and the American People, September 20, 2001

When the Japanese attacked Pearl Harbor that infamous December long ago, they were led by a man who understood well what his nation was getting into. Admiral Yamamoto was a Harvard alumnus. He had spent time traveling and exploring young and energetic America and had seen firsthand the enormity of its resources and industrial power. He was more than a little concerned about the folly that had seduced the leaders of his own country believing that their nation's disciplined warriors could, with one mighty blow, decimate America's Pacific Fleet and frighten the United States from interfering with their plans of an Empire in the Western Pacific.

Nevertheless, Fleet Admiral Isoroku Yamamoto was a good officer and he did what good officers do: he obeyed orders. His leaders did not believe they could win a war against America unless they opened with a devastating surprise attack. Admiral Isoroku Yamamoto was instructed to plan an attack to destroy America's sleeping Pearl Harbor armada. He did as best as he could. Observing America's fascination with Hollywood's dreamland, and believing that the US Navy's officers were more concerned about prowess on the golf course than on the ocean waves, Japan's

CHARLES EDMUND COYOTE

government thought the US was soft and would not take a stand against the terrible sword of Japan's disciplined military culture. But as Yamamoto prepared his ships and planes for their sinister plan, he wrote a friend:

> Now that things have come to this pass, I'll throw everything I have into the fight. I expect to die in battle. By that time, I imagine, Imperial Tokyo will have been set on fire, and Japan reduced to a pitiful state. I don't like it.

> Admiral Isoroku Yamamoto

Yamamoto had told his superiors that he could be certain of victory in battle against the Great Britain and United States only during the first six to twelve months of war. If the conflict were to continue beyond that, he said, he could have no expectation of long term success considering the realities of his own nation's limited access to iron and oil and the mustering of America's industrial power.

A Combined Fleet under the command of Admiral Chuichi Nagumo left port from northern Japan in late November 1941 for the intended strike position, 4 degrees 27 minutes latitude north of Pearl Harbor, on the Hawaiian Island of Oahu. The Fleet consisted of Japan's six largest carriers, with more than 400 fighters, bomber, and other assorted aircraft, along with 2 battleships, 3 cruisers, 9 destroyers, 8 tankers, and 27 submarines. The aircrews were ordered to concentrate their attack on the American battleships for maximum psychological effect.

Radar operators at US Army training post on the northern tip of Oahu saw the waves of incoming aircraft on their screens. 'Don't worry,' they were told.

'*They must be American*'. Six B-17 bombers had been scheduled to fly in to the island that morning on what was essentially the same inbound course. The islanders waved to the hundreds of aircraft flying low over their fields racing on toward the south, but the pilots of the aircraft did not wave back.

The defenders at Pearl Harbor, Hickam Field, Wheeler, Bellows, and the battleship moorings at Ford Island woke unprepared on that lazy Sunday morning to the sounds of exploding torpedoes, bombs, gunfire, and the searing knowledge that '*THIS IS NO DRILL*'. [1]

Japanese torpedo and horizontal bombers swarmed the 30,000 ton, USS Arizona, within minutes. Shortly after 08:00 am, the ship was attacked by 10 Nakajima B5N torpedo bombers carrying modified 16 inch armor-piercing 1,760 lb bombs. The battleship took four of these massive bombs, the first three causing relatively minor damage.

The last bomb hit at 08:06 in the vicinity of the forward turret, penetrating the armored deck near the ammunition magazines. Seconds after it hit, the magazines detonated sending cataclysmic shock waves outward through the sides of the ship. These waves destroyed much of the Arizona's forward structure, conning tower, and foremast. The explosion showered the nearby area with wreckage, sank the ship, and killed 1,177 of the 1,400 crewmen that were on board. 2,403 American lives were lost during the attack. [2]

The intent of the Japanese was to force America to the negotiating table.

It didn't work.

CHARLES EDMUND COYOTE

On the evening following the attack, America's radio networks carried the newsman's announcement: *"To-night, America is a nation in shock and anger"*. The nation's President had foreseen the necessity for his country to become involved in the world-wide struggle against fascism. Roosevelt's eloquent address the next morning asked Congress to formalize the reality that in every state and city and town throughout the country *'the American people in their righteous might'* were already lining up to fight. A state of War existed between the Empire of Japan and the People of the United States which both were going to pursue until one would 'gain the inevitable triumph':

> *Mr. Vice President, Mr. Speaker, members of the Senate and the House of Representatives:*
>
> *Yesterday, December 7th, 1941 – a date which will live in infamy – the United States of America was suddenly and deliberately attacked by naval and air forces of the Empire of Japan....*
>
> *...As Commander-in-Chief of the Army and Navy I have directed that all measures be taken for our defense, that always will our whole nation remember the character of the onslaught against us.*
>
> *No matter how long it may take us to overcome this premeditated invasion, the American people, in their righteous might, will win through to absolute victory.*
>
> *I believe that I interpret the will of the Congress and of the people when I assert that we will not only defend ourselves to the uttermost but will make it very certain that this form of treachery shall never again endanger us.*
>
> *Hostilities exist. There is no blinking at the fact that our people, our territory and our interests are in grave danger.*
>
> *With confidence in our armed forces, with the unbounding determination of our people, we will gain the inevitable*

triumph. So help us God.

> *I ask that the Congress declare that since the un-provoked and dastardly attack by Japan on Sunday, December 7th, 1941, a state of war has existed between the United States and the Japanese Empire.*
>
> President Franklin D. Roosevelt, 8 December 1941 [3]

Japan fought with ferocious savagery. It was brutal to its enemies, and loyal, to the death, to the designs of its leaders. But, they had underestimated the Americans and the American dream: the ability for the common to become extraordinary. Four months after Pearl Harbor, Lieutenant Colonel 'Jimmy' Doolittle launched B-25 Mitchell Bombers from sixteen carriers to drop bombs over Tokyo, Yokohama, Yokosuka, Nagoya, Kobe and Osaka on the Japanese mainland. Six months after Pearl Harbor, the United States Navy inflicted irreparable damage on the Imperial Japanese Fleet at the Battle of Midway in one of *'the most decisive blows in naval history'.* [4]

Crucial to Yamamoto's Pearl Harbor plan was the sinking of most of the US aircraft carriers, a goal he did not realize due to poor intelligence. His sneak attack had only stirred the sleeping giant of an economically depressed America and filled its people with the awesome resolve that would reduce Japan's imperial militarism to ruin and bring atomic fire upon its homeland.

Three years and nine months after Pearl Harbor, the might of Hitler's Germany and Tojo's Japan had been reduced to smoking rubble. Their nation's focus shifted to the far better future that awaited them in quality manufacturing and world trade. Germany and Japan, having failed as elitist empires, began to flourish as egalitarian states. [5] In short order, former enemies stood as friends. The Japanese soon seemed hungry for everything American, and the Germans became our partners in helping to build a free and peaceful Europe.

For America, World War II and the peace that followed brought many dividends. The dollar became the world's currency. Henry Ford's contributions to mass-production and fair wages helped transform the country's broad rural expanse into the most pros-perous industrial power the world had ever seen. Edward Bernays made conformity more seductive than ever. Elvis Presley electrified the nation and Marilyn Monroe enticed it into a previously veiled sensuality. Dr. Martin Luther King lived his life so that others could live his dream, while J. Edgar Hoover made sure nobody got too far out of line. Bill Gates took play and productivity to another level, and Rush Limbaugh preached the virtues of rugged individualism to mil-lions of dittoheads.

America fought wars, big, small and often, but always somewhere else. Since the bloody Civil War, which had shattered and reunited the nation a century be-fore, the United States had been blessed. Aside from that one horrendous Hawaiian Sunday, it had had little experience of conflict on its own soil. Americans wrestled with social equality, good dance tunes, and how to make a buck, all the while paying homage to liberty and justice for all on the appropriate holidays. The country, after making it through the Cold War with-out a nuclear winter, took on an ever expanding role in the world.

Washington, in the District of Columbia, liked it that

way. Named after the nation's first president, the nation's capital was a monument to the greatness of its leading Founder, even as it paid less attention to the humility that made that greatness possible. D.C. became the seat of *'Pax Americana,'* and there was serious money to be made.

Most Americans, however, were more concerned about their government's sometimes overbearing influence on their own lives than about its sometimes overbearing influence on the rest of the world. Therefore, when passenger jets exploded through the walls and columns of three of the country's greatest buildings on that clear September morning, most had no idea why a score of young men from distant lands had become so goaded by rage that they were willing to spend years plotting to seize control of those planes and ride them to their fiery destruction.

As the planes were hijacked, America's trillion dollar military seemed strangely unresponsive. Regulations required the North American Aerospace Defense Command to be informed immediately. However, FAA air traffic controllers – aware of the strange behavior of American Airlines Flight 11 since 8:14 am, and certain since 8:24 am it had been hijacked – did not report the problem to the NORAD until 8:38 am. This was just eight minutes before the Boeing 767 crashed into the World Trade Center's North Tower. [6], [7] The Pentagon was struck at 9:38 am, more than an hour into the attack. There was still no military response.

As the structures of America's great buildings went down under attack, the nation's President lingered, strangely unresponsive, over a children's story in a Florida elementary school. Though told of the unfolding disaster

CHARLES EDMUND COYOTE

in New York, he remained in the classroom until some 30 minutes after the national news services began reporting the events at the World Trade Center and high level officials in Washington had begun to discuss the attack. That morning, Air Force One would fly unprotected for almost two hours with the President on board, the country under attack, and the situation far from clear. The President's plane left Sarasota at 9:55 am and flew on its own until 11:41 am, shortly before landing at Barksdale Air Force Base near Shreveport, Louisiana. [8] The National Guard F-16 fighters that finally did arrive from Ellington Field Air Force Base in Texas to protect Air Force One had the capacity to be airborne in 10 minutes.

In the White House that morning, the National Security Council's Chief Counter-Terrorism Advisor, Richard Clacke, remained in the West Wing's Situation Room watching events unfold in New York:

> *I kept thinking of the words from 'Apocalypse Now,' the whispered words of Marlon Brando, when he thought about Vietnam. 'The horror. The horror.' Because we knew what was going on in New York. We knew about the bodies flying out of the windows. People falling through the air. We knew that Osama bin Laden had succeeded in bringing horror to the streets of America.*
>
> *Richard Clarke, former White House counter-terrorism adviser, 21 March 2004* [9]

Above Washington D.C., a Boeing 757 of American Airlines Flight 77 was commandeered by the poorly skilled Hani Hanjour and four other al-Qaeda terrorists. They swooped in from the north, executed a difficult 330 degree turn, and descended 2,200 feet to slam, ground-level, into the western face of the Pentagon at 530 miles an hour. In eight-tenths of a second it ripped through more than 300 feet of the outer three ring sections of the building bursting into a massive fireball and disintegrating the lives of 189 people.

In the beautiful late summer skies above Shanksville, Pennsylvania, a group of passengers determined to provide a moment of resistance to the devastating attacks on the American spirit. Their plane, United Flight 93, was off course and not responding to air traffic control. It had been seized that morning at 9:28 by four hijackers with box cutters and knives. One of the terrorists carried a small package tied around his upper body, which he claimed was a bomb. Their pilot, Ziad Jarrah, had turned the flight back toward the East Coast, presumably toward Washington, D.C.

UAL 93's takeoff from Newark, New Jersey, had been delayed more than 40 minutes that morning because of congested airport traffic. By the time it reached the Cleveland area in Ohio, around 9:30 am, the other two doomed planes had already slammed their passengers into the World Trade Center. Inside UAL 93, four Arab men stood, tied red bandannas around their heads, and killed the cabin crew.

Most of Flight 93's passengers were then herded back to the rear seats. Because several had cell phones or could use the onboard GTE Airfones, they were able to reach their families and other ground personnel. The hijackers did not seem to care, but through these contacts the passengers were learning that their own hijacking was not an isolated incident.

The passengers took a vote and, deciding they had nothing to lose, determined that they would try to take their plane back before it too ended up a suicidal

CHARLES EDMUND COYOTE

missile. Todd Beamer, attempting to call his wife, Lisa, from a seatback phone in the rear of the plane, had instead been routed to GTE phone operator Lisa Jefferson. Beamer told the operator about the hijacking and the vote the passengers had taken to *'jump on'* the skyjackers before they could carry out their plans. Operator Jefferson could hear the screams and commotion in the background as other passengers prepared boiling water to throw on their hijackers. She joined Beamer and his seatmates in a recitation of the Lord's Prayer. As the plane fitfully lurched and swayed, Beamer and others recited the 23rd Psalm: *"Yea, though I walk through the valley of the shadow of death, I will fear no evil..."* At about 9:55 a.m., Jefferson heard someone ask, *"Are you ready?"* Beamer got Jefferson to promise she would call his family and then heard what Todd's wife, Lisa, believes were her husband's last words: *"Let's roll."* [10]

The revolt on Flight 93 began at 9:57 am, as the group of salespeople, corporate executives, lawyers, a retired ironworker, a waiter going to his son's funeral, a fish-and-wildlife officer, a former judo champion, a retired paratrooper, a weightlifter, a former policewoman, and others, rose up to confront the gruesome fate that had been thrown their way. The cockpit voice recorder preserved the last minutes of the death struggle as the passengers rushed the first class section where the hijackers were anxiously waiting. Voices screamed and cursed in English and Arabic and the plane swayed, rolled and dove toward the earth. [11]

The hijackers in the cockpit exclaimed, *"Is there something? A fight? Yeah?"* A passenger shouts, *"Let's get them!"* An Arabic voice screams, *"They're coming!"*

Grabbing a service cart, the passengers attempted to batter in the cockpit door. Jarrah responded by rolling the airplane sharply right and left, trying to knock them off balance. *"Hold, hold from the inside. Hold from the inside. Hold,"* he shouted at a fellow hijacker. When the assault continued through the rolling, Jarrah tried to throw them off by violently pitching the aircraft's nose up and down. [12]

At 10:01 am, with the passengers only seconds away from breaking through the cabin, Jarrah was told by another hijacker to crash the plane rather than lose control of it: *"Is that it?"* Jarrah asked. *"I mean, shall we pull it down?"*; "Yes, put it in it, and pull it down," was the response.

Jarrah rolled hard to the right turning the plane upside down into a 45 degree dive. Descending 8,000 feet in about 20 seconds, Jarrah ripped into the earth at 580 miles an hour near Shanksville, Pennsylvania, about 125 miles from Washington, D.C.

As the twin-engine Boeing 757 – heavily laden with fuel – was swallowed into the ground, it ejected a powerful fireball across hundreds of acres of nearby woodland, setting many of the trees on fire. Human remains and other debris were found as far as eight miles from the crash site. Its fuselage impacted so forcefully that one of its 'black boxes' was found underneath 25 feet of soil and rock.

The passengers, crew and hijackers were cremated instantly. Only bits of scorched tissue would ever be recovered from the small smoking crater and nearby acreage. There were no bodies, only an unplanned cemetery that stretched to the nearby ridge and woods.

CHARLES EDMUND COYOTE

[13], [14], [15], [16], [17], [18], [19], [20]

CHAPTER 1 REFERENCES

[1] "AIR RAID ON PEARL HARBOR. THIS IS NO DRILL.";
Telegram from CINCPAC to all ships in: Hawaiian area, 7
December 1941;
http://www.archives.gov/exhibits/american_originals/fdr.ht
ml
(SHORTENED URL: http://tinyurl.com/labs83n)

[2] Defining Moments, the Attack on Pearl Harbor, by
Laurie Collier Hillstrom, Omnigraphics;
http://docs.fdrlibrary.marist.edu:8000/tmirhdee.html
(SHORTENED URL: http://tinyurl.com/defmoments)

[3] December 8, 1941 - Franklin Roosevelt asks Congress
for a Declaration of War with Japan, Franklin D. Roosevelt
Presidential Library and Museum - 1941 Declaration of War;
http://docs.fdrlibrary.marist.edu:8000/tmirhdee.html
(SHORTENED URL: http://tinyurl.com/declareswar)

[4] The Battle of Midway, US Navy Documentary Training
Film, 1950;

Part One:
http://www.learningace.com/doc/715575/8a8c54b4861a7f2
424dbd070bcd0a4d2/the-battle-of-midway-part-1-us-navy-
documentary-training-film-1950
(SHORTENED URL: http://tinyurl.com/bamiwa1)

Part Two:
http://www.learningace.com/doc/746891/8304e2249e56f30
5ca496352bf080403/the-battle-of-midway-part-2-us-navy-
documentary-training-film-1950
(SHORTENED URL: http://tinyurl.com/bamiwa2)

[5] How empire ruled the world, by Jane Burbank and
Frederick Cooper, Le Monde diplomatique, January 2012;
http://mondediplo.com/2012/01/13empire

[6] "WE HAVE SOME PLANES", The National Commission on

Terrorist Attacks Upon the United States, 22 July 2004;
http://govinfo.library.unt.edu/911/report/911Report_Ch1.ht
m
(SHORTENED URL: http://tinyurl.com/usancta)

[7] Flight Path Study - Americans Airlines Flight 11,
National Transportation Safety Board, Office of Research
and Engineering, 19 February 2002;
http://www.gwu.edu/~nsarchiv/NSAEBB/NSAEBB196/doc01
.pdf
(SHORTENED URL: http://tinyurl.com/aaflight11)

[8] Clear the Skies, 911review.org;
http://911review.org/Media/air-force-one_September-
11.html
(SHORTENED URL: http://tinyurl.com/911skies)

[9] Clarke's Take On Terror, CBS 60 Minutes Interview, by
Rebecca Leung, March 21, 2004;
http://www.cbsnews.com/stories/2004/03/19/60minutes/m
ain607356.shtml
(SHORTENED URL: http://tinyurl.com/rleung)

[10] United States of America v. Zacarias Moussaoui,
Stipulation Regarding Flights Hijacked on September 11,
2001, pp 9-12, United States District Court for the Eastern
District of Virginia, 1 March 2006;
http://www.vaed.uscourts.gov/notablecases/moussaoui/exh
ibits/prosecution/ST00001A.pdf
(SHORTENED URL: http://tinyurl.com/mebaka)

[11] We Have Some Planes, National Commission on
Terrorist Attacks Upon the United States, 21 August 2004;
http://govinfo.library.unt.edu/911/report/911Report_Ch1.ht
m
(SHORTENED URL: http://tinyurl.com/l8wzens)

[12] United Airlines Flight #93 Cockpit Voice Recorder
Transcript, Government Exhibit P200056T 01-455-A (ID);
http://i.a.cnn.net/cnn/2006/images/04/12/flight93.transcrip
t.pdf
(SHORTENED URL: http://tinyurl.com/cockrec)

CHARLES EDMUND COYOTE

14

[13] Hallowed Ground, by Peter Perl, 12 May 2002;
http://old.911digitalarchive.org/crr/documents/4532.pdf
(SHORTENED URL: http://tinyurl.com/hosona)

[14]

(a) First attack on WTC 1, YouTube;
https://www.youtube.com/watch?v=7iSwpLGMl80
(SHORTENED URL: http://tinyurl.com/fetak1)

(b) https://www.youtube.com/watch?v=oG58-Vs838M
(SHORTENED URL: http://tinyurl.com/fetak2)

(c) September 11 2001, As It Happened - CNN Live 8.40
am – 10.11 am;
https://www.youtube.com/watch?v=rsIWPPw-JzU
(SHORTENED URL: http://tinyurl.com/fetak3)

[15] Inside the Twin Towers - Plane Impact Survivor,
YouTube;http://www.youtube.com/watch?v=zMelmLspMP0
&feature=related
(SHORTENED URL: http://tinyurl.com/twito)

[16] 911 The Falling Man, YouTube;
http://www.youtube.com/watch?v=wqp22Vhq_DQ&feature
=related
(SHORTENED URL URL: http://tinyurl.com/fallmen)

[17] Kevin Cosgrove's LIVE 911 call as he DIES, YouTube;
http://callerids.blogspot.com/2012/03/kevin-cosgrove-live-
911-call-as-he-dies.html
(SHORTENED URL: http://tinyurl.com/lidico)

[18] South Tower Collapsing, YouTube;
http://www.youtube.com/watch?v=x4sRi5stG10&feature=fv
wrel
(SHORTENED URL: http://tinyurl.com/souco)

[19] North Tower Slow Motion Collapse, YouTube;
http://www.youtube.com/watch?v=-ib93ktc454
(SHORTENED URL: http://tinyurl.com/norcol)

[20] When the World Stopped Turning: A 9/11 tribute, Alan
Jackson; http://www.youtube.com/watch?v=AW8puRqE4Sc
(SHORTENED URL: http://tinyurl.com/worstop)

IRAQ WAR 2003

CHAPTER 2

THE STATE OF OUR UNION

My fellow citizens, for the last nine days, the entire world has seen for itself the state of our Union – and it is strong.

> *George W. Bush, Address to a Joint Session of Congress and the American People, September 20, 2001*

The President's plane flew on to a secure location at Barksdale Air Force Base near Shreveport, Louisiana, where it stopped at about 11:45 am. It then continued a couple of hours later on to the highly secure US Strategic Underground Command Center at Offutt Air Force Base near Omaha, Nebraska, where it landed shortly before 3:00 pm. [1] From Omaha, President Bush returned to Washington, D.C. at 6:34 pm, and gave a nationally televised address to the American people a couple of hours later. During that talk, the President first outlined what would become known as the Bush Doctrine:

> *We will make no distinction between the terrorists who committed these acts and those who harbor them.*
>
> *George W. Bush, 11 September 2001* [2]

Things were moving fast at the Pentagon where Defense Secretary Donald Rumsfeld, returning to his office after a few minutes of assisting the injured at the Flight 77 crash site, began to send notes to his aids instructing them to get the *"best info fast. Judge whether good enough hit S.H. at same time. Not only UBL"*. The initials SH and UBL were used to identify Saddam Hussein and Osama bin Laden, respectively. Rumsfeld told the team *to "Go massive,"* and *"Sweep it all up. Things related and not."* [3], [4]

CHARLES EDMUND COYOTE

As the sun set on New York that evening, a television reporter walked amongst the pulverized dust scattered about a deserted sunset Manhattan street and told her national audience that, *"Tonight, America is a nation in shock and terror."* The words were a slight, yet significant, modification of those the radioman had told his country on the evening following the attack on Pearl Harbor: *"Tonight, America is a nation in shock and anger."* Nevertheless, the children of that Greatest Generation began to prove they were not that different from their elders. A focused hush took possession of the country and summoned its might. Someone had just pissed off the Big Dog. The American people remembered what they had in common and there would be hell to pay.

Except for a couple of flights carrying members of the bin Laden family and other well-connected Saudis from Tampa, Florida to Lexington, Kentucky and then back to Saudi Arabia, the empty sky took on the shade of brilliant deep blue it had not worn for decades. [5] On the streets below, the blare and noise of rude traffic hushed into quiet, common courtesy. Strangers became neighbors, and the neighbors reassembled themselves into a great nation.

From almost every passing car and corner, the red, white and blue of millions of flags began to flutter. The children and grandchildren of those who had assembled themselves 60 years before had come together as one people and awaited orders. The words *"Let's Roll!"* from the last downed plane became the battle cry of a nation, with its President from atop a crushed fire truck in the devastation at *'Ground Zero'* telling the clean-up crews and the listening world:

I can hear you. The rest of the world hears you. And the people who knocked these buildings down will hear all of us soon.

President George W. Bush, 14 September 2001 [6]

Shocked by the violent murder of the innocent thousands, the world responded. The citizens of 80 nations, with particularly large numbers from Great Britain, Israel and India, were among those that were killed in the attacks. America's friends, along with the billions who believed the world could be a better place, turned to solidarity with the people of the United States. At London's Buckingham Place, Berlin's Brandenburg Gate, and on the streets of Paris, near the Eiffel Tower, bands assembled to play the US national anthem. It was now their hymn. In Russia, Vladimir Putin attended a candlelight memorial service. In Iran, young people assembled by the thousands to condemn the mass murders.

Throughout Canada, Greenland, and Iceland, strangers, families, and friends took in American citizens and the many others stranded by the abrupt cancellation of flights following the hijackings. In France, Doublet of Lillie – one of the largest manufacturers of flags in the world – was swamped with orders for Stars and Stripes. In mosques throughout the Muslim world, voices rose in prayer for the United States. Iran used its contacts with Afghanistan's Northern Alliance to encourage them to work with the American and British Special Forces to take on Osama bin Laden and the Taliban. [7], [8] Libyan leader Muammar Gadhafi ordered his intelligence agents to turn over the extensive files they had gathered on al-Qaeda cells. Japan and South Korea offered extraordinary levels of logistical support to the assembling counterterrorist efforts. [9] China,

CHARLES EDMUND COYOTE

New Zealand, the Philippines, Singapore, and Thailand reached for assistance. [10] Russia's government froze the bank accounts of those connected to al-Qaeda and opened up old Soviet military bases in Central Asia, just north of Afghanistan, to be used by the US armed forces. A special Russian team was sent to CIA Headquarters in Langley, Virginia, to make available the extensive store of military intelligence the U.S.S.R. had gathered during their own Afghan War in the 1980s. This intelligence included wide-ranging information about the caves and topography of the country where bin Laden and his organization were centered.

On September 20, 2001, President Bush addressed a Joint Session of Congress and the American people. He observed that the American people had already fulfilled his own obligation to report on the State of the Union, having done so by virtue of the courage, the decency, and the strength that they had demonstrated during the previous nine days. The state of the American union was strong, and the country's grief and shock became a collective resolution:

THE PRESIDENT: Mr. Speaker, Mr. President Pro Tempore, members of Congress, and fellow Americans:

In the normal course of events, Presidents come to this chamber to report on the state of the Union. Tonight, no such report is needed. It has already been delivered by the American people.

We have seen it in the courage of passengers, who rushed terrorists to save others on the ground – passengers like an exceptional man named Todd Beamer. And would you please help me to welcome his wife, Lisa Beamer, here tonight. (Applause.)

We have seen the state of our Union in the endurance of rescuers, working past exhaustion. We have seen the unfurling of flags, the lighting of candles, the giving of *blood, the saying of prayers – in English, Hebrew, and Arabic. We have seen the decency of a loving and giving people who have made the grief of strangers their own.*

My fellow citizens, for the last nine days, the entire world has seen for itself the state of our Union – and it is strong. (Applause.)

Tonight we are a country awakened to danger and called to defend freedom. Our grief has turned to anger, and anger to resolution. Whether we bring our enemies to justice, or bring justice to our enemies, justice will be done. (Applause.)

George W. Bush, September 20, 2001 [11]

The President then identified a loosely connected assortment of terrorist organizations known as al-Qaeda and declared that its leader, Osama bin Laden, was responsible for the attacks on New York, Washington, and over Pennsylvania. He talked about the relationship between al-Qaeda and Afghanistan's Taliban leadership and gave the Taliban an ultimatum to hand Osama bin Laden over to the United States. He also instructed the Taliban to release and protect the foreigners present in their country, and to allow the United States full access to any terrorist camps in its territory to put them out of operation:

These demands are not open to negotiation or discussion. The Taliban must act, and act immediately. They will hand over the terrorists, or they will share in their fate.

George W. Bush, September 20, 2001 [12]

Americans were ready to roll.

CHARLES EDMUND COYOTE

CHAPTER 2 REFERENCES

[1] Remarks by the President Upon Arrival at Barksdale Air Force Base Barksdale Air Force Base, Louisiana, 11 September 2001;
http://remember911.albertarose.org/Bush9-11_Barksdale.htm
(SHORTENED URL: http://tinyurl.com/freednot)

[2] Statement by President George W. Bush in His Address to the Nation, 11 September 2001 - 8:30 P.M. EDT;
http://remember911.albertarose.org/Bush9-11_National-Address.htm
(SHORTENED URL: http://tinyurl.com/readre)

[3] Plans for Iraq Attack Began on 9/11, CBS NEWS, September 4, 2002;
http://www.cbsnews.com/stories/2002/09/04/september11/main520830.shtml
(SHORTENED URL: http://tinyurl.com/plansfor)

[4] 'Rumsfeld', by Andrew Cockburn, The New York Times, March 25, 2007;
http://www.nytimes.com/2007/03/25/books/chapters/0325-1st-cockb.html?ref=books&pagewanted=all
(SHORTENED URL: http://tinyurl.com/rumcock)

[5] Saving the Saudis, by Craig Unger, Vanity Fair, October 2003;
http://www.vanityfair.com/politics/features/2003/10/saving-the-saudis-200310
(SHORTENED URL: http://tinyurl.com/savsa)

[6] Bush Encourages N.Y. Rescuers, by Edward Walsh, washingtonpost.com, September 15, 2001;
http://old.911digitalarchive.org/crr/documents/1126.pdf
(SHORTENED URL: http://tinyurl.com/bushen)

[7] Iran weighs up its options, BBC NEWS: World: Middle East, 16 September 2001;
http://news.bbc.co.uk/2/hi/middle_east/1546882.stm
(SHORTENED URL: http://tinyurl.com/iranwei)

*[8] Showdown With Iran, Public Broadcasting System -
Frontline;
http://topdocumentaryfilms.com/showdown-with-iran/
(SHORTENED URL: http://tinyurl.com/showira)*

*[9] The National Security Strategy of the United States of
America, September 2002 - viii. Develop Agendas for
Cooperative Action with the Other Main Centers of Global
Power, globalsecurity.org;
http://www.globalsecurity.org/military/library/policy/nation
al/nss-020920.pdf
(SHORTENED URL: http://tinyurl.com/natisec)*

*[10] G8 - Sommet Evian summit 2003; G8 counter-
terrorism cooperation since September 11th backgrounder;
http://www.g8.fr/evian/english/navigation/g8_documents/a
rchives_from_previous_summits/kananaskis_summit_-
_2002/g8_counter-
terrorism_cooperation_since_september_11th_backgrounde
r.html
(SHORTENED URL: http://tinyurl.com/G8som)*

*[11] President George W. Bush, Address to a Joint Session
of Congress and the American People, September 20, 2001,
United States Capitol, Washington, D.C.;
http://www.fas.org/irp/news/2001/09/gwb092001.html
(SHORTENED URL: http://tinyurl.com/seecon)*

*[12] President George W. Bush, Address to a Joint Session
of Congress and the American People, September 20, 2001,
United States Capitol, Washington, D.C.;
http://www.fas.org/irp/news/2001/09/gwb092001.html
(SHORTENED URL: http://tinyurl.com/seecon)*

CHARLES EDMUND COYOTE

CHAPTER 3

I WANT JUSTICE

I want justice. There's an old poster out west, as I recall, that said, "Wanted: Dead or Alive."

> *George W. Bush, Remarks by the President to Pentagon Employees, 17 September 2001*

Resolution wears eloquent words giving it dignity and the strength to move that which needs to be moved. Shock turned to anger and anger became unity. The American people heard their charge, *"Let's Roll!"* from the air above Shanksville Pennsylvania, and the world got ready to roll with them.

At least that was the passion. But the next day a still, small voice spoke:

All governments lie; yours only less than most.

Afghanistan! Rudyard Kipling described it as *'the place where Empires go to die'*. Perhaps no nation on earth had seen more come and go. It was a natural fortress. In the eastern part of the country, the Hindu Kush Mountains topped out at over twenty thousand feet. Their name was taken from the old Persian word *'kush'*, meaning *'killing'*, and was a reference to the vast numbers of Hindus that had died on their snowy slopes at the hands of Islamic invaders. The mountain passes that allowed entrance through them from the Pakistani border carved their way through those slopes at about ten thousand feet above the very far distant sea.

From the time of the ancient Aryans and the Indo-Iranian tribes through Zoroaster and the Persian Empire,

Alexander the Great, Asoka, and the Islamic caliphate, past Genghis Khan and Tamerlane, the native Bactrian and Pashtun kingdoms had woven the rich texture of the world's history into their own and survived to confront their modern invaders, first the British, then the Soviets, and now the Americans.

In 1842, during the century of Britain's imperial power, the entire British army that was advancing into the remote land of Afghanistan had in the course of seven mere days been gnawed down to one sole survivor. [1]

The modern Soviet military sent as many as 118,000 troops to Afghanistan in December of 1979 to join 300,000 Afghan Soviet soldiers. There they battled for 3,339 days, from December 27, 1979 to February 15, 1989. They fought over 200,000 opponents, most of whom were Afghan mujahedeen insurgents. The rebels were backed by significant financial and military aid from Pakistani, Saudi Arabia, and the United States as well as foreign fighters from throughout the Muslim world, including about 10-15 thousand Arab volunteers during the nine years of the war. [2], [3], [4]

The mujahedeen waged an effective resistance that drained the Soviet military power and its already strained economy, contributing to the coming demise of the Communist state. [5] One of the Arabs that came to help was a 22 year old son of one of the wealthiest families in Saudi Arabia, Osama bin Laden.

Osama bin Laden had been born in Riyadh, Saudi Arabia on March 10, 1957, the only son of Muhammad bin Laden's tenth wife. His father, a businessman of extraordinary wealth, had been for decades a friend

CHARLES EDMUND COYOTE

and associate of the Saudi Royal Family. The family business, the Saudi Binladin Group (SBG), was considered to be the largest construction firm in the world and had built the US military bases in Saudi Arabia after the 1991 Gulf War. Osama's older half-brother, Salem bin Laden, eldest son of Muhammad, had invested $50,000 in George W. Bush's 1979 oil adventure, Arbusto Energy. On September 11, 2001, another half-brother of Osama, Shafig bin Laden, had been present at the Ritz-Carlton Hotel in Washington, D.C., along with former US Secretary of Defense Frank Carlucci, former Secretary of State James Baker III, and former President George H.W. Bush, for the annual investor conference of the Carlyle Group, one of the most well-connected private equity firms in the world. [6]

Described as hard-working and a pious student of his faith, bin Laden had studied economics and business administration at King Abdul-Aziz University in Saudi Arabia before joining the mujahedeen effort. He contributed money and organizational effort to the Afghan opposition and tested himself in combat against the Soviets. Over time, Osama and the net-work of Arab fighters struggling with the Afghan resistance fighters would eventually evolve into al-Qaeda, a term derived from a CIA file meaning *'the base'*. After the Soviets withdrew, Osama bin Laden returned home to Saudi Arabia as a hero of the Afghan struggle. In 1990, when Iraq invaded Kuwait, bin Laden tried to persuade Saudi Arabia's Crown Prince to let his mujahedeen, rather than the US military, pro-tect Saudi Arabia from any potential invasion by Saddam Hussein.

Upset with the Saudi Arabia's ruling family allowing their

nation to be occupied by American troops, as well as with their suppression of the Islamist movement, bin Laden became more and more critical of the Saudi monarchy. The Saudi Royals first tried to silence him through their connections with his family. Failing in that, they expelled him from the country in 1994 and revoked his citizenship. The bin Laden family followed these actions by disowning him for his activities and cutting him off from the $7 million yearly allowance he had been receiving. [7]

Osama bin Laden then moved to Khartoum, in the nearby African country of Sudan, where he continued to become more radicalized, supporting a 1995 attempt by the Egyptian Islamic Jihad to assassinate Egyptian President Hosni Mubarak. In retribution, an assassination attempt was launched against bin Laden. When that failed, Saudi officials, encouraged by the US, convinced the Sudanese government to expel bin Laden.

According to the *National Commission on Terrorist Attacks Upon the United States* (the 9/11 Commission), US Ambassador to Sudan, Timothy Carney, asked the Sudanese to expel bin Laden. However, there is no credible evidence that the government of Sudan ever offered to hand bin Laden over to the United States. At that early date (late 1995), there was yet no perception that Osama bin Laden was a danger to the United States. [8] Even as of 1997, the CIA's Counterterrorist Center continued to regard him only as an *'extremist financier'*.

After being expelled from Sudan, bin Laden returned to Afghanistan in May, 1996, and began to pursue a close relationship with the nation's new rulers, the Taliban and their spiritual leader, the fundamentalist scholar Mullah Mohammed Omar. [9] Both had been active in the anti-Soviet struggle, Mullah Omar having lost an eye and most of his sons in battle.

The word *'Taliban'* means *'religious students'* in the Pashto language of Central Asia. Following the 1992 collapse of the Afghan Communist government, civil War and lawlessness had taken control of the country. The Taliban arose in 1994, with vows by Mullah Omar and his students to rid Afghanistan of the bandit gangs that plagued the civilian population and commerce. Their vow was supported by powerful criminal organizations in Pakistan and the ISI (Pakistan's Interservices Intelligence Agency), which was concerned about the civil disorder north of their common border. [10]

The Taliban rapidly grew in power in the impoverished, war weary nation, absorbing many of the country's warlords and their armed fighters. By the summer of 1996, Mullah Omar and his supporters had taken control of most of the country and its capital city, Kabul, establishing the Islamic Emirate of Afghanistan. From its popular beginnings as a law and order government, the Islamic Emirate quickly transformed itself into an authoritarian fundamentalist state, whipping the population into an ultra-conservative observance of Sharia law and Pashtun tribal custom. [11] Their rule included a severe assault on the status of women in Afghan society. [12], [13] In 1999 the Taliban dismayed the world by dynamiting the 1,500-year-old Buddhist statues at Bam yam, and by severely assaulting the status of women. [14]

The Taliban created a world in which bin Laden felt at home and provided its leadership with fine automobiles and large amounts of money. The wealthy Saudi paved the streets of Kandahar, and sent two of his fighters to eliminate Ahmed Shah Massoud, just two days before 9/11. Massoud had been the progressive leader of Afghanistan's Northern Alliance and Mullah Omar's only serious opponent for control of the country. [15] In return for these favors, Mullah Omar provided Osama with the safe harbor he needed to build his insurgent and terrorist training camps for the holy war he had declared against the United States for its support of Israel, its military presence in Saudi Arabia, and its decimation of the Iraqi people through the UN sanctions. [16]

Bin Laden began to train thousands of young Muslim fundamentalists, preparing them for guerrilla warfare and giving instruction in terrorist techniques to those who demonstrated greater dedication and proficiency. In February 1998, he released another declaration of war against the United States, announcing, in concert with Ayman al Zawahiri of the Egyptian Islamic Jihad and others from Pakistan and Bangladesh, the formation of a *World Islamic Front for Jihad against the Crusaders and Jews'*. [17] This *'Jihad Against Jews and Crusaders'* continued to fulminate against the United States for its support to Israel, activities in the Arabian Peninsula, and the devastation of the Iraqi people. [18]

> *He's been pretty consistent about why he's attacking the United States. It's because of American foreign policies. He did not say anything about Madonna, Hollywood, drugs, sex, or any of the kind of cultural issues you might expect him to be concerned with. It's all about what America is doing in his backyard, as he sees it. He sees this as a defensive war responding to a record of hu-miliation that began after the end of World War I when the Ottoman Empire was carved up by the British and the French. And bin Laden believes that today Muslims*

CHARLES EDMUND COYOTE

are still being humiliated whether it is in Kashmir or Palestine or in Iraq. As far as he's concerned, his war is about humiliation and reclaiming Muslim pride.

> *Peter Jouvenal, cinematographer and producer of CNN's story about Osama bin Laden, which aired in May 1997* [19]

In August of 1998, simultaneous car bomb explosions at the American embassies in the African capitals of Dar es Salaam in Tanzania, and Nairobi in Kenya killed 223 people and injured thousands. US President Clinton responded by authorizing bin Laden's arrest or assassination and launching cruise missile strikes against al-Qaeda training camps in Afghanistan and a Sudanese pharmaceutical factory. Bin Laden's organization was unaffected by the American missiles, but the destruction of the Sudanese factory resulted in the deaths of thousands of Sudanese who were thereby deprived of essential pharmaceutical supplies. [20]

In October 1999, with the United Nations Security Council Resolution 1267, the UN began to apply financial, military, and travel sanctions against the Taliban in an effort to pressure them to turn Osama bin Laden over to American authorities for trial and close down al-Qaeda's training camps. [21] That and other UN Resolutions, however, had little impact on the Taliban, who regarded bin Laden as an honored guest to whom, by the dictates of Pashtun custom, they were obligated to grant asylum and hospitality. Nevertheless, the resolutions brought increased hardship to the people of Afghanistan, who were dependent on food aid from the international community. [22]

Osama bin Laden began planning to use Afghanistan as a base from which he could strike at the United

States, seeking thereby to drag it into a confrontation with the Islamic world. [23] Realizing that the Achilles heel of the American superpower was its very high-priced military, bin Laden believed he could wear down America's wealth by forcing it to invade and fight for years against an inexpensive insurgency in their native land. He was certain that the cost and duration of such a fight would drain the American economy and lead the US to abandon the Middle East, just as the Soviet Union had done 20 years before. He anticipated that such a conflict in the Middle East, which supplies most of the world's oil, would destabilize the region and cause energy prices to soar, further degrading the American economy and forcing the US to withdraw support to Israel and other anti-Islamist regimes in the region.

> *Our ultimate objective of these painful strikes against the head of the serpent was to prompt it to come out of its hole. This would make it easier for us to deal consecutive blows to undermine it and tear it apart. It would foster our credibility in front of our nation and the beleaguered people of the world. A person will react randomly when he receives painful strikes on his head from an undisclosed enemy. Such strikes will force the person to carry out random acts and provoke him to make serious and sometimes fatal mistakes. This is what actually happened.*
>
> *Sayf Adel, al Qaeda military commander* [24]

Seeking to provoke such an American response, in October 2000 al-Qaeda carried out a suicide bombing of the guided missile destroyer, U.S.S. Cole, while it was refueling in the Yemeni port of Aden, blowing a 40x40 foot hole in the ship's port side and killing 17 of its crewmen. Though an attack on a Navy ship is considered an act of war, the Cole attack did not produce the fierce US response al-Qaeda was hoping to get. This was due in part because al-Qaeda's responsibility, though strongly suspected, was not definitively established until February 2001. Stung by the cruise missile mistakes of August 1998, the Clinton administration wanted to be certain this time it was making the right moves. [25]

In February 2001, a source reported that an individual whom he identified as the big instructor (probably a reference to Bin Ladin) complained frequently that the United States had not yet attacked. According to the source, Bin Ladin wanted the United States to attack, and if it did not he would launch something bigger. [26]

By the following summer, al-Qaeda, frustrated over the initial failure to bring about the desired American invasion of Afghanistan, was positioning itself inside the United States, readying for a more spectacular attack. American intelligence began picking up evidence of al-Qaeda's preparations:

> *The incident that had gotten everyone's attention was a conversation between two members of Al Qaida. And they had been talking to one another, supposedly expressing disappointment that the United States had not chosen to retaliate more seriously against what had happened to the Cole. And one Al Qaida operative was overheard saying to the other, "Don't worry; we're planning something so big now that the US will have to respond."*
>
> *Judith Miller, New York Times, Pulitzer Prize winning Reporter* [27]

By carrying out a highly visible strike against the United States, al-Qaeda also intended to signal their emergence as the new Islamist leadership opposing the Anglo-Zionist alliance on which many Middle Easterners blamed the region's problems. Al-Qaeda's leaders saw themselves as forerunners to a worldwide movement that would inspire political upheaval and eventually bring down the Arab dictatorships that had been cooperating with the US and its allies. In planning since 1996, the attacks against the World Trade Center and the Pentagon were being organized by Khaled Sheikh Mohammed, an al-Qaeda associate, who had persuaded bin Laden to fund them.

Al-Qaeda believed that the major America military response to these spectacular attacks on US soil would make it easier to bleed America in the Middle East and significantly enhance al-Qaeda's position within the region. [28] It also believed that the powerful, and inevitably clumsy, military response from the last remaining superpower was sure to offend the Muslim world and rally millions of angry youth to the Islamist banner. The destabilization through a prolonged major military action was expected to send oil prices, heretofore cheap, spiraling upward, further damaging the American economy while it prospered the Middle East. [29]

Sure that God was on their side, al-Qaeda believed victory would ultimately be theirs and that America's gargantuan appetite for Middle Eastern oil would prove to be its undoing, bankrupting it through unending conflict and increasing energy costs.

> A U.S. campaign against Afghanistan will cause great long-term economic burdens [on the United States], which will force America to resort to the former Soviet Union's only option: withdrawal from Afghanistan, disintegration, and contraction.
>
> Osama bin Laden, October 3, 2001 [30]

CHARLES EDMUND COYOTE

In a captured computer document dated October 3, 2001, bin Laden refers to a survey that found seven out of ten Americans had experienced psychological problems immediately following the New York and Washington attacks. It appears he thought that America was no longer the nation that had once, in relatively short order, brought down such powerful opposition as the Nazi German and Imperial Japanese War machines. Perhaps, as a fan of international television news, he had seen the uncertain television reporter proclaiming *'shock and terror'* to the air waves, rather than the *'shock and anger'* of the generation before. Was something now perceived to be missing in a great nation at the height of world power?

> *Recognition of the falsity of material wealth as the standard of success goes hand in hand with the abandonment of the false belief that public office and high political position are to be valued only by the standards of pride of place and personal profit; and there must be an end to a conduct in banking and in business which too often has given to a sacred trust the likeness of callous and selfish wrongdoing. Small wonder that confidence languishes, for it thrives only on honesty, on honor, on the sacredness of obligations, on faithful protection, on unselfish performance; without them it cannot live.*

> *Franklin Delano Roosevelt, March 1933* [31]

Though hardly a well-kept secret, the higher levels of the US government chose not to see the 9/11 attacks coming. [32] When the attacks came, their impact on the American people was not dissimilar to the shock that awoke the sleeping giant of their parents and grandparents 60 years before. In Afghanistan, the fundamentalist Taliban government of Mullah Omar appears not to have advance awareness of al-Qaeda's

9/11 plans. However their close ties to bin Laden led them to refuse US requests for bin Laden's extradition, absent the presentation of clear evidence of his involvement. [33] Their demand for evidence set the stage for the American attack and subsequently swift collapse of the Taliban government.

With equal swiftness, bin Laden soon learned that he had almost catastrophically misjudged the character and power of the American response he had long sought to provoke. Instead of the massive ground invasion he had wanted, the US and UK campaigned against him with about 400 American and British Special Forces and CIA agents on the ground, along with about 40,000 Northern Alliance and the mercenary fighters of various warlords, all supported by substantial American airpower. [34]

The al-Qaeda Salafists – having once held their own against better equipped and numerically superior Soviet forces – saw their training camps destroyed and the freedom to operate on Afghan soil quickly reduced to a small patch of mountain slopes. From the White Mountains of Tora Bora, Osama bin Laden would soon be heard on the radio asking forgiveness of his followers for leading them down a dead end as a small team of nearby CIA agents and Special Forces directed a pulverizing bombing attack against his best fighters and closed in on a *'Mission Accomplished'*. [35]

CHAPTER 3 REFERENCES

[1] First Afghan War - Battle of Kabul and the retreat to Gandamak, BritishBattles.com;
http://www.britishbattles.com/first-afghan-war/kabul-

gandamak.htm
(SHORTENED URL: http://tinyurl.com/warkab)

[2] The Osama bin Laden I Know, An Oral History of al
Qaeda's Leader, by Peter L. Bergen; © 2006, Free Press, a
Division of Simon & Schuster, Inc., p 49.

[3] The Zarqawi Generation, by Vicken Cheterian,
Counterpunch, December 11, 2008;
http://www.counterpunch.org/cheterian12112008.html
(SHORTENED URL: http://tinyurl.com/countpun)

[4] Interview of Zbigniew Brzezinski, Le Nouvel
Observateur pp 76, 15-21 January 1998, Scribd.com;
http://www.scribd.com/doc/44537431/Interview-With
Zbigniew-Brzezinski-From-Le-Nouvel-Observateur-Jan-1998
(SHORTENED URL: http://tinyurl.com/scrint)

[5] Soviet afghan war, 36 min documentary, Apr 29, 2006;

1. http://www.youtube.com/watch?v=w8Vmx9Pg5Js
(SHORTENED URL: http://tinyurl.com/sovaf1)

2. http://www.youtube.com/watch?v=zoXo9eVO1x0
(SHORTENED URL: http://tinyurl.com/sovaf2)

3. http://www.youtube.com/watch?v=ISyeBbV3tPg
(SHORTENED URL: http://tinyurl.com/sovaf3)

4. http://www.youtube.com/watch?v=KN-we7SszL8
(SHORTENED URL: http://tinyurl.com/sovaf4)

5. http://www.youtube.com/watch?v=Gl6Wb1TH1iE
(SHORTENED URL: http://tinyurl.com/sovaf5)

[6] Carlyle's way; Making a mint inside "the iron triangle"
of defense, government, and industry, by Dan Briody,
REDHERRING.com, January 8, 2002;
http://web.archive.org/web/20030607113821/http://redher
ring.com/vc/2002/0111/947.html
(SHORTENED URL: http://tinyurl.com/carlyma)

[7] Osama bin Laden, Wikipedia, the free encyclopedia;
http://en.wikipedia.org/wiki/Osama_bin_Laden
(SHORTENED URL: http://tinyurl.com/enbin)

[8] Responses to Al Qaeda's Initial Assaults, Section 4.1, p

110; The 9-11 Commission Report, Final Report of the National Commission on Terrorist Attacks Upon the United States, Official Government Edition;
http://www.gpoaccess.gov/911/

[9] Profile: Mullah Mohammed Omar, BBC NEWS: World: South Asia, 18 September, 2001;
http://news.bbc.co.uk/2/hi/south_asia/1550419.stm
(SHORTENED URL: http://tinyurl.com/mumoham)

[10] Operation Enduring Disaster, by Tariq Ali, Tomgram: Tariq Ali, Flight Path to Disaster in Afghanistan, TomDispatch.com;
http://www.tomdispatch.com/post/175003/tariq_ali_flight_path_to_disaster_in_afghanistan
(SHORTENED URL: http://tinyurl.com/endis)

[11] Taliban, From Wikipedia, the free encyclopedia; Life under the Taliban regime, Treatment of women, Prohibitions on culture, Ethnic massacres and persecution;
http://en.wikipedia.org/wiki/Taliban#cite_note-55
(SHORTENED URL: http://tinyurl.com/talwipe)

[12] US Department of State; Afghanistan, Country Reports on Human Rights Practices - 2001; Released by the Bureau of Democracy, Human Rights, and Labor; March 4, 2002;
http://www.state.gov/g/drl/rls/hrrpt/2001/sa/8222.htm
(SHORTENED URL: http://tinyurl.com/humris)

[13] Revolutionary Association of the Women of Afghanistan (RAWA);
http://www.rawa.org/index.php

[14] Why the Taliban are destroying Buddhas, by W.L. Rathje, USA TODAY, 03/22/2001;
http://www.usatoday.com/news/science/archaeology/2001-03-22-afghan-buddhas.htm
(SHORTENED URL: http://tinyurl.com/talbub)

[15] PBS Frontline: The Dark Side: Interviews by Gary C. Schroen;
http://www.pbs.org/wgbh/pages/frontline/darkside/intervie

CHARLES EDMUND COYOTE

ws/schroen.html
(SHORTENED URL: http://tinyurl.com/dargary)

[16] Text of Osama bin Laden's Declaration of Jihad, Aug. 23, 1996; Declaration of War Against the Americans Occupying the Land of the Two Holy Places; HOMELAND SECURITY, GlobalSecurity.org; http://www.globalsecurity.org/security/profiles/osama_bin_l aden_declares_jihad_text.htm
(SHORTENED URL: http://tinyurl.com/declaji)

[17] Jihad Against Jews and Crusaders, World Islamic Front Statement, 23 February 1998; http://www.fas.org/irp/world/para/docs/980223-fatwa.htm
(SHORTENED URL: http://tinyurl.com/jijecru)

[18] The Concept and Practice of Jihad in Islam, by Michael G. Knapp, From Parameters, US Army War College Quarterly - Spring 2003, from Parameters, Spring 2003, pp. 82-94; http://www.carlisle.army.mil/USAWC/Parameters/Articles/0 3spring/knapp.htm
(SHORTENED URL: http://tinyurl.com/carminap)

[19] The Osama bin Laden I Know, An Oral History of al Qaeda's Leader, by Peter L. Bergen; © 2006, Free Press, a Division of Simon & Schuster, Inc., p 182.

[20] The National Security Archive: Pre-9/11 US Attempts to Drive Bin Laden Out of Afghanistan Repeatedly Unsuccessful, Edited by Barbara Elias; Posted August 18, 2005; http://www.gwu.edu/~nsarchiv/NSAEBB/NSAEBB134/index 2.htm
(SHORTENED URL: http://tinyurl.com/nased)

[21] S-RES-1267 (1999) Security Council Resolution 1267 (1999), UNdemocracy.com; http://www.undemocracy.com/S-RES-1267(1999)
(SHORTENED URL: http://tinyurl.com/undemse)

[22] Why Bombing and Warnings Are Not Working, by Hasan Jafri and Lewis Dolinsky, San Francisco Chronicle, 16

October 2001;
http://www.commondreams.org/views01/1016-09.htm
(SHORTENED URL: http://tinyurl.com/bomnot)

[23] The Osama bin Laden I Know, An Oral History of al
Qaeda's Leader, by Peter L. Bergen; © 2006, Free Press, a
Division of Simon & Schuster, Inc., p 193.

[24] The Osama bin Laden I Know, An Oral History of al
Qaeda's Leader, by Peter L. Bergen; © 2006, Free Press, a
Division of Simon & Schuster, Inc., pp 309.

[25] National Commission on Terrorist Attacks Upon the
United States, Chapter 6 - From Threat To Threat, pp 193-
196;
http://govinfo.library.unt.edu/911/report/911Report_Ch6.p
(SHORTENED URL: http://tinyurl.com/nacosta)

[26] National Commission on Terrorist Attacks Upon the
United States, Chapter 6 - From Threat To Threat, p 191;
http://govinfo.library.unt.edu/911/report/911Report_Ch6.p
df
(SHORTENED URL: http://tinyurl.com/nattera)

[27] The 9/11 Story That Got Away, by Rory O'Connor and
William Scott Malone, posted 18 May 2006, AlterNet;
http://www.alternet.org/story/36388/?page=entire
(SHORTENED URL: http://tinyurl.com/storor)

[28] The Goals of the New York Strike, Al Qaeda:
Statements and Evolving Ideology, Congressional Research
Service, Prepared for Members and Committees of Congress
by Christopher M. Blanchard, Analyst in Middle Eastern
Affairs, Foreign Affairs, Defense, and Trade Division,
Updated July 9, 2007, CRS-5&6;
http://www.fas.org/sgp/crs/terror/RL32759.pdf
(SHORTENED URL: http://tinyurl.com/gofaste)

[29] FLASHBACK: Ten Years Ago, Bin Laden Demanded
Barrel Of Oil Should Cost $144, by Faiz Shakir, July 5, 2008,
Think Progress;
http://thinkprogress.org/2008/07/05/bin-laden-144-oil/
(SHORTENED URL: http://tinyurl.com/thinprog)

CHARLES EDMUND COYOTE

38

[30] The Osama bin Laden I Know, An Oral History of al Qaeda's Leader, by Peter L. Bergen; © 2006, Free Press, a Division of Simon & Schuster, Inc., p 316.

[31] First Inaugural Address of Franklin D. Roosevelt, 4 MARCH 1933; The Avalon Project, Lillian Goldman Law Library, Yale Law School;
http://avalon.law.yale.edu/20th_century/froos1.asp
(SHORTENED URL: http://tinyurl.com/avafinad)

[32] "THE SYSTEM WAS BLINKING RED", 9-11 Commission Report, Chapter 8, National Commission on Terrorist Attacks Upon the United States;
http://govinfo.library.unt.edu/911/report/911Report_Ch8.htm
(SHORTENED URL: http://tinyurl.com/gocha8)

[33] The Osama bin Laden I Know, An Oral History of al Qaeda's Leader, by Peter L. Bergen; © 2006, Free Press, a Division of Simon & Schuster, Inc., pp 316-317.

[34] The Osama bin Laden I Know, An Oral History of al Qaeda's Leader, by Peter L. Bergen; © 2006, Free Press, a Division of Simon & Schuster, Inc., p 311.

[35] TORA BORA REVISITED: HOW WE FAILED TO GET BIN LADEN AND WHY IT MATTERS TODAY, A Report To Members Of The Committee On Foreign Relations United States Senate, John F. Kerry, Chairman, 30 November 2009;
www.foreign.senate.gov/imo/media/doc/Tora_Bora_Report.pdf
(SHORTENED URL: http://tinyurl.com/tobora)

CHAPTER 4

BEFORE THE JOB IS DONE

The only way we can win is to leave before the job is done.
George W. Bush, Greeley, Colorado, November 4, 2006

Only 2 months after September 11, America was closing in on bin Laden's Islamists with a swiftness no one on either side had expected. Since the late 1990s, the Central Intelligence Agency had been working on plans to penetrate and disrupt bin Laden's Afghan operations. This planning had positioned them to respond quickly after 9/11. The Bush Administration knew that removing bin Laden's sanctuary meant they would have to tackle Afghanistan with troops on the ground, but the commanding general of the *US Central Command* (CENTCOM), Tommy Franks, said he had no immediately useable plans on hand to go after such an objective. [1]

The CIA, however, already had portions of their own *'Plan'* in place. With bases in adjacent countries, information gathering already ongoing, and more than 100 agents on the ground, the agency's headquarters in Langley, Virginia, already had most the country of Afghanistan under surveillance. Back in 1999, the Director of Central Intelligence, George Tenet, had requested his counter-terrorism division to develop a plan for penetrating bin Laden's operations. He put Cofer Black in charge. The *'Plan'* they developed focused on the collection of intelligence from within al-Qaeda in order to compromise planned attacks against the United States as they were being prepared. The Counter Terrorism Center's *'Plan'* involved surrounding Afghanistan with secret operations bases, sending agents

CHARLES EDMUND COYOTE

from those bases to penetrate bin Laden's sanctuaries, and building ties to the Northern Alliance, the indigenous military/political organization that was uniting various Afghan groups opposed to the Taliban.

CTC Director Black flew to Russia to brief its government on the American plans to attack Afghanistan. After initially expressing reservations based on their own experience two decades before, Black's determination won over their respect:

> *After the meeting was over, two senior Russian officials, whom I will not name, said to me, "Mr. Black, finally America is acting like a superpower!" They'd been to the rodeo and they lost. They had a hell of a fight in Afghanistan. It was a great expression of solidarity in our moment of need. We needed their support and their cooperation, and we got it. They too were the enemies of Al Qaeda and the Taliban; they just had to be assured that we had no ulterior motivations.*
>
> Cofer Black, October 17, 2008 Interview [2]

The CIA *'Plan'* involved getting agents as close as possible to bin Laden and, in that proximity, recruiting other proxies to help conduct operations. Director Black was looking for teams that could blend into the local Muslim populations. In October 1999, Black arranged for a CIA team headed by *'Richard'*, the newly appointed chief of the Counter Terrorism Center's Bin Laden Station, to visit Northern-Alliance leader Ahmed Shah Massoud to discuss operations. Richar's mission was codenamed *'Jawbreaker-5'*.

CTC Chief Cofer Black and Richard Clarke, the White House's Coordinator for Security and Counter-Terrorism, were strong advocates of the Air Force's program of arming *Predator Unmanned Aerial Vehicles* (UAVs) with Hellfire missiles that would be able to attack un-suspecting terrorists from thousands of feet in the air. [3] On both September 7 and September 28, 2000, the unarmed Predator UAV reconnaissance tests con-ducted in Afghanistan had spotted a tall man in white robes surrounded by a security detail at al-Qaeda's Tarnak Farm location close to Kandahar. The intel-ligence community believed those Predator video feeds to be real-time images of Osama bin Laden. [4]

On September 9, 2001, the CIA submitted a formal, high level National Security Directive proposal for the elimination of al-Qaeda to Condoleezza Rice and President Bush. [5] This plan for action had been drafted along the lines of the 1999 CTC *'Plan'* by Cofer Black and George Tenet and consisted of a three-year strategy of increasing pressure on the Taliban be-ginning with an ultimatum to hand over Osama bin Laden. [6] If the Taliban were to reject that, pressure would then be gradually increased by channeling mili-tary aid to anti-Taliban groups, bringing armed Pre-dator UAVs into play, and persuading other nations to become involved in a world-wide round-up of al-Qaeda suspects. If these options ultimately fell short, Ame-rican military power would be used to take down the Taliban government and remove bin Laden's safe harbor. [7]

The proposed Presidential Directive became the precursor of the initial plan put into action after the September 11 attacks. [8] In March 2001, *Jane's Security News* – a respected British publisher specializing in open source military intelligence – observed that the United States, India, Iran and Russia were already co-operating, through bases in Tajikistan and Uzbekistan, to support the Northern Alliance with both information and logistics support in its fight against the Taliban. [9]

The former Foreign Secretary of Pakistan, Niaz Naik, told the BBC that he had been informed by the Americans, during a July 2001 meeting of senior Iranian, Pakistani, Russian and US diplomats, that military action would be initiated against the Taliban by the middle of October. Mr. Naik said Washington planned to launch military operations from bases in Tajikistan where it already had advisors in place. [10] In the months before September 11, US Army Rangers inside Kyrgyzstan were training special troops. Other reports held that Tajik and Uzbek troops were also being trained on US territory in Alaska and Montana. By the end of summer, 2001, the US also had military advisors in Tajikistan and Uzbekistan. [11]

At a September 15, 2001 Camp David meeting of the National Security Council chaired by the President, George Tenet proposed sending additional CIA teams and Special Operations units from the military into Afghanistan to mount covert operations. The President approved and the CIA took the lead during the first couple months of the 2001 US ground attack on al-Qaeda and the Taliban. [12] On September 26, 2001, a seven member Liaison Team, led by CIA agent Gary Schroen, slipped into Afghanistan to link up with the Northern Alliance's 40,000 troops. [13] In short order, they were joined by US Army Special Forces.

Mullah Omar does not appear to have known that bin Laden was involved in the September 11 attacks. [14] Despite America's ultimatum that the al-Qaeda leader should be turned over, the Taliban government maintained that until proven otherwise they owed him the protection of Afghanistan. Rejecting the October 7th Taliban offer to put Osama bin laden on trial, the US and UK began bombing Afghanistan with 15 B-52, B-1 & B-2 bombers, 25 carrier-based fighter aircraft and 50 ship and submarine that launched Tomahawk missiles. Their mission was to target air defense sites, airfields, the Taliban's 80 aging combat aircraft and military command centers, the electrical grid and oil supply centers for Kabul and other major cities. [15]

President Bush announced the strikes on national television and stated that food, medicine, and supplies were also being dropped to *"the starving and suffering men, women and children of Afghanistan."* The humanitarian relief missions started that same night as two C-17 Globemasters began to bring in an average of 35,000 Daily Rations and other supplies every 24 hours.

On the war's first night, an unmanned MQ-1 Predator, equipped with imaging radar and an array of infrared and television cameras, identified a procession of cars and trucks fleeing the capital of Kabul carrying Mullah Omar, the Head of the Taliban's Supreme Council'. The Predator's CIA operators were eager to fire the supersonic AGM-114 antitank Hellfire missiles at the Taliban leader, but under a previously worked out agreement, they were required to first ask permission from headquarters at the United States Central Command (CENTCOM) in Tampa, Florida. [16]

While waiting for the authorization to fire, the Predator silently followed the caravan to a building where Omar and about hundred guards paused to take refuge. Immediately, another request was sent out for a full-scale assault on the adjacent structure. As reported by

Seymour Hersh:

> *At that point word came from General Tommy R. Franks, CENTCOM commander, saying, 'My JAG' – Judge Advocate General, a legal officer – 'doesn't like this, so we're not going to fire.' Instead, the Predator was authorized to fire a missile in front of the building, 'bounce it off the front door,' one officer said.*
>
> *Seymour Hersh, The New Yorker, 16 October 2001* [17]

The drone's operators were approved to fire one missile in front of the building where Omar had taken cover, *"bounce it off the front door, and see who comes out, and take a picture,"* said one officer. When the Hellfire was unable to acquire a targeting signature on the dirt in front of the edifice, a decision was made to fire at the parked vehicles that had carried Omar and his guards to the location. [18]

A ground operative later confirmed that Omar had been in the convoy. When the missile obliterated the parked vehicles, Omar's guards assumed that the conflagration had been caused by rocket-propelled grenades fired by nearby Northern Alliance troops. A group from Taliban went looking for the enemy, but found nothing. [19]

By the time F-18s were sent to destroy the building, however, Mullah Omar had moved on. Commenting on the failure, one senior official told Hersh:

> *It's not a fuckup, it's an outrage. This isn't like you're six years old and your mother calls you to come in for lunch and you say, 'Time out.' If anyone thinks otherwise, go look at the World Trade Center or the Pentagon.*
>
> *Seymour Hersh, The New Yorker, 16 October 2001* [20]

Other officers blamed the pattern of stalled attacks, which continued especially during the beginning of the war, on a sluggish bureaucratic culture and an atmosphere of political correctness. [21] This climate in the early months of the War was balanced by otherwise stunning successes that did much to boost morale among the American people. Even by the second day, October 8, the Taliban's ability to defend its airspace and communicate with its forces had been effectively obliterated. B-2 stealth bombers, flying almost two days from Whiteman Air Force Base in the state of Missouri, were used in the initial targeting of Taliban air defenses. That was followed by B-52 and B-1B bombers flying a 5,000 mile round trip up and back again from airfield facilities on the Indian Ocean atoll of Diego Garcia. Seven hundred miles away, in the Arabian Sea, the supercarrier USS Enterprise and its battle group were joined by three additional carriers, among them the USS Kitty Hawk which was utilized for special operations helicopters. [22]

Because of the opening degradation of the military infrastructure, no western aircraft carriers were lost to Taliban or al-Qaeda activity. Once that phase was done, selection shifted from preplanned stationary objectives to time-sensitive, moving targets such as military columns, formations and leadership. As thousands of Pashtun fighters began to pour in from Pakistan to help the Taliban, Apache helicopters, carrier based F/A-18 Hornets, and AC-130 gunships shifted to support the Northern Alliance's mostly Tajik and Uzbek militias, giving them the firepower needed to break the Taliban's strongholds and numerical advantage. Western air-ground controllers operating with the Alliance directed precision firepower against tanks and

CHARLES EDMUND COYOTE

artillery pieces and brought in B-52 dropping cluster bombs against concentrations of field troops. Americans on horseback were directing 50 to 100 airstrike sorties a day. [23] The Taliban was totally unprepared to deal with the precision munitions, cluster bombs, and the 15,000-pound BLU-82s used against them by the American Air Force. [24]

Despite its finicky use on the war's first day, the MQ-1A armed version of the UAV Predator, having become available shortly after 9/11, quickly proved a valuable resource. Earlier in the year, the Air Force had fired Hellfire antitank missiles from a *Predator Unmanned Aerial Vehicle* in a series of successful tests; now the CIA was using them to track and attack key targets in Afghanistan. [25] During the first month of war, various Predators fired some 40 Hellfire missiles. Flying as high as 25,000 feet the Predator is inconspicuous and the supersonic Hellfires give little warning of their attack. [26]

> *A Hellfire missile hitting a T-72 tank – it is an absolute catastrophic destruction. The turret absolutely separates and blows off a hundred feet in the air, a hundred yards away.*
>
> > Colonel John Le Moyne, 24th Infantry Division, 1st Brigade, 22 May 2000 [27]

In early November, attacks were concentrated on Taliban and al-Qaeda forces near Mazar-e Sharif, in the Central north, and Kabul, the capital. On November 4, aircraft dropped two BLU-82 15,000-pound bombs on Taliban troops. Used for psychological effect as well as destructive power, when dropped, the BLU-82 releases a cloud of inflammable ammonium nitrate and aluminum dust that detonates to create a firestorm incinerating an area the size of several football fields and sucking the oxygen from the lungs of anyone within a quarter mile, creating a shockwave that can destroy internal organs. [28]

By early November resistance was collapsing and the Northern Alliance was marching on the capital of Kabul. On November 9, the city of Mazari-e Sharif in northern Afghanistan fell after the Americans carpet bombed the Taliban defenders waiting at the city's entrance. The withdrawal of Taliban forces from the city severed their supply lines and opened up the flow of supplies to the Northern Alliance. The following day, the Northern Alliance moved swiftly through the nearby provinces as local ethnic Tajik commanders switched sides instead of continuing to fight for the southern Pashtun Taliban. Mullah Omar's ability to control the country was rapidly withering away.

The morning of November 12 saw the end of the Taliban's control of Kabul as B-52 strikes pounded Taliban positions around the capital. [29] In the afternoon, Northern Alliance armor and infantry moved down the *"Old Road"* toward the city sweeping through the remnants. Fleeing Taliban fighters discarded what they could, and ran for their lives as their government collapsed. On November 13, the Northern Alliance took control of Kabul and began to set up police functions.

General Tommy Franks described the month of fighting during which the Taliban's hold on Afghanistan had been broken:

> *We have said that it's all about condition setting, followed by our attaining our objectives. The first thing we did*

CHARLES EDMUND COYOTE

was set conditions to begin to take down the tactical air defense and all of that. So we set conditions and then we did that. The next thing we did was set conditions with these special forces teams and the positioning of our aviation assets to be able to take the Taliban apart or fracture it. And we did that.

CENTCOM Commander General Tommy Franks, November 15, 2001 [30]

Above the fleeing partisans armed Predator drones flew high and undetected, each keeping a close eye on a hundred square miles of territory at a time. [31], [32] Among those dispersing to the countryside was al-Qaeda's senior military leader, Mohammad Atef. On November 15 an al-Qaeda group gathered at a 3-story hotel outside Gardez, about 60 miles south of Kabul. A Predator silently broadcast the meeting to the US Central Command in Tampa, Florida, to CIA headquarters in Langley, Virginia, and to the Pentagon in Washington DC. Seizing the opportunity, a coordinated attack, consisting of three US Air Force F-15s each dropping a 2,500 lb GBU-15 smart bomb and two Hellfire missiles fired from the Predator, was launched to incinerate the building and pickup trucks parked outside. The resulting inferno killed Atef, a man who was a key lieutenant and close friend of Osama bin Laden, and several other high-ranking members of al-Qaeda. [33]

The Northern Alliance took its pursuit of the Taliban and al-Qaeda into their remaining strongholds of Kandahar in the south, and Kunduz in the north near the border with Tajikistan. Shortly before the fall of Kunduz, hundreds of Pakistani Inter-Services Intelligence agents, who had been helping the Taliban and al-Qaeda fight the United Front/Northern Alliance and

American forces, were airlifted out of Kunduz to safety in Northern Pakistan at the request of Pakistani President Pervez Musharraf and the permission of US Vice President Dick Cheney. Among them were hundreds, if not thousands, of additional Taliban and al-Qaeda fighters. From the surrounding hills, American Special Operation Forces helplessly watched the operation and called it *"Operation Evil Airlift."* [34], [35], [36]

On November 20, about 1,000 Taliban fighters at Kunduz surrendered to the Northern Alliance and by the 26th Kunduz was occupied. Yet, although Afghanistan was slipping from Taliban control, only a fraction of its top leadership had been captured or killed.

East of Kabul, about 30 miles southwest of Jalalabad and seven miles from the Pakistan border, stretch the Mountains of Spin Ghar, and an area known to the West as Tora Bora. What was left of al-Qaeda in Afghanistan by mid November was now retreating to the refuge of bunkers and caves the fighters had maintained in that high, rugged area of the White Mountains, not far from the famous Khyber Pass. It was there, during that 1980s, that a little over a hundred Arab mujahidin had managed to fend off with 50 helicopters and jets an attacking Soviet and Afghan Communist force more than forty times as large. Knowing that the Soviet Union and the US had held each other in an apparently equally matched superpower stalemate for more than forty years, al-Qaeda believed that they would once again be able to hold their own and fight off the Americans just as once they had done with the Soviet Union.

On his way to al-Qaeda's mountain fortress, bin Laden paused briefly at the Saudi funded Institute for Islamic

CHARLES EDMUND COYOTE

studies in Jalalabad to give a speech to those who admired him as a benefactor of the Afghan resistance to the Soviet Union. After his talk, bin Laden passed out cash to those whose help he might soon need, and then beat a hasty exit for the mountain slopes in a convoy of 25 Toyota Land Cruisers. [37]

CHAPTER 4 REFERENCES

[1] WAR TIME, 9-11 Commission Report, Chapter 10, National Commission on Terrorist Attacks Upon the United States;
http://govinfo.library.unt.edu/911/report/911Report_Ch10.htm
(SHORTENED URL: http://tinyurl.com/warep)

[2] Cofer Black, Out of the Shadows, Interviewed by Kevin McMurray, Men's Journal, 17 October 2008;
http://www.mensjournal.com/cofer-black
(SHORTENED URL: http://tinyurl.com/mecocke)

[3] How the Predator UAV Works, by Robert Valdes;
http://science.howstuffworks.com/predator3.htm
(SHORTENED URL: http://tinyurl.com/preuav)

[4] The 9-11 Commission Report, Final Report of the National Commission on Terrorist Attacks Upon the United States, Official Government Edition, Chapter 6, FROM THREAT TO THREAT, 6.2 Post-Crisis Reflection: Agenda for 2000, p 190; http://www.gpoaccess.gov/911/pdf/sec6.pdf
(SHORTENED URL: http://tinyurl.com/corefina)

[5] Bush team 'agreed plan to attack the Taliban the day before September 11', by Julian Borger, guardian, co.uk, 24 March 2004;
http://www.guardian.co.uk/world/2004/mar/24/september11.usa2
(SHORTENED URL: http://tinyurl.com/attatali)

[6] The 9-11 Commission Report, Final Report of the

National Commission on Terrorist Attacks Upon the United States, Official Government Edition, Chapter 6, FROM THREAT TO THREAT, 6.5 THE NEW ADMINISTRATION'S APPROACH, pp 210-214;
http://www.gpoaccess.gov/911/pdf/fullreport.pdf
(SHORTENED URL: http://tinyurl.com/corefull)

[7] A Strategy's Cautious Evolution, by Barton Gellman, Washington Post Staff Writer, Sunday, January 20, 2002; p A01;
http://www.maxstandridge.net/911BushColebackdown.html
(SHORTENED URL: http://tinyurl.com/lidima)

[8] US sought attack on al-Qaida, by Jim Miklaszewski and Alex Johnson, msnbc, May 16, 2002;
http://www.msnbc.msn.com/id/4587368/
(SHORTENED URL: http://tinyurl.com/wabagel)

[9] India joins anti-Taliban coalition, by Rahul Bedi, Jane's Security News, 15 March 2001, AFGHANISTAN NEWS CENTER;
http://www.afghanistannewscenter.com/news/2001/march/mar19f2001.html
(SHORTENED URL: http://tinyurl.com/tarabe)

[10] US 'planned attack on Taleban', by George Arney, BBC News SOUTH ASIA, 18 September, 2001;
http://news.bbc.co.uk/2/hi/south_asia/1550366.stm
(SHORTENED URL: http://tinyurl.com/planatta)

[11] Attack and counter-attack, by David Leigh, Guardian Unlimited, September 26, 2001;
http://www.guardian.co.uk/Archive/Article/0,4273,4264545,00.html
(SHORTENED URL: http://tinyurl.com/countdav)

[12] The 9-11 Commission Report, Final Report of the National Commission on Terrorist Attacks Upon the United States, Official Government Edition, Chapter 10. Wartime, 10.2 Planning for War, pp 330-334;
http://www.gpoaccess.gov/911/

[13] Gary Schroen, Wikipedia Encyclopedia;

CHARLES EDMUND COYOTE

http://en.wikipedia.org/wiki/Gary_Schroen
(SHORTENED URL: http://tinyurl.com/wigars)

[14] *The Osama bin Laden I Know, An Oral History of al Qaeda's Leader, by Peter L. Bergen;* © 2006, Free Press, a Division of Simon & Schuster, Inc., p 317.

[15] *Defense officials: Air operation to last 'several days', CNN.com,* October 7, 2001;
http://archives.cnn.com/2001/US/10/07/ret.attack.pentagon/
(SHORTENED URL: http://tinyurl.com/defofic)

[16] *An Air War Like No Other, by Rebecca Grant, Contributing Editor, AIR FORCE Magazine,* November 2002, Vol. 85, No. 11;
http://www.airforcemagazine.com/MagazineArchive/Pages/2002/November%202002/1102airwar.aspx
(SHORTENED URL: http://tinyurl.com/warlino)

[17]
(a) *The New Yorker: Annals of National Security, King's Ransom: How vulnerable are the Saudi royals? by Seymour M. Hersh,* 22 October 2001;
http://www.newyorker.com/archive/2001/10/22/011022fa_FACT1#ixzz1pPwHQE3Q
(SHORTENED URL: http://tinyurl.com/nasekin)

(b) *Free Republic, FreeRepublic.com;*
http://www.freerepublic.com/focus/f-news/549600/posts
(SHORTENED URL: http://tinyurl.com/ferepub)

[18] *An Air War Like No Other, by Rebecca Grant, Contributing Editor, AIR FORCE Magazine,* November 2002, Vol. 85, No. 11;
http://www.airforcemagazine.com/MagazineArchive/Pages/2002/November%202002/1102airwar.aspx
(SHORTENED URL: http://tinyurl.com/warlinot)

[19] *The New Yorker: Annals of National Security, King's Ransom: How vulnerable are the Saudi royals? by Seymour M. Hersh,* 22 October 2001;
http://www.newyorker.com/archive/2001/10/22/011022fa_FACT1#ixzz1pPwHQE3Q

IRAQ WAR 2003

(SHORTENED URL: http://tinyurl.com/norkann)

[20] The New Yorker: Annals of National Security, King's Ransom: How vulnerable are the Saudi royals? by Seymour M. Hersh, 22 October 2001; http://www.newyorker.com/archive/2001/10/22/011022fa FACT1#ixzz1pPwHQE3Q (SHORTENED URL: http://tinyurl.com/norkan2)

[21] Early June-September 10, 2001: Armed Drone Ready to Hit Bin Laden, but Bureaucratic Concerns Prevent Its Use, History Commons, War in Afghanistan, US Military Strategies and Tactics; http://www.historycommons.org/context.jsp?item=a0601pr edatorready#a0601predatorready (SHORTENED URL: http://tinyurl.com/dronred)

[22] KILLING AL QAEDA: THE NAVY'S ROLE, © 2002 the Lexington Institute; http://www.lexingtoninstitute.org/library/resources/docume nts/NavalStrikeForum/killing-al-qaeda-the-navys-role.pdf (SHORTENED URL: http://tinyurl.com/kilagar)

[23] An Air War Like No Other, by Rebecca Grant, Contributing Editor, AIR FORCE Magazine, November 2002, Vol. 85, No. 11; http://www.airforcemagazine.com/MagazineArchive/Pages/ 2002/November%202002/1102airwar.aspx (SHORTENED URL: http://tinyurl.com/warlino)

[24] BLU-82, digplanet, YouTube; http://www.digplanet.com/wiki/BLU-82 (SHORTENED URL: http://tinyurl.com/digplan)

[25] Predator missile launch test totally successful, by Sue Baker Aeronautical Systems Center Public Affairs, 27 February 2001, WRIGHT-PATTERSON AIR FORCE BASE, Ohio; http://www.fas.org/irp/program/collect/docs/man-ipc-predator-010228.htm (SHORTENED URL: http://tinyurl.com/miletan)

[26] HELLFIRE - Getting the Most from a Lethal Missile

CHARLES EDMUND COYOTE

54

System, by Captain Adam W. Lange, ARMOR Magazine
January-February 1998;
http://www.fas.org/man/dod-
101/sys/missile/docs/1helfire.pdf
(SHORTENED URL: http://tinyurl.com/helgemon)

[27] Overwhelming Force, by Seymour Hersh, The New
Yorker, 22 May 2000, cryptome.org;
http://cryptome.org/mccaffrey-sh.htm
(SHORTENED URL: http://tinyurl.com/cryptom)

[28] BLU-82 Daisy Cutter, YouTube;
http://www.youtube.com/watch?v=_upy14pesi4
(SHORTENED URL: http://tinyurl.com/vakuba)

[29] November 2001 Timeline, September 11 News.com;
http://www.september11news.com/DailyTimelineNov.htm
(SHORTENED URL: http://tinyurl.com/novtile)

[30] An Air War Like No Other, by Rebecca Grant,
Contributing Editor, AIR FORCE Magazine, November 2002,
Vol. 85, No. 11;
http://www.airforce-
magazine.com/MagazineArchive/Pages/2002/November%20
2002/1102airwar.aspx
(SHORTENED URL: http://tinyurl.com/rebgra)

[31] Predator Drones, YouTube;
http://www.youtube.com/watch?v=nMh8Cjnzen8
(SHORTENED URL: http://tinyurl.com/predron)

[32] US Air Force Predator UAV Engages Insurgents In
Afghanistan, YouTube;
http://www.youtube.com/watch?v=IXgGCH36fzM
(SHORTENED URL: http://tinyurl.com/zatobe)

[33] Death of Bin Laden's deputy, by Stephen Grey, The
London Times, November 18, 2001;
http://www.sweetliberty.org/issues/war/remote.htm
(SHORTENED URL: http://tinyurl.com/bindepu)

[34] The Getaway: Questions surround a secret Pakistani
airlift, by Seymour M. Hersh, The New Yorker - Annals of
National Security, 28 January 2002;

http://www.newyorker.com/archive/2002/01/28/020128fa
FACT?currentPage=all
(SHORTENED URL: http://tinyurl.com/getaqu)

[35] *The 'Airlift of Evil', Michael Moran, msnbc.com, 29 November 2001, Council on Foreign Relations Op-Ed;*
http://www.cfr.org/pakistan/airlift-evil/p10301
(SHORTENED URL: http://tinyurl.com/airevil)

[36] *Pakistan: "The Taliban's Godfather"? Documents Detail Years of Pakistani Support for Taliban, Extremists - The National Security Archives, George Washington University;*
http://www.gwu.edu/~nsarchiv/NSAEBB/NSAEBB227/index.htm
(SHORTENED URL: http://tinyurl.com/pagodfa)

[37] *How bin Laden got away, by Philip Smucker, The Christian Science Monitor, March 4, 2002;*
http://www.csmonitor.com/2002/0304/p01s03-wosc.html
(SHORTENED URL: http://tinyurl.com/binaday)

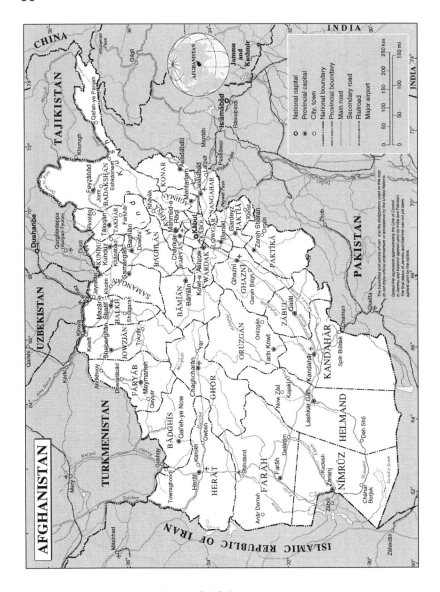

Map of Afghanistan
United Nations Department of Public Information
November 2000

CHAPTER 5

IT'S NOT OUR PRIORITY

I don't know where bin Laden is. I have no idea and really don't care. It's not that important. It's not our priority.

George W Bush, Washington, D.C., March 13, 2002

At Spin Ghar (Pashto for 'White Mountains'), in the 1980s a group of 120 to 130 Arab mujahedeen had once fought off an attacking Soviet force of 2,000 soldiers supported by a fleet of 50 helicopters and MiG fighter jets and an additional 2,000 Afghan communist troops. [1] Known to the West as Tora Bora, the rugged mountains, slopes, and caves, located halfway between the capital cities of Kabul and Islamabad, made a natural fortress. The Spin Ghar range, with the important Khyber Pass on its eastern end, forms a natural border between Pakistan and Afghanistan, the boundary of which is running along the almost unbroken 14,000-foot summit wall that towers over the surrounding hills. If worse came to worse for al-Qaeda, their decades-old encampment afforded an excellent opportunity to escape since they knew the rugged trails to the nearby border with Pakistani, just seven miles away.

It was a place that Osama bin Laden knew well, the area from which he had fought the Soviets at Jaji, the battle that helped build his reputation as a defender of the Muslim world. His sons would later complain of the rugged hikes on which their father would take them to the nearby border with Pakistan while instructing them to learn every rock along the way. He would tell them: *"We never know when war will strike. We must know our way out of the mountains."* [2]

CHARLES EDMUND COYOTE

By November 14, 2001, according to varied reports, somewhere around a thousand al-Qaeda and Chechen fighters, including Osama bin Laden and his mentor Dr. Ayman al Zawahiri, were taking up positions in the caves and bunkers of Tora Bora, about 9,000 feet above sea level. The furious response of the Americans to the 9/11 attacks had not gone well for the jihadists, but they hoped their White Mountain retreat would enable them to turn the tide.

> *The Americans had a plan to invade, but if we are united and believe in Allah, we'll teach them a lesson, the same one we taught the Russians.*
>
> *Osama bin Laden, November 10, 2001* [3]

By the end of November, Kandahar – the birthplace of the Taliban – had had become their last stronghold in Afghanistan. Their leader, Mullah Omar, was now reduced to moving from house to house to avoid airstrikes while calling on his followers to fight to the death. Outside the city, 3,000 fighters led by Hamid Karzai and Gul Agha Sherzai were severing its supply lines. They were joined by additional United Front troops coming in from the north and, later on the 25th of the month, by over twelve hundred US Marines coming up from the Arabian Sea to capture the airport south of the city.

Mullah Omar's forces were losing control under the heavy bombardment and ground pressure. Denied amnesty by the US government, Mullah Omar signaled Karzai he was ready to surrender and then pulled a ruse to slip out of town in a convoy of motorcycles heading north toward the central mountains. [4]

> *I don't want bin Laden and his thugs captured, I want them dead... They must be killed. I want to see photos of their*

heads on pikes. I want bin Laden's head shipped back in a box filled with dry ice. I want to be able to show bin Laden's head to the president. I promised him I would do that.

CIA counterterrorism chief Cofer Black, September 19, 2001 [5]

One of the men sent to Afghanistan with those instructions from Cofer Black was CIA officer Gary Berntsen. He had been helicoptered to Northeastern Afghanistan in late September with a team of 10 operatives and a large trunk crammed with eleven million dollars in $100 dollar bills. He was regarded by his superiors as both *'difficult'* and *'exactly the kind of guy you want to have'*. The trunk full of money enabled him to pay out as needed to carry out the assignment. [6] After the fall of Kabul, Berntsen learned that bin Laden had traveled to the Southeastern Province of Nangarhar in a convoy of several hundred vehicles. [7] Although the US was bombing heavily all around the provincial capital of Jalalabad, somehow the large caravan was overlooked. [8] Berntsen dispatched a team of 8 to find bin Laden.

You had a very small number of Americans inside a province alone and the Afghans that we're working with were Pashtuns, who had previously been allied with the Taliban and with al Qaeda. So, we are paying off warlords to try to get them to switch sides. This is dangerous for my team; I was always concerned about the fact that some of our allies could turn on us at any moment.

Gary Berntsen, January 2006 [9]

Berntsen's team arrived in Jalalabad, then split into two 4-man groups to find bin Laden's force. Following the trail into the mountains, on November 16, they came upon an encampment of about 1,000 al-Qaeda fighters and began to call in air strikes. The Battle of Tora Bora had begun.

While al-Qaeda was readied for the fight, American commanders had their field operatives patch together a mercenary force of around 2,500 Afghan locals to battle on the ground for them. America's hired force in Nangarhar would be led by two warlords: Hazret Ali, the Eastern Shura's *'Minister for Law and Order'* who was paid $250,000 for his help, and Haji Ghamsharik, a major heroin dealer the CIA had recently flown back from exile in France. The two warlords did not like one another, but the Americans let them work their fractious relationship out for themselves.

> *The Americans can bomb all they want, they'll never catch Osama.*
>
> *Maulvi Younus Khalis, Jalalabad patriarch, November 25, 2001* [10]

On November 29, Vice President Dick Cheney told the American people on ABC Television's Primetime Live program that he believed bin Laden was in that location:

> *I think he was equipped to go to ground there. He's got what he believes to be a fairly secure facility. He's got caves underground; it's an area he's familiar with.*
>
> *Vice President Dick Cheney, November 29, 2001*

During late November and early December, while Berntsen's small but growing team used laser designators to target al-Qaeda positions for the incoming bombers, America's Afghan mercenaries crawled over the rugged slopes, firing their weapons aimlessly at bin Laden's best. Come early evening, the muhj hiked down off the mountains and headed home to break their

Ramadan fast and get a good night's sleep. [11] Al-Qaeda then retook most of the ground lost during the day. Eventually, a few old Soviet-era tanks were brought up to blast away at bin Laden's higher-up fortifications, but it was clear to Berntsen and the other Westerners at the scene that the Afghans were not really interested in doing away with the local hero, bin Laden, or their fellow Muslims fighters in al-Qaeda.

During the month-long battle, the number of US and British agents and Special Forces increased from the original four to about five or six dozen. But it wasn't going to be enough to prevent bin Laden's escape, so by late November Berntsen was urgently calling for 600-800 US Army Rangers to be sent in. [12]

> I'd made it clear in my reports that our Afghan allies were hardly anxious to get at al-Qaeda in Tora Bora.
>
> Gary Berntsen, 2005 [13]

By late November significant contingents of US Marines were arriving in theater and some were getting ready for deployment to the Kandahar region under the command of Brigadier General James Mattis. The total number of Marines in the Arabian Sea area now numbered more than 4,000. [14] At an old Soviet airbase in Uzbekistan, a thousand soldiers of the 10th Mountain Division, specially trained to fight in rugged terrains, had been stationed; hundreds of them were already deployed to Bagram Air Base 40 miles north of Kabul. [15] In Washington, CIA Deputy Counter Terrorism Director, Hank Crumpton, was urging General Tommy Franks and other CENTCOM leaders to send the Marines scheduled for Kandahar to Tora Bora instead. Unless the US personally sealed off al-Qaeda's escape routes, Crumpton argued, US would lose the chance to get bin Laden and much of al-Qaeda's senior leadership. [16]

> *I'd sent my request for 800 US Army Rangers and was still waiting for a response. I repeated to anyone at headquarters who would listen: We need Rangers now! The opportunity to get bin Laden and his men is slipping away.*
>
> *Gary Berntsen, CIA Field Commander at Tora Bora* [17]

In Kabul Berntsen was shouting at a US Army general, trying to get him to attend to what was happening on the Tora Bora slopes. The general, however, was more concerned about not offending America's Afghan allies than offending bin Laden. [18] The US Central Command at MacDill Air Force Base, taking its time before responding to Berntsen, now began offering excuses for not sending American troops up to the 9,000 foot high al-Qaeda encampment:

> *'The altitude's too high. It's too cold.' It's this; it's that – makes up a lot of reasons.*
>
> *Gary Berntsen, on PBS Frontline, January 20, 2006* [19]

300 miles away, in Kandahar Province, Marine Corps Brigadier General James Mattis understood what was going on up in the mountains and wanted to do something about it. [20] Freshly landed in Afghanistan with 1,200 of his Marines, General Mattis had a history of expressing too much enthusiasm for his job. He had announced his arrival and seizure of the Kandahar airstrip with the words, *"We have landed and we now own terrain in south Afghanistan"*. This remark had public relations at the Pentagon in a dither over concerns that, even while the US Air Force and Navy were in the process of bombing the Islamic Emirate of Afghanistan

into nonexistence, America ought to not appear overly aggressive. [21] During the first week of December 2001, Mattis aggressively lobbied his superiors, trying to convince them to let him take his Sikorsky CH-53E Helicopters and Expeditionary Forces up to the Af-Pak border to seal the fate of bin Laden. [22]

Cofer Black's deputy, Hank Crumpton, was now taking his case for a significant American ground presence at Tora Bora directly to President Bush and Vice President Cheney. Meeting one-on-one in the White House, Hank Crumpton told them that the 15 square mile area around bin Laden's camp had many tunnels and escape routes and that the Afghan muhj fighting there for the US were *"just not invested in getting bin Laden"*. When the President asked about the troops that Pakistan's President Pervez Musharraf had promised to send to the border passes, Crumpton showed him a map of the rugged expanse on the Pakistani side of the border over which Musharraf's government had only limited control and said that satellite images were showing the promised troops had not arrived and were not likely to do so anytime soon.

The Deputy Director strongly recommended the Marine expeditionary force the US was sending to Kandahar should instead be immediately redirected to Tora Bora. Cheney listened and said nothing. The President asked, *"How bad off are these Afghani forces, really? Are they up to the job?"* Crumpton answered, *"Definitely not, Mr. President. Definitely not."* [23]

No marines were sent.

Centcom finally radioed back to Berntsen that no large numbers of US Forces were going to be sent to Tora

Bora and the warlords already provided would be sufficient for whatever ground fighting was needed. He was also told not to bother headquarters anymore; it had other things to think about. Unknown to the personnel fighting in Afghanistan, Secretary of Defense Donald Rumsfeld had just ordered the Head of US Central Command, General Tommy Franks, to begin intensive planning for the Iraq Invasion.

The CIA continued to press President Bush to send troops to the White Mountains where bin Laden and much of his leadership were located, submitting daily intelligence that warned him the 'the back door is open' for al-Qaeda's escape and that Pakistani army units were not gathering at the nearby border to the south.

Pressured by the Bush administration, Musharraf reassured the White House that troops were on their way. The assurance received high level misgivings within the US government. Bush, Cheney, and Rumsfeld, however, continued to believe President Musharraf would follow through on his guarantee. [24]

Berntsen had been pushing hard for an American troop deployment to catch bin Laden, but suddenly, on December 9, he was pulled off the operation and sent back to Latin America. [25] Berntsen was not happy with the unexpected change of orders and his team threatened to leave with him.

> *It felt as though someone had just thrown a bucket of cold water in my face. I couldn't believe they were doing this in the middle of the most important battle of the war.*
>
> *Gary Berntsen, 2005* [26]

Hands-on responsibility for Tora Bora was passed to

an Army Delta Force major freshly sent in by helicopter with about three dozen Special Force-Delta
commandos, a dozen British Royal navy Special Boat
Service personnel, a dozen US Green Berets, and another
dozen or so CIA and Air Force Signals Operators. Writing
about the experience later under the pen name 'Dalton
Fury', the Delta team commander found he too would
have to adjust to considerable interference from up
the chain of command. He also would be allowed few
options apart from advising Afghan muhj and calling in
air strikes.

Trying to deal with the situation at hand without the
extra troops needed, Major 'Fury' proposed an assault
by using oxygen masks to climb over the 14,000-foot
peaks on their southern rear. He was denied permission. When he requested that hundreds of GATOR
mines be dropped in the mountain escape routes,
NATO's commanders would refuse authorization. When
he closed in on bin Laden's position, with the estimated one thousand fighters protecting him, the
Afghan mercenaries would not help. [27] "How often
does Delta come up with a tactical plan that's dis-
approved by higher headquarters?" CBS News would
later ask 'Fury'. "In my experience, in my five years at
Delta, never before," he responded. [28]

Throughout the battle the bombing was intense.
Between December 4 and 7 alone, the US dropped 350
tons of depleted uranium ordinance. On December 9,
a BLU-82 was dropped, but the use of different
coordinate systems by different branches of service
caused it to miss its target by more than half a mile.
The massive 15,000 lb bomb, however, was immediately followed by three or four B-52 strikes, each

CHARLES EDMUND COYOTE

66

plane dropping twenty-five 500-lb bombs. The BLU-82 bombing injured bin Laden who appeared on a videotape released a few weeks later. Both stunned and depressed, bin Laden did not move the left side of his body the entire 34 minutes of the recording. [29], [30]

Wearied by the constant bombing, al-Qaeda's Arabs began looking for a way out. Having been paid a fortune by the US Government, America's muhj remained reluctant to kill fellow Muslims. As long as the Afghans were being paid to fight the Taliban, they had a common cause with the Americans. Fighting al-Qaeda, however, was a different matter, for al-Qaeda's fighters and bin Laden, in particular, were heroes to the mujahedeen: the latter having abandoned a life of luxury and privilege to share the struggle of the impoverished Afghans against Soviet communism. The bond the wealthy bin Laden had made with the Pashtun people of southern Afghanistan, to whom honor was everything, was not something western money could easily set aside. [31]

The opportunity for the local Afghans to make money from both sides of combatants was also part of the equation of America's slipping opportunity. In the lobby of a Jalalabad hotel on December 3, an American journalist overheard Hazret Ali making a deal to help three members of al-Qaeda escape the battle. [32] Ali and Ghamsharik were quietly beginning negotiations to allow al-Qaeda to slip away to the government-free regions of Northwest Pakistan.

Taking payments from both the CIA and bin Laden's organization, the double-dipping warlords quietly helped the instigators of 9/11 slip away to the safe haven of Pakistan's Tribal Areas, only 7 miles away.

Ali's fighters were very familiar with the area, but, for extra cash, were quite willing to help out with al-Qaeda's escape. Bin Laden's soldiers were better armed and supplied than Ali's and Ghamsharik's, and were willing to fight to their death. Out-positioned by al-Qaeda's entrenched high ground and unimpressed by the strange restraint that disallowed American participation apart from their many bombs, the Afghan militia's reluctance to kill the Arabs and their own festering animosities wore away their already marginal commitment to the fight.

> *We are not interested in killing the Arabs. They are our Muslim brothers.*
>
> *Awul Gul, military commander for Younus Khalis, patriarchal leader of the Jalalabad area*

In November, President Pervez Musharraf had assured the US that he would seal the Afghan border in exchange for almost a billion dollars in economic aid. Following the agreement, Musharraf spent two weeks negotiating with tribal chieftains in the Federally Administered Areas before starting to deploy his soldiers. Finally, on December 10, several thousand Pakistani troops began to take positions along the border. But important areas were still left unguarded, and the CIA started to intercept messages between Pakistani officers signaling them to not hinder the foreign fighters coming in to the area. [33] That same day, Special Ops picked up the voice of Salah Uddin, one of bin Laden's sons, on a radio taken from a dead al-Qaeda fighter: *"Father is trying to break through the siege line."* [34]

On December 12, despite CENTCOM's objections, the warlords enforced a temporary cease-fire, so al-Qaeda could ostensibly attempt to negotiate terms of surrender to the United Nations rather than the US. Haji

Ghamsharik, who had told the Arabs they must either leave or surrender, was a major player in setting up the observance. [35] When Delta Forces decided to disregard the unauthorized truce and move on al-Qaeda by themselves, their Afghan mercenaries drew weapons to hold the small American team at gunpoint. [36] Al-Qaeda said they would get back the next morning with their decision, but, that night, some 800 of bin Laden's fighters, and likely bin Laden himself, took full advantage of the lull and positioned themselves to steal away. [37]

Arabic-speaking members of the US team listen in on captured radios as Osama bin Laden urged his remaining followers to fight to the death. Then, on December 13, they heard the al-Qaeda's leader praying with his supporters about their diminishing fortunes and apologizing for getting them exposed to the almost relentless airstrikes.

> *Our prayers were not answered. Times are dire and bad. We did not get support from the apostate nations who call themselves our Muslim brothers. Things might have been different. I'm sorry for getting you involved in this battle, if you can no longer resist, you may surrender with my blessing.*
>
> > *Osama bin Laden's last radio transmissions at Tora Bora, December 13, 2001 as reported by Delta Force commander 'Dalton Fury'* [38]

Bin Laden's last reported broadcast, seemly pre-recorded, was on December 14. The al-Qaeda leader and his bodyguards had made their escape, helped along the way by many sympathetic Pashtun residents on both sides of the border. [39]

> *The border with Pakistan was the key, but no one paid any attention to it. And there were plenty of landing*

areas for helicopters, had the Americans acted decisively. Al Qaeda escaped right out from under their feet.

Pir Baksh Bardiwal, Eastern Shura Chief of Intelligence [40]

Only three days after Pakistan's troops had arrived at their side of the border, gunmen from a radical Islamist group, which was connected to the Pakistani government's Directorate for Inter-Services Intelligence (ISI), stormed into India's Parliament building in New Delhi. Fourteen people are left dead and India's military raised the possibility of war, leading President Musharraf to redeploy troops intended for the autonomous tribal region to the Indian border instead. [41] As the Battle of Tora Bora came to an end, only 100 stragglers crossing the AfPak border were captured by Pakistani troops. Most of these were soon allowed to escape.

Eventually a videotape emerged that showed bin Laden walking on a mountain trail along the Afghan-Pakistan border toward the end of the Tora Bora battle. In the distance an American bomb explodes. *"We were there last night,"* he says calmly noting the explosion, as he explains to his bodyguards how to dig holes in the ground to safely hide at night. [42]

On December 17, 2001, with 21 prisoners taken and a couple of hundred killed, the US declared victory at Tora Bora. Two months after that, President Bush decided to pull out most of the *special ops* and corresponding CIA units out of Afghanistan in order to begin preparations for the war in Iraq. Comfortably established in the wilderness of northwestern Pakistan, bin Laden and the Taliban began pulling themselves back together.

CHARLES EDMUND COYOTE

Instead of a dramatic and powerful close to the opening chapters of the Bush administration's *'War on Terror'*, the US would now have to fight the *'Long War'*. That seems not to have bothered the White House at all.

> And again, I don't know where he [bin Laden] is. I - I'll repeat what I said. I truly am not that concerned about him.
>
> President George W Bush, March 13, 2002 [43]

CHAPTER 5 REFERENCES

[1] *The Osama bin Laden I Know, An Oral History of al Qaeda's Leader*, by Peter L. Bergen; © 2006, Free Press, a Division of Simon & Schuster, Inc., pp 329-330.

[2] *The Battle for Tora Bora*, by Peter L. Bergen, The New America Foundation; The New Republic, 22 December 2009; http://www.newamerica.net/publications/articles/2009/the_battle_for_tora_bora_25531
(SHORTENED URL: http://tinyurl.com/battora)

[3] *How bin Laden got away*, by Philip Smucker, The Christian Science Monitor, 4 March 2002; http://www.csmonitor.com/2002/0304/p01s03-wosc.html
(SHORTENED URL: http://tinyurl.com/phismuck)

[4] *War in Afghanistan (2001-present)*, Wikipedia; http://en.wikipedia.org/wiki/War_in_Afghanistan_%282001%E2%80%93present%29
(SHORTENED URL: http://tinyurl.com/warawi)

[5] *September 26, 2001: First CIA Operatives Arrive in Afghanistan to Launch War against Taliban*, History Commons; http://www.historycommons.org/context.jsp?item=a092601jawbreakercash#a092601jawbreakercash
(SHORTENED URL: http://tinyurl.com/opara)

[6] Knocking on Osama's Cave Door, by Richard Leiby, washingtonpost.com, February 16, 2006; http://www.washingtonpost.com/wp-dyn/content/article/2006/02/15/AR2006021502717.html (SHORTENED URL: http://tinyurl.com/knockosa)

[7] How bin Laden got away, by Philip Smucker, The Christian Science Monitor, 4 March 2002; http://www.csmonitor.com/2002/0304/p01s03-wosc.html (SHORTENED URL: http://tinyurl.com/binlapi)

[8] November 13, 2001: Al-Qaeda Convoy Flees to Tora Bora; US Fails to Attack, History Commons; http://www.historycommons.org/context.jsp?item=a111401 convoyflees#a111401convoyflees (SHORTENED URL: http://tinyurl.com/fletobo)

[9] 'Jawbreaker'; The Hunt for Bin Laden, National Public Radio, Host Steve Inskeep, 19 January 2006; http://www.npr.org/templates/story/story.php?storyId=516 2925 (SHORTENED URL: http://tinyurl.com/jawhost)

[10] How bin Laden got away, by Philip Smucker, The Christian Science Monitor, 4 March 2002; http://www.csmonitor.com/2002/0304/p01s03-wosc.html (SHORTENED URL: http://tinyurl.com/philsmu)

[11] HOW BIN LADEN GOT AWAY, by Stephen Lynch, NEW YORK POST, 4 October 2008; http://www.nypost.com/seven/10042008/news/worldnews/ how_bin_laden_got_away_132109.htm (SHORTENED URL: http://tinyurl.com/stely)

[12] The Dark Side, FRONTLINE Interviews Gary Berntsen, 20 January 2006; http://www.pbs.org/wgbh/pages/frontline/darkside/intervie ws/berntsen.html (SHORTENED URL: http://tinyurl.com/froga)

[13] November 26, 2001: US Marines Land in Kandahar instead of Tora Bora, History Commons; http://www.historycommons.org/context.jsp?item=a112601

CHARLES EDMUND COYOTE

marineskandahar#a112601marineskandahar
(SHORTENED URL: http://tinyurl.com/usmala)

[14] Campaign Chronologies of the United States Marine
Corps, Global War on Terrorism: 2001-2008, United States
Marine Corps, History Division;
http://www.tecom.usmc.mil/HD/Chronologies/Campaign/G
WOT_2001-2008.htm
(SHORTENED URL: http://tinyurl.com/cobano)

[15] The Battle for Tora Bora, by Peter L. Bergen, The New
America Foundation; The New Republic, 22 December 2009;
http://www.newamerica.net/publications/articles/2009/the_
battle_for_tora_bora_25531
(SHORTENED URL: http://tinyurl.com/babeber)

[16] The One Percent Doctrine: Deep Inside America's
Pursuit of Its Enemies Since 9/11, Ron Suskind, 2006, p 58;
http://www.amazon.com/exec/obidos/ASIN/0743271092/ce
nterforcoop-20
(SHORTENED URL: http://tinyurl.com/onedep)

[17] Flight to Tora Bora, Other Voices, Same Conclusion;
Tora Bora Revisited: How We Failed To Get Bin Laden And
Why It Matters Today, A Report To Members Of The
Committee On Foreign Relations United States Senate, 30
November 2009, GlobalSecurity.org;
http://www.globalsecurity.org/military/library/congress/200
9_rpt/091130_tora-bora_ubl-1c.htm
(SHORTENED URL: http://tinyurl.com/torarev)

[18] The Attack on Bin Laden and Al Qaeda: A Personal
Account by the CIA's Key Field Commander, by Gary
Berntsen with Ralph Pezzullo, 2005, pp 296-297;
http://www.amazon.com/exec/obidos/ASIN/0307237400/ce
nterforcoop-20
(SHORTENED URL: http://tinyurl.com/attabin)

[19] The Dark Side, FRONTLINE Interviews by Gary
Berntsen, 20 January 2006;
http://www.pbs.org/wgbh/pages/frontline/darkside/intervie
ws/berntsen.html
(SHORTENED URL: http://tinyurl.com/darsiga)

IRAQ WAR 2003

[20] Lost at Tora Bora, by Mary Anne Weaver, The New York Times, September 11, 2005; http://www.nytimes.com/2005/09/11/magazine/11TORABORA.html?_r=1&oref=slogin&...&oref=slogin (SHORTENED URL: http://tinyurl.com/losbora)

[21] Marines wanted to surround Tora Bora, TOPDOG08.COM; http://www.topdog08.com/2005/10/marines_wanted.html (SHORTENED URL: http://tinyurl.com/maboto)

[22] The Battle for Tora Bora, by Peter L. Bergen, The New America Foundation; The New Republic, 22 December 2009; http://www.newamerica.net/publications/articles/2009/the_battle_for_tora_bora_25531 (SHORTENED URL: http://tinyurl.com/amifod)

[23] Late November 2001: CIA Advises Bush and Cheney That Allies Won't Help Trap Bin Laden, but No Action Is Taken, History Commons; http://www.historycommons.org/context.jsp?item=alate1101allieswonthelp#alate1101allieswonthelp (SHORTENED URL: http://tinyurl.com/alnohe)

[24] Early December 2001: CIA Again Warns Bush 'Back Door Is Open' for Bin Laden to Escape Tora Bora, History Commons; http://www.historycommons.org/context.jsp?item=a1201backdooropen#a1201backdooropen (SHORTENED URL: http://tinyurl.com/ciabil)

[25] The Dark Side, FRONTLINE Interviews Gary Berntsen, 20 January 2006; http://www.pbs.org/wgbh/pages/frontline/darkside/interviews/berntsen.html (SHORTENED URL: http://tinyurl.com/darbest)

[26] December 9, 2001: CIA's Bin Laden Unit Boss Becomes New Chief of CIA's Kabul Station during Tora Bora Battle, History Commons; http://www.historycommons.org/context.jsp?item=a120901richbkabul&scale=0#a120901richbkabul (SHORTENED URL: http://tinyurl.com/debinla)

CHARLES EDMUND COYOTE

[27] *Kill Bin Laden: A Delta Force Commander's Account of the Hunt for the World's Most Wanted Man, by Dalton Fury; http://www.amazon.com/Kill-Bin-Laden-Commanders-Account/dp/0312547412/ref=la_B001J93AUS_1_3?ie=UTF8 &qid=1343443951&sr=1-3 (SHORTENED URL: http://tinyurl.com/delfoco)*

[28] *Kill Bin Laden, CBS News 60 Minutes, 12 July 2009; http://www.cbsnews.com/video/watch/?id=5153449n (SHORTENED URL: http://tinyurl.com/mijul)*

[29] *Bin Laden's great escape: How the world's most wanted man made fools of elite troops who'd trapped him in his mountain lair, by Guy Walters, Mail Online, 30 April 2011; http://www.dailymail.co.uk/news/article-1382011/Bin-Ladens-great-escape-How-worlds-wanted-man-fools-elite-troops-whod-trapped-mountain-lair.html#ixzz20fh9bKm6 (SHORTENED URL: http://tinyurl.com/damabin)*

[30] *The Osama bin Laden I Know, An Oral History of al Qaeda's Leader, by Peter L. Bergen; © 2006, Free Press, a Division of Simon & Schuster, Inc., p 335.*

[31] *Bush pledges to get bin Laden, dead or alive, USATODAY.com, 12/14/2001; http://www.usatoday.com/news/sept11/2001/12/14/bush-binladen.htm (SHORTENED URL: http://tinyurl.com/pegebi)*

[32] *How bin Laden got away, by Philip Smucker, The Christian Science Monitor, 4 March 2002; http://www.csmonitor.com/2002/0304/p01s03-wosc.html (SHORTENED URL: http://tinyurl.com/philsmuc)*

[33] *December 10, 2001: Pakistani Troops Start to Guard Parts of Tora Bora Border but Then Withdraw, History Commons; http://www.historycommons.org/context.jsp?item=a121001 paktroops#a121001paktroops (SHORTENED URL: http://tinyurl.com/depakis)*

[34] *HOW BIN LADEN GOT AWAY, by Stephen Lynch, NEW*

YORK POST, 4 October 2008;
http://www.nypost.com/seven/10042008/news/worldnews/
how_bin_laden_got_away_132109.htm
(SHORTENED URL: http://tinyurl.com/binstely)

[35] How bin Laden got away, by Philip Smucker, The
Christian Science Monitor, March 4, 2002;
http://www.csmonitor.com/2002/0304/p01s03-wosc.html
(SHORTENED URL: http://tinyurl.com/binladil)

[36] Kill Bin Laden, CBS News 60 Minutes, 12 July 2009;
http://www.cbsnews.com/video/watch/?id=5153449n
(SHORTENED URL: http://tinyurl.com/bilanew)

[37] The Battle for Tora Bora, by Peter L. Bergen, The New
America Foundation; The New Republic, 22 December 2009;
http://www.newamerica.net/publications/articles/2009/the_
battle_for_tora_bora_25531
(SHORTENED URL: http://tinyurl.com/amfoda)

[38] Elite Officer Recalls Bin Laden Hunt, CBS News 60
Minutes, 13 July 2009;
http://www.cbsnews.com/stories/1998/07/08/60minutes/m
ain4494937.shtml?tag=cbsnewsSidebarArea.0
(SHORTENED URL: http://tinyurl.com/elrica)

[39] Lost at Tora Bora, by Mary Anne Weaver, The New
York Times, September 11, 2005;
http://www.nytimes.com/2005/09/11/magazine/11TORABO
RA.html?_r=1&oref=slogin&...&oref=slogin
(SHORTENED URL: http://tinyurl.com/lotobora)

[40] How bin Laden got away, by Philip Smucker, The
Christian Science Monitor, March 4, 2002;
http://www.csmonitor.com/2002/0304/p01s03-wosc.html
(SHORTENED URL: http://tinyurl.com/3fxra)

[41] December 13, 2001: ISI-Connected Militants Attack
Indian Parliament, History Commons;
http://www.historycommons.org/context.jsp?item=a121301
indianparliament#a121301indianparliament
(SHORTENED URL: http://tinyurl.com/isicomi)

[42] Bin Laden Trail 'Stone Cold', by Dana Priest and Ann

Scott Tyson, The Washington Post, 10 September 2006;
http://www.washingtonpost.com/wp-
dyn/content/article/2006/09/09/AR2006090901105_pf.html
(SHORTENED URL: http://tinyurl.com/toneco)

[43] How Bush blew it in Tora Bora, by Pepe Escobar, Asia
Times Online, October 27, 2004;
http://atimes.com/atimes/Central_Asia/FJ27Ag02.html
(SHORTENED URL: http://tinyurl.com/petili)

CHAPTER 6

YOU REALLY SNATCHED DEFEAT

And so, General, I want to thank you for your service. And I appreciate the fact that you really snatched defeat out of the jaws of those who are trying to defeat us in Iraq.

George W. Bush, Washington, D.C., March 3, 2008

With the 9/11 attacks, al-Qaeda sought to provoke the United States into mounting a large and clumsy military retaliation likely to alienate and destabilize the Middle East and send the price of oil skyrocketing. The long years and high costs associated with operating a modern military against a local and inexpensive insurgency would surely drain the US economy and contribute to its bankruptcy much as had happened with the Soviet Union two decades before.

The Bush administration was happy to oblige, but it almost did not happen. The plans Cofer Black and CIA's Counterterrorism Center had been developing to break bin Laden in his sanctuaries proved to be almost devastating to his organization. The CIA's fast moving, inexpensive, and overwhelming counterattack had almost destroyed bin Laden and his organization within months of 9/11.

In December 2001, injured and dispirited, bin Laden contemplated his transience and prepared his will telling his children:

I have chosen a road fraught with dangers and for this sake suffered from hardships, embitterment, betrayal, and treachery. I advise you not to work with al Qaeda and the Front.

CHARLES EDMUND COYOTE

Osama bin Laden, 14 December 2001 [1]

The collapse of the Taliban government had come with shocking swiftness. Even Tora Bora was unable to provide refuge for bin Laden, Zawahiri, and their cadre of fighters. Two months after al-Qaeda had finally succeeded in drawing the US out, they were almost done in. Such an ending would have been a stunning lesson for any others who might consider offending Pax Americana.

But the Bush administration had other priorities, and it would not be long until bin Laden got what he wanted. After a narrow brush with annihilation, al-Qaeda would soon be able to operate where it had never had gone before and would even, for a brief time, be seen by millions throughout the Muslim world as a heroic defender of their homelands. President Bush's lack of resolve – saying first that he was determined to bring bin Laden to justice, then, a few months later that he really didn't care – represented an agenda only portions of which would be played out in the public eye in the next few months and years. The Bush administration was turning its attention to Iraq. By 2005, the CIA's Bin Laden Unit (Bin Laden Issue Station or Alec Station), which had been dedicated to tracking Osama bin Laden since 1996, would no longer exist.

The acts of devastation committed on 9/11 inflicted greater damage on American soil than any foreign power had ever managed to accomplish previously. If capturing bin Laden, the man behind those acts, was not important to the President, then what was? Why would the United States, having come so close to grasping those who had attacked its symbols of strength by murdering thousands of its citizens along with hundreds of foreign guests, suddenly held back those trying to deliver its justice? If America had allowed its warriors to complete the job done in Afghanistan on the slopes of Tora Bora, it would have been free to return to the peace and prosperity it had known during the twentieth century's closing decade. Why trade swift victory for 'The Long War'?

> Thus, though we have heard of stupid haste in war, cleverness has never been seen associated with long delays. In all history, there is no instance of a country having benefited from prolonged warfare. Only one who knows the disastrous effects of a long war can realize the supreme importance of rapidity in bring it to a close. It is only one who is thoroughly acquainted with the evils of war who can thoroughly understand the profitable way of carrying it on.
>
> Sun Tzu, The Art of War [2]

The Bush Administration began to shift intelligence resources and Special Forces teams toward Iraq and Saddam Hussein. Instead of keeping the focus on bin Laden – founder and chief of an organization that had demonstrated the capacity to murder thousands of innocent civilians and shown the intent to acquire the weapons of mass destruction that would enable it to kill many more – the Bush Administration began to shift Intelligence resources and Special Forces teams toward a nation and a leader that posed no threat to the American people, unlike the clear intent of al-Qaeda. American military forces would now be divided: one to take on the Islamists who had bloodied our country's nose, and another to take on an enemy of those Islamists.

The American leaders that emerged from the fires of 9/11 chose to disregard the good will of most of the

CHARLES EDMUND COYOTE

rest of the world and began to insist that other cultures and nations adopt America's agendas and modes of government. Richard Clarke, chief counterterrorism adviser to the National Security Council under both Presidents Bill Clinton and George W. Bush, was aghast at the new strategy. Neither he, nor the intelligence community he worked with knew of any relationship between the secular dictatorship of Saddam Hussein and the religious radicals who had carried out the 9/11 attacks. In the eyes of Islamists such as bin Laden, Saddam Hussein's secular Ba'athists were unholy, because they advocated literacy, employment opportunities and greater equality for the women of Iraq, and favored maintaining a climate of religious freedom, making Iraq the only country in the Persian Gulf not ruled by Sharia Law.

Although Vice President Dick Cheney would menacingly tell the American people that bin Laden and Saddam Hussein were working together to destroy America, this was simply not the case. Considerable documentation exists to show bin Laden's dislike of Saddam even before he invaded Kuwait in 1990. In his book, *The Osama bin Laden I know* (2006), a collection of perspectives on the al-Qaeda leader from people who had met him, counterterrorist expert Peter Bergen includes sources personally familiar with bin Laden's animosity for Hussein.

On page 112, Prince Turki, the former Chief of Saudi Intelligence and Ambassador to the United States, in a November 7, 2001 interview for the newspaper, *Arab News*, discusses bin Laden's desire to confront Saddam Hussein:

> [After Iraq's invasion of Kuwait in August 1990] it was

not [bin Laden] alone who offered their services [for jihad against Saddam Hussein]. Other personalities in the Arab world did the same. They wanted to show that there are Arabs capable of fighting and defeating Saddam.

> *Prince Turki bin Faisal Al Saud, former Chief of Saudi Intelligence, 7 November 2001* [3]

On the same page, Abu Jandal, bin Laden's former chief bodyguard, during an interview for the *Al Quds al Arabi* newspaper, talked about bin Laden's hostility to Saddam:

His intentions were geared toward ending the Iraqi occupation of Kuwait and rescuing the Iraqi people from the domination of the Ba'th Party (Saddam Hussein's nationalist-socialist organization). Sheikh Osama bin Laden was dreaming of this.

> *Nasir Ahmad Nasir al-Bahri (Abu Jandal) Osama bin Laden's former bodyguard* [4]

On page 170 of Peter Bergen's book, Abdel Bari Atwan, the editor of *Al Quds al Arabi*, discussing his November 1996 interview of Osama bin Laden, said:

He didn't like him and he told me he wanted to kick him out of Iraq, as he considered, the Ba'ath (Iraqi socialist) regime [to be an] atheist regime. He considered Saddam Hussein as an atheist, and he hates an atheist.

> *Abdel al-Bari Atwan, editor-in-chief of London-based pan-Arab newspaper Al-Quds Al-Arabi* [5]

The old aphorism that *'the enemy of my enemy is my friend'*, was not one George W. Bush seemed interested in heeding. Whereas the administration of President Ronald Reagan, as with previous administrations, had found Saddam Hussein to be useful, George Bush, Jr., who liked to think of himself as

Reagan's political heir, would ignore Reagan's real-politik approach to conserving American resources in the Middle East, and choose instead to place a profligate burden on American blood and treasure. Of this misstep, Ronald Reagan's former National Security Agency Director, Lieutenant General William Odom, would say:

> *The Iraq War may turn out to be the greatest strategic disaster in American history. In a mere 18 months we went from unprecedented levels of support after 9-11... to being one of the most hated countries. Turkey used to be one of strongest pro-US regimes, now we're so unpopular, there's a movie playing there-Metal Storm, about a war between US and Turkey. In addition to producing faulty intel and ties to Al Qaida, Bush made preposterous claim that toppling Saddam would open the way for liberal democracy in a very short time... Misunderstanding the character of American power, he dismissed the allies as a nuisance and failed to get the UN Security Council's sanction...*
>
> *Lieutenant General William E. Odom, April 7, 2006* [6]

How did it come about?

Saddam Hussein Abd al-Majid al-Tikriti was born April 28, 1937, to a family of shepherds living about 8 miles from the Central North Iraqi town of Tikrit. Five months before Saddam was born, his father passed away from cancer. Only a few months later, his 12 year old brother lost his life to the disease. Saddam's mother was so traumatized by the losses that she tried to abort Saddam and kill herself. Rescued from these actions by a Jewish family, his mother gave him the name 'Saddam' at his birth, which means in Arabic 'He who confronts'. She wanted nothing to do with her newborn infant, however, and sent him away to Baghdad to stay with the family of her brother, Khairallah

Talfah, a Ba'ath Party official and author of a widely circulated anti-Iranian, anti-Jewish tract entitled: *'Three Whom God Should Not Have Created: Persians, Jews, and Flies.'* [7]

> *Of all of the leaders I've profiled, his background is assuredly the most traumatic. His troubles can really be traced back to the womb.*
>
> > Dr. Jerrold M. Post, founder of the Central Intelligence Agency's Center for the Analysis of Personality and Political Behavior [8]

At the age of three, Saddam Hussein reunited with his mother, after her remarriage to Ibrahim al-Hassan, a distant relative. His new stepfather, however, physically and psychologically abused him, so at the age of nine Saddam escaped back to the home of his uncle, Khairallah.

> *So that would produce in psychoanalytic terms what we call 'the wounded self'. Most people with that kind of background would be highly ineffective as adults and be faltering, insecure human beings. But there is an alternative path that a minority of wounded selves take: 'malignant narcissism'.*
>
> > Dr. Jerrold M. Post, founder of the CIA's Center for the Analysis of Personality and Political Behavior [9]

Malignant narcissism is a personality disorder driven by an extraordinary need for admiration, a lack of empathy for other people, and an encompassing pattern of grandiosity. The narcissist is preoccupied with power and prestige and is ensnarled by traits of paranoia and self-centeredness. [10] The absence of conscience, the psychological need for power, and a distorted sense of importance (grandiosity) are salient characteristics. The malignant narcissist lacks beha-

CHARLES EDMUND COYOTE

vioral regulation and manifests joyful cruelty. Psychology regards malignant narcissism as part of a pathology spectrum ranging from the merely irritating narcissistic personality disorder to the psychopath's moral insanity and inability to reform. [11]

Dr. Jerrold Post, quoted above, spent more than 20 years profiling world leaders for the Central Intelligence Agency. Dr. Post has pointed out that Saddam Hussein - through the encouragement of his uncle Khairallah Talfah - was able to rise out of his difficult childhood to become a *'ruthless political calculator'* instead of the helpless, faltering adult the difficult circumstances of his early years might have led him to become. [12]

Khairallah's outlook on life became the basis of Saddam's political views and his oldest daughter, Sajida, became Saddam's first wife. Saddam studied at an Iraqi law school for three years in his late teens. Dropping out at the age of twenty, he joined the revolutionary pan-Arab Ba'ath Party and supported himself as a secondary school teacher.

In the 1950s, the Middle East seethed with revolutionary sentiment as progressives and socialists assailed traditional colonial bureaucrats and monarchists, along with landowners, wealthy mechants, and tribal chiefs. The instability within Iraq once led CIA Director Allan Dulles to describe it as *"the most dangerous spot in the world."* In this environment, Saddam honed his survival skills, profoundly influenced by the pan-Arab nationalism of Egypt's Gamal Abdel Nasser and the colonel's stand against the English and French during the Suez Crisis of 1956. In July 1958, Iraqi army officers, led by General Abdul

Karim Qassim, overthrew the British installed Hashe-
mite monarchy of King Faisal II in what has been described as *"a horrible orgy of bloodshed."* [13]

During his 40 years in politics, Saddam often worked
with American interests, becoming first involved with
US intelligence in 1959 as part of an unsuccessful CIA
plot to assassinate General Abdul Qasim. [14] Qasim,
had become Prime Minister of Iraq following the coup,
but had upset Washington by taking Iraq out of the
anti-Soviet Baghdad Pact, the Middle East equivalent
of NATO.

Iraq was considered very important to the West during
the Cold War and had become the headquarters of the
anti-Soviet Baghdad Pact of Middle Eastern nations
after it was formed in 1955. Prime Minister Qasim's
sudden decision to withdraw from the anti-communist
league four years later dismayed Washington. The US
government determined to put an end to Qasim who
had begun to purchase military arms from the Soviet
Union and advance communists into positions of power
in the Iraqi government.

Attempting to undermine Qasim, the CIA allied itself
with the anti-communist Baath Party and Saddam
Hussein, then only 22 years of age, became part of
the US plot to get rid of the General. Saddam's handler
was an Iraqi dentist who worked for both the CIA and
Egyptian intelligence. To keep an eye on the Prime
Minister's comings and goings, he put young Saddam
in an apartment on Baghdad's al-Rashid Street directly
opposite Qasim's office in the Iraqi Ministry of Defense.
In October 1959, a badly executed assassination attempt was carried out against Qasim in which Saddam
lost his nerve and began firing too soon, killing the

CHARLES EDMUND COYOTE

driver of Qasim's car, but only wounding the Prime Minister. Another member of the team had brought bullets that did not fit his gun, while a third one wrestled with a hand grenade that had gotten stuck in the lining of his coat. [15]

Saddam, with his leg grazed by the bullet of another member of the bungling assassins, was able to escape with the help of CIA and Egyptian intelligence. He fled first to Tikrit, where he hid in the same foxhole where the US forces found him in December 2003, and from there to Syria. From Syria he was transferred by Egyptian agents to Beirut, Lebanon. In Beirut, the CIA paid for his apartment, put him through brief training, and then helped him get to Cairo, Egypt, where he spent the next four years. [16]

In Cairo, Saddam settled in an apartment in an upper class neighborhood, spending his time associating with the local Ba'ath Party student cell and playing dominos in the Indiana Café, watched over by CIA and Egyptian intelligence agents. During those years, Saddam made frequent visits to the American Embassy, meeting with resident CIA specialists. A former US government official, who knew Saddam at that time, said he was *"...known as having no class. He was a thug – a cut-throat."* [17]

In February 1963, the Ba'ath Party finally succeeded in killing Qasim. The unexpected coup took the CIA by surprise, but the agency quickly took advantage of the situation, making sure the Ba'athists were given the names of anyone even suspected of Marxist associations. They began hunting down and jailing Iraq's communists many of whom were interrogated and killed in the *Qasr al-Nehayat*, the *'Palace of the End'*, an

incarceration facility directly under Saddam Hussein'
supervision. [18]

> We were frankly glad to be rid of them. You ask that they
> get a fair trial? You have to get kidding. This was serious
> business.
>
> Former senior US State Department official speaking
> anonymously about the 1963 mass killings of Iraq's
> communists [19]

CHAPTER 6 REFERENCES

[1] The Osama bin Laden I Know, An Oral History of al
Qaeda's Leader, by Peter L. Bergen; © 2006, Free Press, a
Division of Simon & Schuster, Inc., p 384.

[2] Sun Tzu, The Art of War, Edited by James Clavell, p 13,
Dell Publishing a division of Bantam Doubleday Dell
Publishing Group, Inc, 1540 Broadway New York, New York,
Copyright © 1983 by James Clavell.

[3] The Osama bin Laden I Know, An Oral History of al
Qaeda's Leader, by Peter L. Bergen; © 2006, Free Press, a
Division of Simon & Schuster, Inc.

[4] The Osama bin Laden I Know, An Oral History of al
Qaeda's Leader, by Peter L. Bergen; © 2006, Free Press, a
Division of Simon & Schuster, Inc.

[5] The Osama bin Laden I Know, An Oral History of al
Qaeda's Leader, by Peter L. Bergen; © 2006, Free Press, a
Division of Simon & Schuster, Inc.

[6] NSA DIRECTOR ODOM DISSECTS IRAQ BLUNDERS, by
Michael Hammerschlag, HAMMERNEWS, April 8, 2006;
http://hammernews.com/odomspeech.htm
(SHORTENED URL: http://tinyurl.com/hamodo)

[7] He dreamed of glory but dealt out only despair, by
David Blair, The Telegraph, 18 March 2003;

http://www.telegraph.co.uk/news/1424980/He-dreamed-of-glory-but-dealt-out-only-despair.html?pageNum=1
(SHORTENED URL: http://tinyurl.com/repori)

[8] Was a Tyrant Prefigured by Baby Saddam? by Elisabeth Bumiller, The New York Times, May 15, 2004;
http://www.nytimes.com/2004/05/15/arts/15POST.html?pagewanted=all
(SHORTENED URL: http://tinyurl.com/tibasa)

[9] Was a Tyrant Prefigured by Baby Saddam? by Elisabeth Bumiller, The New York Times, May 15, 2004;
http://www.wehaitians.com/was%20a%20tyrant%20prefigured%20by%20baby%20saddam.html
(SHORTENED URL: http://tinyurl.com/elisabu)

[10] Saddam Hussein of Iraq: A Political Psychology Profile, Jerrold M. Post, M.D., Case Western Reserve University School of Law;
http://law.cwru.edu/saddamtrial/documents/saddam_hussein_political_psychology_profile.pdf
(SHORTENED URL: http://tinyurl.com/sahuraq)

[11] Narcissistic Personality Disorder - Who is a Malignant Narcissist? Sam Vaknin, Ph.D., © 2009 EzineArticles.com;
http://ezinearticles.com/?Narcissistic-Personality-Disorder---Who-is-a-Malignant-Narcissist?&id=32647
(SHORTENED URL: http://tinyurl.com/narpedis)

[12] "SADDAM IS IRAQ: IRAQ IS SADDAM", by Jerrold M. Post, M.D. and Amatzia Baram, Ph.D.; The Counterproliferation Papers, Future Warfare Series No. 17; USAF Counterproliferation Center, Air University, Maxwell Air Force Base, Alabama; November 2002;
http://www.au.af.mil/au/awc/awcgate/cpc-pubs/postbaram.pdf
(SHORTENED URL: http://tinyurl.com/saraqi)

[13] Saddam Key in Early CIA Plot, upi.com, April 10, 2003, © 2003 by United Press International;
http://www.upi.com/Business_News/Security-Industry/2003/04/10/Exclusive-Saddam-key-in-early-CIA-

plot/UPI-65571050017416/ l
(SHORTENED URL: http://tinyurl.com/sakemi)

[14] Saddam Key in Early CIA Plot, by Richard Sale, United Press International, April 10, 2003;
http://www.globalpolicy.org/security/issues/iraq/history/20 03/0410saddam.htm
(SHORTENED URL: http://tinyurl.com/saripa)

[15] Saddam Key in Early CIA Plot, upi.com; April 10, 2003; Copyright 2003 by United Press International;
http://www.upi.com/Business_News/Security-Industry/2003/04/10/Exclusive-Saddam-key-in-early-CIA-plot/UPI-65571050017416/ l
(SHORTENED URL: http://tinyurl.com/sakemi)

[16] A Tyrant 40 Years in the Making, by Roger Morris, New York Times, March 14, 2003;
http://query.nytimes.com/gst/fullpage.html?res=9505EFDB 103EF937A25750C0A9659C8B63&scp=1&sq=sadaam%20m orris&st=cse
(SHORTENED URL: http://tinyurl.com/timaro)

[17] Saddam Key in Early CIA Plot, by Richard Sale, United Press International, April 10, 2003;
http://www.globalpolicy.org/security/issues/iraq/history/20 03/0410saddam.htm
(SHORTENED URL: http://tinyurl.com/sakepo)

[18] Saddam Key in Early CIA Plot, by Richard Sale, United Press International, April 10, 2003;
http://www.globalpolicy.org/security/issues/iraq/history/20 03/0410saddam.htm
(SHORTENED URL: http://tinyurl.com/sadaki)

[19] Saddam Key in Early CIA Plot, upi.com, April 10, 2003, © 2003 by United Press International;
http://www.upi.com/Business_News/Security-Industry/2003/04/10/Exclusive-Saddam-key-in-early-CIA-plot/UPI-65571050017416/ l
(SHORTENED URL: http://tinyurl.com/sakemi)

CHAPTER 7

FREE NATIONS DON'T DEVELOP WMD

See, free nations are peaceful nations. Free nations don't attack each other. Free nations don't develop weapons of mass destruction.

George W. Bush, Milwaukee, Wisconsin, October3, 2003

In September 1980, Iraq's Ba'athist Party leader, Saddam Hussein, initiated a war with Iran over increasing concerns that the leaders of Iran's 1979 Revolution were trying to win over Iraq's majority Shia population. The United States of America, frustrated and angry over the ongoing hostage crises at the US embassy in Tehran, quietly encouraged Saddam to attack. [1] Since their overthrow of the Shah the previous year, Iran's new Shia leaders had been encouraging Iraq's 60 percent Shia population to break away from Baghdad's control and join their revolution. Saddam Hussein regarded these activities as a violation of the 1975 Algiers Peace Accord under which Iraq had given Iran access to the important Shatt al-Arab waterway to the Persian Gulf in exchange for Iran's promise not to meddle in Iraq's internal affairs. [2]

Saddam launched the Iran-Iraq War with a major campaign near the city of Basrah designed to recapture the Shatt al-Arab waterway. Despite its recent revolution, Iran, a nation three times the size of Iraq, proved more resilient than anticipated, and Saddam's attack became a significant factor in uniting the disparate Iranian peoples behind their new rulers. Within 6 months Saddam's advance was stalled, and in another year his troops were forced to retreat when Iran struck back with massive suicidal human wave attacks. The two countries then spent most of the 1980s fighting a seesaw war that became one of the 20th Century's bloodiest conflicts.

By 1982, the situation for Iraq was dire. US President Ronald Reagan decided America could not afford to let Iran's militant Shia gain control over the oil-rich southern portion of Iraq. Over the objections of both Congress and Secretary of State Alexander Haig, the White House removed Iraq from the State Department's list of terrorist-supporting nations. The United States began backing Hussein with significant amounts of economic and military aid, as well as intelligence and material for the development of biological and chemical weapons of mass destruction [WMDs]. A November 1983 National Security Directive stated that the United States would do *"whatever was necessary and legal"* to prevent Iraq from losing the war with Iran. [3] The massive provision to Saddam Hussein of the knowledge and material needed for the production of WMDs was illegal under American export policy and was carried out largely with the knowledge of only a few officials in the US government.

At the beginning of the war, Iraq was equipped mostly with weapons purchased from the Soviet Union and its Warsaw bloc countries. But as the conflict continued, Iraq bought tens of billions of dollars of additional weapons not only from the Soviet Union, but also from the People's Republic of China, France, India, Israel, North Korea, the United Kingdom, and the United States, as well as other sources. [4] Weapons purchased from France, the UK, and the US included equipment and facilities for making biological and chemical WMDs and for undertaking initial steps toward the development of nuclear weapons. As noted by US Senator Don Riegle:

> *The executive branch of our government approved 771 different export licenses for sale of dual-use technology to Iraq. I think it's a devastating record.*
>
> > *Don Riegle, Chairman of the Senate Committee on Banking, Housing and Urban Affairs with Respect to Export Administration; 103d Congress, 25 May 1994* [5]

The effort the US Government was making to facilitate Iraq's acquisition of those weapons was highly compartmentalized and restricted to a very few on a *'need to know'* basis only. [6] Even the President was not informed of the particulars of the support he had authorized for the Iraqi regime. Though the source of Iraq's WMDs was not obvious to the world, a US State Department memorandum confirmed Iraqi use of chemical weapons as early as 1982. [7]

Donald Rumsfeld, who had been Secretary of Defense in the Ford Administration, served as an envoy for the Reagan Administration's developing relationship with Saddam. At the time, Rumsfeld was the Chairman of G.D. Searle & Company, a multinational pharmaceutical corporation involved in the development and marketing of such products as Aspartame, Dramamine, and Metamucil. During his career in private industry, Rumsfeld continued to serve on federal commissions and his high level contacts in the government made him very useful to both the Reagan White House and G.D. Searle. [8] Rumsfeld visited with President Saddam Hussein and Foreign Minister Tariq Aziz in Baghdad in December 1983 and March 1984 – at a time when Iraq was using chemical weapons on an almost daily basis. The well-known video photograph was taken during those meetings.

Video of Donald Rumsfeld in Iraq meeting with Saddam Hussein in December, 1983 [9]

The first meeting between Donald Rumsfeld and Saddam Hussein took place on the same day the UN released a report on Iraq's use of mustard gas and tabun nerve agent against Iranian troops. The US government, as indicated in declassified documents, knew that Iraq had begun using chemical WMDs almost daily in its conflict with Iran. [10] Nevertheless American diplomats pronounced themselves satisfied with Iraq and suggested that normal diplomatic ties had been established in all but name. [11]

The American firm Alcolac International was found to be supplying to both Iraq and Iran the mustard-gas precursor, thiodiglycol. This was in violation of export laws, since the Department of Justice served a 1988

CHARLES EDMUND COYOTE

indictment on the company for exports only to Iran. According to an Iraqi report filed with the UN following the 1991 Persian Gulf War, the knowledge and material enabling it to develop chemical WMDs came principally from France, the People's Republic of China, the United Kingdom, the United States, and West Germany. The National Security Archive, a private research foundation, maintains (through the Freedom of Information Act) electronic links to National Security Agency Documents that provide an extensive record of US involvement in supplying arms to Iraq during the 1980s war. [12]

In 1984, the CIA began secretly supplying intelligence information, gathered from Saudi AWACS (Airborne Warning and Control System) surveillance planes, to Iraq to enable it to better direct attacks – including mustard gas attacks – against Iranian positions. In August that same year, the Central Intelligence Agency established a direct Washington-Baghdad link and assigned as many as 90 US military advisors to help Iraq pick bombing and missile targets. [13] By 1985, the CIA was also supplying satellite reconnaissance data to Baghdad. [14] The CIA and DIA (Defense Intelligence Agency) assisted Saddam's February 1988 assault on the al-Fao peninsula by blinding Iranian radar for three days. [15]

That same year, the Center for Disease Control and Prevention in Atlanta sent three shipments of West Nile virus to Iraq for research purposes. From 1985 to 1989, the US Department of Commerce licensed 70 biological exports to Iraq, including at least 21 shipments of lethal anthrax. [16] According to U.N. records, a Virginia based non-profit bio-resource center named *American Type Culture Collection* (ATCC) sent shipments to Iraq that included anthrax bacteria and microorganisms capable of causing botulism, influenza, lung failure and meningitis. [17]

During the Iran-Iraq War, the US and other nations also sold Iran considerable quantities of conventional military equipment. Part of the funding the US obtained thereby was used, in violation of US law, to funnel aid to the right-wing Contras in Nicaragua. At one point US officials involved in the operation were unable to raise the money they wanted; after all, Iran felt it had all the armaments it needed. CIA Chief William Casey then arranged for Vice President H.W. Bush to undertake a quiet Middle Eastern mission, in the summer of 1986, to encourage Iraq to step up its attacks on Iran. The purpose of the mission was to make the Iranians feel vulnerable and more inclined to make weapon purchases. [18] The Vice President's mission offered enhanced military intelligence and used Jordan's King Hussein and Egypt's President Mubarak as go-betweens to urge Saddam Hussein to undertake more aggressive bombing operations. [19] The Iraqis had been disinclined to listen to US urging to escalate their bombing raids because they feared losing too many planes, but, by mid-1986 their own pressing needs for additional American help, money and weapons led them to step up their efforts against Iran.

> During the 48 hours after Bush's visit with Mubarak, Iraq flew 359 missions over Iran. Over the next few weeks, Iraqi planes continued to strike deep into Iran, bombing oil refineries, including the oil facilities on Sirri Island, 460 miles from the border, a daring feat for Iraqi pilots who were running out of fuel.
>
> Craig Unger, American journalist and writer, April 20,

CHARLES EDMUND COYOTE

2006 [20]

Officials in the United States were as disinterested in Saddam Hussein and the Ba'athist Party's Pan-Arab nationalism as they were in the Ayatollah Khomeini's Shia fundamentalism. Washington had no problem with the two countries fighting their way to an exhausted stalemate. [21]

The extent of US involvement in supplying Iraq with Weapons of Mass Destruction sheds some light on why Washington's neocons may have felt so secure in claiming that Saddam Hussein was in possession of WMDs – it hadn't been that long since they had been selling them to him! [22] In his February 5, 2003 address to a full session of the UN Security Council, Secretary of State Colin Powell claimed, *"To support its deadly biological and chemical weapons program, Iraq procures needed items from around the world using an extensive clandestine network."* Although Iraq had not possessed such a clandestine network since the 1991 Persian Gulf War, it was a network that the United States had played a significant role in creating previous to the First Gulf War. [23]

In his book, The Spider's Web: *The Secret History of How the White House Illegally Armed Iraq*, investigative reporter Alan Friedman exposed many of the details of this network:

> At the time the United States, using the power of the White House with particular interest by Vice President George Herbert Walker Bush, using the intelligence services and the Pentagon, was embarked upon a tilt to Iraq. Nobody really liked Saddam Hussein. Everybody knew that he was a dictator who had gassed his own people but the United States made the decision to back Iraq in order to use Saddam Hussein as a – you know,

as a cynical balance of power against Iran. The tragic result, of course, was that as the United States armed Iraq in the early 1980's, a war continued throughout the 1980's between Iran and Iraq, that cost the lives of more than 1 million people. What really happened then is as the 1980's progressed, and as George Herbert Walker Bush moved from the vice presidency in the Reagan administration to the White House himself, the war in Iraq – the war between Iraq and Iran ended, and, of course, what had been created was a kind of auto pilot, if you will.

Alan Friedman, economics writer, December 17, 2003
[24]

From 1985 to 1990, the US Department of Commerce, under the supervision of George H.W. Bush, licensed more than $1.5 billion worth of sensitive exports to Iraq. Most of it was dual-use items that could be diverted from civilian purposes into nuclear weapons or long-range missiles. Total American funding for Saddam's military and WMD programs were quietly underwritten by $35-$40 billion dollars' worth of loans, courtesy of the US taxpayers. These loans would be forgotten after the 1991 Persian Gulf War. Following that War, ABC Television's Nightline news program reported:

> *It is becoming increasingly clear that George Bush Sr., operating largely behind the scenes throughout the 1980s, initiated and supported much of the financing, intelligence, and military help that built Saddam's Iraq into (an aggressive power).*

Ted Koppel, ABC Nightline, June 9, 1992 [25]

As the George W. Bush's Administration rushed toward its 2003 war with Iraq, Saddam Hussein's government attempted to comply with UN weapons inspection requirements. [26] On December 8, 2002, Iraq filed an

CHARLES EDMUND COYOTE

11,800 page Weapons Declaration listing the corporations, countries, and individuals that had supplied a total of 17,602 tons of chemical weapon precursor agents for Saddam's WMD programs. [27]

Claiming the need to protect sources and withhold information useful for the development of chemical weapons, the US edited out approximately 8,500 pages of Iraq's dossier before passing it on to the 10 non-permanent members of the UN Security Council. [28], [29] The remaining declaration showed that more than half of the equipment used in producing Iraq's chemical weapons came from a US firm through the intermediary of a German company. The rest came mostly from Austria, France, and Spain.

Sixty tons of Dimethyl Methyl Phosphonate (DMMP), a chemical used to make sarin nerve gas, was delivered to Iraq by the Al Haddad trading company of Tennessee, an Iraqi front company owned by Sahib Abd al-Amir al-Haddad, an Iraqi-born US citizen. In 1984, Customs at New York's Kennedy Airport stopped an order placed by Al-Haddad Enterprises for 74 drums of potassium fluoride to be sent to the Iraqi State Enterprise for Pesticide Production. Potassium fluoride is also used in the production of sarin gas, a neurotoxin which would later be implicated in the Gulf War Syndrome, the illness that has affected about 250,000 of the personnel involved in the 1991 Persian Gulf War. At the time of that war, Czech chemical-detection equipment – one of the best in the world – affirmed American soldiers had been exposed to mustard gas and sarin nerve-gas, much of it having been indiscriminately released with the bombing of Iraqi targets. The owner of Al-Haddad Enterprises, Sahib al-Amir al-Haddad, was arrested in Bulgaria in November 2002 for conspiring to purchase equipment for the manufacture of the Iraqi super-cannon.

Howard Teicher, a former Director of the Office of Political-Military Affairs of the White House National Security Council (NSC), has stated that 31 Bell helicopters given to Iraq by the US were used to deliver chemical WMDs. Teicher also testified in a 1995 court affidavit that former CIA director William Casey used Cardoen, a Chilean based company, to supply cluster bombs to Iraq for use against Iran's human wave attacks. [30]

In March 1986, the United Sates, in partnership with the United Kingdom, blocked the UN Security Council from adopting resolutions that condemned Iraqi's use of chemical weapons. On March 21 of that year, the US became the only country refusing to sign a Security Council denunciation of Iraqi use of chemical weapons, despite the fact that the US government knew the Ba'ath Party was using these weapons to suppress ethnic rebellion.

Saddam had begun using chemical weapons to strike back against the Kurds for their support for Iran during the war. Kurdish rebels had taken advantage of the conflict to assume control of 23,000 square miles of mountain homelands in northeastern Iraq. [31] The Ba'ath Party's 1986–1989 al-Anfal campaign against the Kurds used aerial bombardment, chemical warfare, concentration camps, firing squads, ground offensives,

and mass deportations to destroy more than 2,000 Kurdish villages and cities. Much of it was carried out with equipment, money, and supplies provided un knowingly by the American taxpayer.

CHARLES EDMUND COYOTE

According to Middle East Watch – a component of the Human Rights Watch organization – the principal targets of the al-Anfal campaign were Kurdish men of 'battle-age'. The attacks reached their peak between February and September 1988, during the final months of the Iraq–Iran War. At that time the Iraqi Government diverted as many as 200,000 soldiers with air support to the genocidal operation against the Kurdish and their defending Patriotic Union of Kurdistan (PUK) Peshmerga guerrilla forces. [32] The attacks destroyed thousands of Kurdish villages in vast areas of northern Iraq and displaced at least 30 percent of the country's Kurdish population. This caused an estimated 50,000 to 180,000 deaths and created as many as 100,000 widows and an even larger number of orphans. [33]

On March 15, 1988, after 2 days of artillery shelling, the Kurdish town of Halabjah, 9 miles from the Iranian border, was taken from Iraqi government forces by PUK fighters and Iranian revolutionary guards. Believing Iraqi forces were likely to counterattack, the PUK guerrillas held the civilian population as human shields, preventing the town's 75,000 inhabitants and refuges from leaving for safer locations. [34]

The following evening, March 16, 1988, about 20 Iraqi MiG-23 fighter-bombers and Mirage aircraft swooped down on Halabjah. Again and again throughout the night, the aircraft conducted sorties, dropping mixtures of hydrogen cyanide, mustard gas, sarin, tabun and VX on the town as thousands of its people blistered, burned, vomited greenish fluids, and dropped dead. The mixed variety of nerve gas and poison chemicals made treatment of the initial survivors very difficult. About 5,000 people, mostly women and children, met death in a hideous manner that night, with an estimated 9,000 more left seriously impaired. Thousands passed away from horrifying complications in the years that followed the 1988 attack. [35]

As a Senator from Tennessee – future US Vice President and Nobel Peace Prize winner – Al Gore twice tried to stop the United States from continuing to supply Saddam Hussein with the material and delivery systems for WMD production. Al Gore warned about Iraq's use of poison gas, its support of terrorism, and its interest in developing nuclear weapons, but he was opposed first by the Reagan-Bush administration, then by Bush-Quayle. During Saddam's 1986-1989 Al-Anfal Campaign, the Chairman of the Senate Foreign Relations Committee, Senator Claiborne Pell of Rhode Island, introduced the Prevention of Genocide Act of 1988. Cosponsored by Senators Robert Byrd, Wendell Ford, Albert Gore Jr., Jesse Helms, Carl Levin, and William Proxmire, the bill cited Saddam's use of chemical weapons against his own population. This Act was an attempt to direct the United States government to cut off all loans, military equipment sales, and transfer of controlled items being sent to Iraq until the Iraqi government could demonstrate that it was no longer using chemical weapons to commit acts of genocide against its own people. [36]

The Prevention of Genocide Act of 1988 was aimed at the official $1.5 billion American program supplying Saddam Hussein with arms. A zealous lobbying effort by the White House, backed by the threat of a Presidential veto, defeated the bill. [37] The Executive Branch was determined, not only to restrain the rise of Shiite fundamentalism, but also to punish Iran for its holding of American diplomats during the 79-81 Embassy standoffs.

Just as London juggled the world's powers to maintain the balance it perceived most favorable to its own interests during the 19th century zenith of the British Empire, so did Washington try later to form a world most favorable to American interests. The Al-Anfal campaign and the horrific deaths at Halabja were activities to which the US government, along with many of the other world powers, was an accomplice. For these and other crimes against humanity, the Supreme Iraqi Criminal Tribunal sought the death penalty for Saddam Hussein and other senior officials of his Ba'athist regime.

To their own people, governments represent their activities in the most benign manner possible, and it is sometimes unrealistic not to recognize those policies rise out of the necessity to make difficult choices in a complex world. The US government's role in facilitating the crimes of Saddam Hussein – crimes it would decry only a couple of decades later – was forged at the highest levels of each Presidential administration. Though widely reported in the world's press, the US government's role was not widely understood by the American people. The story of any nation's people and their governments can be told in as many shades of color as the vast number of individuals whose lives have been touched. Our own government would have been truer to its fundamental responsibilities, if its foreign policies decisions had borne fidelity to the ideals of its founding document. [38]

CHAPTER 7 REFERENCES

[1] *Fueling the Iran-Iraq Slaughter, by Larry Everest, Net, September 05, 2002;*
http://www.zmag.org/znet/viewArticle/11715
(SHORTENED URL: http://tinyurl.com/fulira)

[2]

(a) *Iran-Iraq War, Wikipedia;*
http://en.wikipedia.org/wiki/Iran%E2%80%93Iraq_War
(SHORTENED URL: http://tinyurl.com/raraw1)

(b)
http://en.wikipedia.org/wiki/Iran%E2%80%93Iraq_War#Origins
(SHORTENED URL: http://tinyurl.com/raraw3)

[3] *Arming Iraq: A Chronology of US Involvement; by John King, Iran Chamber Society, March 2003;*
http://www.iranchamber.com/history/articles/arming_iraq.php
(SHORTENED URL: http://tinyurl.com/aramira)

[4] *Shaking Hands with Saddam Hussein: The US Tilts toward Iraq, 1980-1984, National Security Archive Electronic Briefing Book No. 82, Edited by Joyce Battle, 25 February 2003, Documents 1 and 2; The National Security Archive, the George Washington University;*
http://www.gwu.edu/~nsarchiv/NSAEBB/NSAEBB82/
(SHORTENED URL: http://tinyurl.com/sakeha)

[5] *The Riegle Report: US Chemical and Biological Warfare-Related Dual Use Exports to Iraq and their Possible Impact on the Health Consequences of the Gulf War, A Report of Chairman Donald W. Riegle, Jr. and Ranking Member Alfonse M. D'Amato of the Committee on Banking, Housing and Urban Affairs with Respect to Export Administration; United States Senate, 103rd Congress, 2nd Session May 25, 1994;*
http://www.gulfweb.org/bigdoc/report/riegle1.html
(SHORTENED URL: http://tinyurl.com/repepo)

[6] *Officers Say US Aided Iraq in War Despite Use of Gas,*

by Patrick E. Tyler, New York Times, 18 August 2002;
http://www.globalpolicy.org/security/issues/iraq/history/20
02/0818officers.htm
(SHORTENED URL: http://tinyurl.com/fisera)

[7] Shaking Hands with Saddam Hussein: The US Tilts
toward Iraq, 1980-1984, National Security Archive
Electronic Briefing Book No. 82, Edited by Joyce Battle, 25
February 2003, The National Security Archive, the George
Washington University;
http://www.gwu.edu/~nsarchiv/NSAEBB/NSAEBB82/
(SHORTENED URL: http://tinyurl.com/sakeha)

[8] Rumsfeld Offered Help to Saddam, by Julian Borgor,
Guardian, December 31, 2002;
http://www.globalpolicy.org/security/issues/iraq/history/20
02/1231rumsfeld.htm
(SHORTENED URL: http://tinyurl.com/helpsad)

[9] Video from Meeting: Shaking Hands with Saddam
Hussein: The US Tilts toward Iraq, 1980-1984; National
Security Archive Electronic Briefing Book No. 82, Edited by
Joyce Battle;
http://www.gwu.edu/~nsarchiv/NSAEBB/NSAEBB82/
(SHORTENED URL: http://tinyurl.com/vemeha)

[10] Iraq's Chemical Warfare Program, DCI Special Advisor
Report on Iraq's WMD, Central Intelligence Agency, 30
September 2004;
https://www.cia.gov/library/reports/general-reports-
1/iraq_wmd_2004/chap5.html
(SHORTENED URL: http://tinyurl.com/rahewa)

[11] Rumsfeld's Handshake Deal with Saddam, by Norman
Solomon, Common Dreams, 8 December 2005;
http://www.commondreams.org/views05/1208-34.htm
(SHORTENED URL: http://tinyurl.com/ruhade)

[12]

(a) Iraqgate: Saddam Hussein, US Policy and the Prelude
to the Persian Gulf War, 1980-1994; National Security
Archive;

http://www.gwu.edu/~nsarchiv/nsa/publications/iraqgate/iraqgate.html
(SHORTENED URL: http://tinyurl.com/sahuto)

(b)
http://www.network54.com/Forum/155335/thread/1039369906/
(SHORTENED URL: http://tinyurl.com/rupegu)

(c) GOOGLE BOOK URL: http://tinyurl.com/sagobo

(d) OPEN LIBRARY: http://tinyurl.com/doperi

[13] US and British Support for Hussein Regime, Global Policy Forum;
http://www.globalpolicy.org/security/issues/iraq/history/husseinindex.htm
(SHORTENED URL: http://tinyurl.com/sahure)

[14] Arming Iraq: A Chronology of US Involvement, John King, March 2003;
http://www.iranchamber.com/history/articles/arming_iraq.php
(SHORTENED URL: http://tinyurl.com/ronolo)

[15] To what extent was the US involved with the Iran-Iraq War (1980-1988)? US - Iraq War, ProCon.org;
http://usiraq.procon.org/view.answers.php?questionID=000901
(SHORTENED URL: http://tinyurl.com/ramali)

[16] US Military Assistance to Saddam Hussein during the Iran-Iraq War, Craig Unger, Global Policy Forum, April 20, 2006;
http://www.globalpolicy.org/security/issues/iraq/history/2006/0420usassistance.htm
(SHORTENED URL: http://tinyurl.com/misahu)

[17] A look at US shipments of pathogens to Iraq, USATODAY - World, 30 September 2002;
http://www.usatoday.com/news/world/2002-09-30-iraq-ushelp-list_x.htm
(SHORTENED URL: http://tinyurl.com/purimo)

[18] US Military Assistance to Saddam Hussein during the

CHARLES EDMUND COYOTE

Iran-Iraq War, Craig Unger, Global Policy Forum, 20 April 2006;
http://www.globalpolicy.org/security/issues/iraq/history/2006/0420usassistance.htm
(SHORTENED URL: http://tinyurl.com/misahu)

[19] US Military Assistance to Saddam Hussein during the Iran-Iraq War, Craig Unger, Global Policy Forum, 20 April 2006;
http://www.globalpolicy.org/security/issues/iraq/history/2006/0420usassistance.htm
(SHORTENED URL: http://tinyurl.com/sahudu)

[20] US Military Assistance to Saddam Hussein during the Iran-Iraq War, Craig Unger, Global Policy Forum, 20 April 2006;
http://www.globalpolicy.org/security/issues/iraq/history/2006/0420usassistance.htm
(SHORTENED URL: http://tinyurl.com/sahudu)

[21] US Had Key Role in Iraq Buildup, by Michael Dobbs, Washington Post, 30 December 2002; Global Policy Forum;
http://www.globalpolicy.org/security/issues/iraq/saddam/2002/1230buildup.htm
(SHORTENED URL: http://tinyurl.com/hakero)

[22] US and British Support for Hussein Regime, Global Policy Forum;
http://www.globalpolicy.org/security/issues/iraq/history/husseinindex.htm
(SHORTENED URL: http://tinyurl.com/sahugi)

[23] DETAILS ON IRAQ'S PROCUREMENT NETWORK, by Henry B. Gonzalez, (TX-20); (House of Representatives – August 10, 1992), Congressional Record US House of Representatives, p H7871;
http://www.fas.org/spp/starwars/congress/1992/h920810g.htm
(SHORTENED URL: http://tinyurl.com/facene)

[24] Spider's Web: The Secret History of How the White House Illegally Armed Iraq; Democracy Now! Interview with Alan Friedman, 17 December 2003;

http://www.democracynow.org/2003/12/17/spiders_web_th
e_secret_history_of
(SHORTENED URL: http://tinyurl.com/tasame)

[25] Arming Iraq: A Chronology of US Involvement, by
John King, March 2003;
http://www.iranchamber.com/history/articles/arming_iraq.p
hp
(SHORTENED URL: http://tinyurl.com/vokema)

[26] Briefing of the Security Council, 14 February 2003: An
update on inspections, by Dr. Hans Blix, Executive
Chairman of UNMOVIC;
http://www.un.org/depts/unmovic/new/pages/security_cou
ncil_briefings.asp#6
(SHORTENED URL: http://tinyurl.com/sekofe)

[27] NucNews, December 9, 2002; NucNews.net;
http://nucnews.net/nucnews/2002nn/0212nn/021209nn.ht
m#032
(SHORTENED URL: http://tinyurl.com/nubena)

[28] Cursor Link Archives, Monday, December 23, 2002;
http://cursor.org/1202_archive.htm
(SHORTENED URL: http://tinyurl.com/budeno)

[29] WAR ON IRAQ - IS OIL OR BIG BUSINESS AN
UNDISCLOSED MOTIVE FOR THE WAR ON IRAQ?: AMERICA
REMOVED 70% OF IRAQ'S WEAPON DECLARATION!, THE
DEBATE, the debate.org;
http://www.thedebate.org/thedebate/iraq.asp
(SHORTENED URL: http://tinyurl.com/bibune)

[30] US Had Key Role in Iraq Buildup, by Michael Dobbs,
Washington Post, 20 December 2002; Global Policy Forum;
http://www.globalpolicy.org/security/issues/iraq/saddam/20
02/1230buildup.htm
(SHORTENED URL: http://tinyurl.com/kerole)

[31] Whatever Happened To The Iraqi Kurds? Human
Rights Watch Report, 1991;
http://www.hrw.org/reports/1991/IRAQ913.htm
(SHORTENED URL: http://tinyurl.com/rakuhu)

CHARLES EDMUND COYOTE

*[32] Gendercide Watch: The Anfal Campaign (Iraqi Kurdistan), 1988;
http://www.gendercide.org/case_anfal.html
(SHORTENED URL: http://tinyurl.com/gekara)*

*[33] Al-Anfal Campaign, Wikipedia Encyclopedia;
http://en.wikipedia.org/wiki/Al-Anfal_campaign#cite_note-hang-6
(SHORTENED URL: http://tinyurl.com/kapedi)*

*[34] The 1988 Chemical Weapons Attack on Halabja, Iraq; Dr. Christine M. Gosden, Testimony before the Senate Judiciary Subcommittee on Technology, Terrorism and Government and the Senate Select Committee on Intelligence on "Chemical and Biological Weapons Threats to America: Are We Prepared?," 22 April 1998;
http://www.fas.org/irp/congress/1998_hr/s980422-cg.htm
(SHORTENED URL: http://tinyurl.com/mikaha)*

*[35] 1988: Thousands die in Halabja gas attack; BBC ON THIS DAY, 16 March;
http://news.bbc.co.uk/onthisday/hi/dates/stories/march/16/newsid_4304000/4304853.stm
(SHORTENED URL: http://tinyurl.com/tosama)*

*[36] 1988 PREVENTION OF GENOCIDE ACT, PDF file, United States Senate, 100th Congress, 2nd Session;
http://www.cbc.ca/fifth/kurds/genocide.pdf
(SHORTENED URL: http://tinyurl.com/vegede)*

*[37] AL GORE, Opposition to US government support of Saddam Hussein;
http://www.solarnavigator.net/embassies/al_gore.htm
(SHORTENED URL: http://tinyurl.com/gomesu)*

*[38] US and British Support for Hussein Regime, Global Policy Forum;
http://www.globalpolicy.org/security/issues/iraq/history/husseinindex.htm
(SHORTENED URL: http://tinyurl.com/sahugi)*

CHAPTER 8
BRING THEM TO JUSTICE

The ambassador and the general were briefing me on the – the vast majority of Iraqis want to live in a peaceful, free world. And we will find these people and we will bring them to justice.

George W Bush, Washington, D.C., October 27, 2003

The Iran-Iraq War lasted from September 1980 to August 1988, making it one of the Twentieth Century's bloodiest conflicts. The number of people killed by the eight year conflict is believed to be in excess of one million, with total economic losses – measured in US dollars – of about a half a trillion to each side. It ended in stalemate, with Iran's Ayatollahs becoming concerned that the US was increasingly taking a role supportive of Iraq, and Iraq concluding it could not sustain any progress in its war efforts.

On August 20, 1988, both sides accepted the UN Security Council Resolution 598 and brought the conflict to an end. [1] Iraq had begun the war with more than $35 billion in reserves and ended it with crippling war debts in the range of $100 billion. Its economy was wrecked as its revenues and human resources had been siphoned off to the war machine. Foreign nationals had to be brought into the country to keep the infrastructure running. [2] Saddam used the war to achieve his objective of militarizing the Iraqi society, but he had accomplished it at the prospect of economic ruin.

A large part of Iraq's debt was owed to the United States. For the Ba'athist advocates of Arab pride and independence, owing so much money to the Americans was a national embarrassment. Faced with a desperate need to emerge from debt and rebuild his nation, Saddam Hussein considered his options. [3]

Kuwait held the largest portion of Iraq's war debt, some $65 to $70 billion. [4] Several of the Sunni Arab sheikdoms, including Kuwait, had encouraged Hussein to block Iran's revolutionary Shia. However, the Al-Sabah family that rules Kuwait, though historically generous with its immense wealth to the rulers of many neighboring countries, refused to forgive Iraq's debts. Kuwait was also preventing OPEC from raising the price of oil, a move Iraq had been requesting to help pay its debts. Iraq also believed Kuwait was stealing oil, through the use of directional drilling, from the huge Rumaila Oil Field between the two nations and selling it at below market prices.

Iraq thought that Kuwait was properly a part of itself. Both nations had been carved out of the collapsing Ottoman Empire by the British and French after the First World War, but the border between the two nations had never been well defined. As major oil fields were discovered in both counties, the boundary contentions that had existed for decades between the two countries were exacerbated by the immense amounts of money at stake. The wealth of the Kuwaiti fields was astounding, providing for the people of that small nation a per capita income that was even higher than that of the United States. Such wealth would be the answer to Saddam Hussein's financial problems.

Iraq was in desperate financially straits, but at the same time it possessed the fourth largest military in the world. Saddam had been on good terms with Washington for decades. The CIA had helped bring him to power, and the US government had loaned him $35 to $40 billion, along with significant military aid, during his eight-year fight with Iran. As he considered his next move, Saddam endeavored to find out how his long-time American allies would view his festering dispute with Kuwait and the plan he was hatching to repay Iraq's debts. On July 25, 1990, in a meeting with April Glaspie, the American ambassador to Iraq, Saddam raised the question. According to the Iraqi transcript of the conversation, Glaspie assured Saddam that Bush *"wanted better and deeper relations,"* and that the US President, *"is not going to declare an economic war against Iraq."* She continued:

> *But we have no opinion on the Arab-Arab conflicts, like your border disagreement with Kuwait. I was in the American Embassy in Kuwait during the late 60's. The instruction we had during this period was that we should express no opinion on this issue and that the issue is not associated with America. James Baker [U.S. Secretary of State January 1989 - August 1992] has directed our official spokesmen to emphasize this instruction. We hope you can solve this problem using any suitable methods via Klibi or via President Mubarak. All that we hope is that these issues are solved quickly.*
>
> *April Glaspie, US Ambassador to Iraq; July 25, 1990*
> [5], [6], [7]

According to FBI agent George Piro, Saddam's interrogator after his December 2003 capture by the US, a personal insult by Jaber al-Sabah, the Emir of Kuwait, finally provoked Saddam to invade the country.

> *What really triggered it for him, according to Saddam, was he had sent his foreign minister to Kuwait to meet with the emir al-Sabah... to try to resolve some of these issues. And the emir told the foreign minister of Iraq that he would not stop doing what he was doing until he*

turned every Iraqi woman into a $10 prostitute. And that really sealed it for him, to invade Kuwait.

FBI Agent George Piro, CBS 60 Minutes interview, 27 January 2008 [8]

Despite ambiguity about Washington's perspective, Saddam guessed that after a four-decade long relationship with the US, his American friends would not stand in his way. He decided to act, and on August 2, 1990 he sent 100,000 troops and 300 tanks into the 6,880 square mile country of Kuwait, seizing control of the nation and declaring it the Nineteenth Province of Iraq.

He guessed wrong.

Within days the United Nations demanded Iraq's immediate withdrawal, and the United States began deploying troops to Saudi Arabia. President George H.W. Bush orchestrated a world-wide coalition against the Iraqi invasion, and by January 1991 had assembled more than 956,000 allied troops from 34 nations in the Gulf region, along with significant financial contributions from Japan and Germany. [9] The massive firepower allied against Saddam also included 8 aircraft carriers (6 of them American carrier battle groups) and more than 2,400 fixed-wing aircraft. On January 17, 1991, the Allied air forces opened with a devastating and sophisticated 37-day bombing campaign on Iraq and its occupation forces. Their military and civilian morale and ability to fight were demolished. By the time the ground troops were unleashed on February 23, Iraq's occupying army was already beaten. Cut off from command and supply by the overwhelming air campaign, thousands of Iraqi soldiers simply gave up. The units that remained and attempted to fight were quickly eliminated by the technologically superior American, British and French forces.

> *My gunner reported targets. We moved closer, discovering the Iraqi soldiers to be young boys and old men. They were a sad sight, with absolutely no fight left in them. Their leaders had cut their Achilles' tendons so they couldn't run away and then left them. What weapons they had were in bad repair and little ammunition was on hand. They were hungry, cold, and scared. The hate I had for any Iraqi dissipated. These people had no business being on a battlefield.*
>
> *1st Lieutenant Greg Downey; 2nd Brigade, 24th Division, XVIII Airborne Corps, US Army, recalling second day of the Persian Gulf ground war* [10]

Within two days, the Iraqi army was fleeing Kuwait, setting fire to more than 700 of its oil wells and enduring massive causalities as they tried to retreat along the main Iraq-Kuwait highway. [11] Alarmed that the world would be shocked and might turn against the war if the decimation were allowed to continue, President Bush ordered a cease-fire to take effect on February 27 to let the surviving Iraqis escape. [12] With Iraq's acceptance of the terms on March 3, 1991, Saddam's war against the outside world came to an end. He faced massive uprisings against his rule in the Kurdish north and Shia south of his own country.

Saddam's second war of conquest had gone even worse than the first. Most estimates place the number of Iraqi military killed in the 1991 Persian Gulf War at somewhere between 25,000-65,000. [13] The US forces of 697,000 in theater personnel suffered 148 killed in action, 1 missing in action, and 121 lost through non-combat incidents. A military force of the same size

CHARLES EDMUND COYOTE

normally experiences more casualties over a similar peacetime period due to the usual amount of non-combat accidents and illnesses.

Sanctions were imposed after the War to force Iraq to relinquish its Biological, Chemical & Nuclear Weapons programs and were successful in that regard, compelling Saddam to essentially terminate WMD possession by 1991. [14], [15] Gradually, the sanctions administration morphed into a regime change agenda. The 1991 War had already destroyed or incapacitated most of Iraq's electric, sewer and water infrastructure, along with its oil installations, which were the nation's only significant source of revenue. After the war all Iraqi-owned international assets were frozen and all known oil exports were placed under the control of the Western nations. The UN Compensation Commission added an additional bill of $248 billion to Iraq's debt problems for the 1990-1991 Persian Gulf War. [16]

By 1995, the sanctioned strangulation of Iraq had drastically reduced the living conditions of the Iraqi people. Before the 1990's, public hospitals in Iraq had been free and 90 percent of the population had access to safe water and modern sanitation. Iraq no longer had any control over what it could sell and purchase on the international markets; all such decisions were placed under the direction of the U.N. Iraq's system of universal education, [17] The pride of the Ba'ath Party, was shrunk to shambles. The once prosperous Iraqi people were reduced to the status of paupers with monthly wages averaging between $5 and $25 a month. In contrast, each member of the international UN staff enforcing the extensive embargo was paid an extra $100 per day allowance in addition to their normal salary. All United Nations expenses were paid out of

Iraqi money. [18]

The US, on the other hand, was jubilant over its stunning victory, and felt militarily reinvigorated for the first time since the lingering malaise of the Vietnam War. Following the Persian Gulf War, details of the long hushed relationship between Saddam Hussein and Washington began to emerge. But America celebrated, fell into an economic recession caused by Savings and Loan deregulation, recovered, and fixed its attention on the OJ Simpson murder trial and related events in Brentwood, California.

In August 1989 in Atlanta, Georgia, an FBI raid on Banca Nazionale del Lavoro (BNL) – a branch of Italy's largest bank – had resulted in charges against branch manager Christopher Drogoul for making illegal loans to Iraq for the purpose of funding chemical and nuclear weapons technology. The *'Iraq-gate'* congressional investigation that followed revealed that BNL had channeled $5 billion in US guaranteed loans to Saddam between 1985 and 1989. But, aside from the observations given by the New York Times, the Los Angeles Times, and ABC Television's Nightline, the channeling of such vast amounts of American taxpayer money to Saddam Hussein during the 1980s was simply not able to compete with OJ for the public's attention.

The tens of billions the US taxpayers had loaned Saddam Hussein were quietly forgotten about after the Persian Gulf War. In Iran, however, deep resentment remains to this day over the fact that the US and other Western countries had secretly sold WMD supplies to Iraq in violation of their own laws and the international laws. The chemical weapons arsenal they had helped

Saddam Hussein to develop was used to kill Iran's soldiers and civilian population by the 10s of thousands. [19], [20] Though democracy only has meaning in the context of a well-informed citizenry, the full extent of American government's support of Saddam Hussein was conducted hidden from the American public, several Federal government agencies, and perhaps even its President. Few cared to know, as long as the content and convenience of high-minded words, such as 'democracy,' 'human rights,' and 'peace' were circulated at times appropriate for public consumption.

The realpolitik that guided US foreign policy can be found in documents of the time. [21] A September 1988 State Department memo from Richard Murphy, Assistant Secretary for Near Eastern and South Asian affairs, states that over the previous decade Saddam's foreign policy had become more agreeable to American interests and therefore US statements on Iraq's use of chemical weapons should avoid 'Iraq-bashing'. He notes:

> The US-Iraqi relationship is... important to our long-term political and economic objectives in the Gulf and beyond... Its oil reserves are second to those of Saudi Arabia.
>
> Richard Murphy, US State Department, September 8, 1988 [22]

At the end of the Persian Gulf War, Iraq's ethnic divisions exploded. Although President George H.W. Bush had encouraged the Iraqis to overthrow Saddam, America did nothing to assist the uprisings that took place because they were perceived by US allies in the region as destabilizing. Turkey, with almost half its territory predominately Kurdish, did not want to see Kurdish independence, and Saudi Arabia feared the spread of Shia fundamentalism. Saddam was left in control of Iraq and allowed to ruthlessly suppress the rebellions.

Iraq never recovered economically or militarily from the Gulf War. The terms of the 1991 cease-fire required Iraq to abandon its WMD programs and allow broad-reaching inspections toward that end. Heavy UN trade sanctions were to remain in effect until Iraq could demonstrate compliance with all the terms of the cease-fire. The nation had been now pushed into ruin and its military, though still one of the largest in the Middle East, had been reduced to less than half its pre-1991 size.

Saddam was embittered by the War. He regarded as treacherous actions of the US leadership, which had pretty much acted as an ally until that time. During a visit by George H.W. Bush to Kuwait in April 1993, he tried to strike back. Kuwaiti authorities found 190 pounds of plastic explosives hidden in a Toyota Landcruiser parked next to the motorcade route the former US President was expected to take. Seventeen people were arrested, and interrogations brought the confession that the Iraqi Intelligence Service (IIS) was involved in the assassination attempt. In May 1993, FBI interviews of the same suspects supported the IIS link obtained from the original confessions. Analysis of the bomb by the CIA found it to be similar to others of Iraqi origin. Relying on the CIA's technical evidence, in particular, the Clinton Administration responded on 26 June, 1993 by firing 23 cruise missiles at the Baghdad headquarters of the Iraqi Intelligence Service, killing several staff members present in the building. The following day US Ambassador to the United Nations,

Madeleine Albright, presented at an emergency session of the UN Security Council evidence in support of the missile response. [23]

Between 1992 and 1995, the US Central Intelligence Agency worked with *The Iraqi National Accord Party* to orchestrate a bomb and sabotage a campaign inside Iraq to undermine Saddam's government. [24] The Iraqi National Accord had been founded in 1990 by Dr. Iyad Allawi, a neurologist and future Iraqi Prime Minister, and Salah Omar Ali al-Tikriti, a popular Iraqi leader and former Ba'athist Party member. The Iraqi National Accord maintained an opposition radio station in Amman, Jordan, planted bombs, sabotaged government facilities, and funneled misleading intelligence to the West, as it plotted to overthrow Saddam. [25] In 1992, Salah Omar broke with Allawi over the latter's connections to the CIA and Britain's MI6 service. [26] The National Accord's largely ineffectual campaign against Iraq's government also struck civilian targets, including a movie theatre and possibly a school bus with children on board. [27] Dr. Allawi later became Iraq's interim Prime Minister, 2004-2005, following the US coalition's removal of Saddam Hussein. [28]

The UN's cease-fire sanctions remained in place during the twelve years between the 1991 Persian Gulf War and the 2003 US-UK invasion, but Iraq's co-operation with the international inspection teams enforcing them was spotty. The United States frequently accused Saddam of violating the agreements and firing, almost daily, on the air patrols enforcing the fixed wing no-fly zones. [29] At one point, oil exports – the foundation of Iraq's once prosperous economy – were banned, bringing immense suffering to the Iraqi people and raising one of bin Laden's grievance points against the United States. [30] The export ban, however, had little effect on Saddam Hussein and his government, and in December 1996, the UN began to allow Iraq to sell limited amounts of oil in exchange for food and medicine. This brought little relief to Iraq's people.

Despite any real evidence, Saddam Hussein was widely believed to be continuing his weapons of mass destruction (WMD) programs. Saddam encouraged these perceptions himself. He admitted during his post 2003 capture interrogations that he believed he had to maintain the appearance of military strength by insinuating he still had a substantial collection of WMD's hidden away, in order to keep his regime safe from Iranian attack. [31] By 1998, Saddam, upset that the CIA had infiltrated the UN weapons inspections teams, was making things so frustrating for the inspectors that their chief, Richard Butler, decided it was necessary to pull his team out of the country. [32] In retaliation, the American and British governments launched four days of heavy cruise missile attacks, targeting Iraq's military installations and Baghdad's command and control centers. [33] Four years later, Iraq reinstated the weapons inspections in a last ditch effort to avert war, following George W. Bush's September 12, 2002 speech to the UN General Assembly on the subject of the supposed WMDs. [34]

During the 1990s, Saddam's government became increasingly repressive, and his sons, Uday and Qusay, carried on a reign of terror. [35] Many Arabs began to feel that while Saddam was often in the wrong, it was not America's place to correct him. Despite his bad reputation, Saddam Hussein began to gain popularity in the Arab world by virtue of having survived his war with America and much of the rest of the world. This perspective was enhanced by Saddam's emerging attempts to portray himself as a devout Muslim.

Saddam's secularism had once gained the support of the Western governments. Now, feeling betrayed by the West, he abandoned the Baath Party's secularization and encouraged the growth of Islamist movements loyal to his state. He added the phrase 'Allahu Akbar' (God is Great) in his own handwriting to the Iraqi flag, and his speeches took on an increasingly religious vocabulary. He appeared on television at prayer, signed decrees as "the humble believer and servant of God," and re-introduced aspects of Sharia law. [36]

Beaten time and again by the military power of Israel and the supporting wealth of the West, the Arab Middle East yearned for a local hero to afford some occasion for pride by being strong enough to challenge Europe and America. If Saddam were not to be that one, then his own attempts at self-transformation might seem a little less cynical. Time and again those with worldly ambitions thwarted have found in religion the source of strength they had not been able to find in themselves.

For the US, the Persian Gulf War was a dramatic demonstration of the military power it had mostly held in restraint all the tense decades of the Cold War. For the American people it was a stunning victory, bringing more drama than Whitney Houston's Super Bowl 'Star-Spangled Banner' and the New York Giant's one-point win in Tampa, Florida, as the opening air campaign unfolded on the other side of the world. [37]

That done, and the Soviet Union gone, American's leaders began to call themselves *'the indispensable nation'* and turn away from much of the humble foresight that had guided Pearl Harbor's Greatest Generation to extend the hand of friendship to vanquished foes: [38]

> *It is logical that the United States should do whatever it is able to do to assist in the return of normal economic health in the world, without which there can be no political stability and no assured peace. Our policy is directed not against any country or doctrine but against hunger, poverty, desperation and chaos. Its purpose should be the revival of a working economy in the world so as to permit the emergence of political and social conditions in which free institutions can exist. Such assistance, I am convinced, must not be on a piecemeal basis as various crises develop. Any assistance that this Government may render in the future should provide a cure rather than a mere palliative. Any government that is willing to assist in the task of recovery will find full co-operation I am sure, on the part of the United States Government. Any government which maneuvers to block the recovery of other countries cannot expect help from us.*
>
> *Secretary of State George C. Marshall, Address at Harvard University Launching the Marshall Program of Aid for war-torn Europe, June 5, 1947* [39]

The people of Iraq would watch as their children, fathers, and husbands died with the stoic familiarity acquired by those accustomed to the weight of ancient days. Gorbachev and his new *'friend'*, Ronald Reagan, had brought their nations further than hoped, though the former, bearing also the heavy weight of history, would sit alone and quiet at the funeral of the latter. A handshake had agreed that Germany could be free to choose and NATO would move no closer to the East.

CHARLES EDMUND COYOTE

Too often, the great must drink hemlock instead of wine. For Gorbachev, Saint Francis mattered more. In Washington, the ivy leaguers drank their wine and pretended gravitas.

Magnanimity in politics is seldom the truest wisdom: and a great empire and little minds go ill together.

Edmund Burke, Second Speech on Conciliation with America, 1775 [40]

CHAPTER 8 REFERENCES

[1] Resolution 598 (1987) Adopted by the UN Security Council at its 2750th meeting, on 20 July 1987, Refworld; http://www.unhcr.org/refworld/docid/3b00f20e64.html (SHORTENED URL: http://tinyurl.com/sotepa)

[2] Human Rights in Iraq, Iraqi Holocaust Files; http://iraqshoahfiles.blogspot.com/ (SHORTENED URL: http://tinyurl.com/huralo)

[3] Cruelty and Strength, by Mona Naggar, the April 2003 issue of World Press Review (VOL. 50, No 4), Worldpress.org; http://worldpress.org/print_article.cfm?article_id=1111&dont=yes (SHORTENED URL: http://tinyurl.com/rumona)

[4] The Kuwait Business, Iraqi Invasion of Kuwait; 1990, by Tom Cooper & Brigadier General Ahmad Sadik (Iraqi Air Force), September 16, 2003, Arabian Peninsula & Persian Gulf Database, Air Combat Information Group; http://www.acig.org/artman/publish/article_213.shtml (SHORTENED URL: http://tinyurl.com/kurava)

[5] Excerpts From Iraqi Document on Meeting with US Envoy (September 22, 1990), THE NEW YORK TIMES INTERNATIONAL SUNDAY, SEPTEMBER 23, 1990, US and British Support for Hussein Regime, Global Policy Forum; http://www.chss.montclair.edu/english/furr/glaspie.html

(SHORTENED URL: http://tinyurl.com/domete)

[6] Excerpts From Iraqi Document on Meeting with US Envoy, Special to The New York Times, September 23, 1990, THE NEW YORK TIMES INTERNATIONAL; http://www.chss.montclair.edu/english/furr/glaspie.html (SHORTENED URL: http://tinyurl.com/sepodo)

[7] Declassified National Security Council Cable from Ambassador April Glaspie summarizing July 25, 1990 Meeting with Iraqi President Saddam Hussein, The Margaret Thatcher Foundation; http://www.margaretthatcher.org/document/0DFD0DDB2BA 34EF59F2570CE7EEE03C8.pdf (SHORTENED URL: http://tinyurl.com/senuku)

[8] FBI Agent: Hussein Didn't Expect Invasion, by Ann Scott Tyson, The Washington Post, January 26, 2008; http://www.spokesman.com/stories/2008/jan/26/fbi-agent-says-saddam-didnt-expect-invasion/ (SHORTENED URL: http://tinyurl.com/huvesa)

[9] Military Statistics - Gulf War Coalition Forces (most recent) by country, NationMaster.com; http://www.nationmaster.com/graph/mil_gul_war_coa_for-military-gulf-war-coalition-forces (SHORTENED URL: http://tinyurl.com/faribe)

[10] OVERWHELMING FORCE, by Seymour Hersh, Source: Hardcopy The New Yorker, May 22, 2000; http://cryptome.info/mccaffrey-sh.htm (SHORTENED URL: http://tinyurl.com/hemifo)

[11] Highway of Death, Wikipedia Encyclopedia; http://en.wikipedia.org/wiki/Highway_of_Death (SHORTENED URL: http://tinyurl.com/hidewi)

[12] The World: Theater of War; The New Face of Battle Wears Greasepaint, by Elaine Sciolino, The New York Times, February 22, 1998; http://www.nytimes.com/1998/02/22/weekinreview/the-world-theater-of-war-the-new-face-of-battle-wears-greasepaint.html?pagewanted=all

CHARLES EDMUND COYOTE

124

(SHORTENED URL: http://tinyurl.com/verada)

[13] CASUALTY FIGURES, The Persian Gulf War (1990-
1991), The History Guy;
http://www.historyguy.com/GulfWar.html
(SHORTENED URL: http://tinyurl.com/pehika)

[14] Regime Strategy and WMD Timeline Events, DCI
Special Advisor Report on Iraq's WMD, Central Intelligence
Agency, 30 September 2004;
https://www.cia.gov/library/reports/general-reports-
1/iraq_wmd_2004/WMD_Timeline_Events.html
(SHORTENED URL: http://tinyurl.com/renoti)

[15] Interview Transcript of part one of Correspondent
Brent Sadler's exclusive interview with Hussein Kamel, CNN
World News, 21 September 1995;
http://www.cnn.com/WORLD/9509/iraq_defector/kamel_tra
nscript/index.html
(SHORTENED URL: http://tinyurl.com/tepako)

[16] International Ignominy: Hans von Sponeck's A
Different Kind of War: The UN Sanctions Regime in Iraq,
Book Review, by Gilles d'Aymery;
http://www.swans.com/library/art13/ga230.html
(SHORTENED URL: http://preview.tinyurl.com/hatira)

[17] Operation Iraqi Freedom, NBC News, Written by Marc
Kusnetz: William M. Arkin; General Montgomery Meigs,
retired: and Neal Shapiro, Andrews McMeel Publishing,
Kansas City, © 2003 by National Broadcasting Company,
Inc., p 107.

[18] International Ignominy, Hans von Sponeck's A
Different Kind of War: The UN Sanctions Regime in Iraq,
Book Review, by Gilles d'Aymery;
http://www.swans.com/library/art13/ga230.html
(SHORTENED URL: http://tinyurl.com/havone)

[19] Iran-Iraq War in Pictures, 1980-1988; Iran Chamber
society;
http://www.iranchamber.com/history/iran_iraq_war/war_pi
ctures/war_pictures.php

(SHORTENED URL: http://tinyurl.com/ramaso)

[20] Examples of Known Iraqi Use of CW, Iraq's Chemical Warfare Program, DCI Special Advisor Report on Iraq's WMD, Central Intelligence Agency, 30 September 2004; https://www.cia.gov/library/reports/general-reports-1/iraq_wmd_2004/chap5.html
(SHORTENED URL: http://tinyurl.com/bisemi)

[21] US and British Support for Hussein Regime, Global Policy Forum; http://www.globalpolicy.org/security/issues/iraq/history/husseinindex.htm
(SHORTENED URL: http://tinyurl.com/tisahu)

[22] Profile: Richard W. Murphy, History Commons; http://www.historycommons.org/entity.jsp?entity=richard_w._murphy
(SHORTENED URL: http://tinyurl.com/rihico)

[23] US Strikes Iraq for Plot to Kill Bush, David Von Drehle & R. Jeffrey Smith, Washington Post, June 27, 1993; http://www.washingtonpost.com/wp-srv/inatl/longterm/iraq/timeline/062793.htm
(SHORTENED URL: http://tinyurl.com/vokebu)

[24] THE REACH OF WAR: NEW PREMIER; Ex-C.I.A. Aides Say Iraq Leader Helped Agency in 90's Attacks, Joel Brinkley, The New York Times; June 9, 2004; http://query.nytimes.com/gst/fullpage.html?res=9403E3D91630F93AA35755C0A9629C8B63&sec=&spon=&pagewanted=all
(SHORTENED URL: http://tinyurl.com/besile)

[25] Salah Omar Al-Ali, Years in opposition; Wikipedia Encyclopedia; http://en.wikipedia.org/wiki/Salah_Omar_Al-Ali
(SHORTENED URL: http://tinyurl.com/sapodi)

[26] Ayad Allawi, Allawi "Intelligence" Reports; SourceWatch, 10 August 2008; http://www.sourcewatch.org/index.php?title=Ayad_Allawi
(SHORTENED URL: http://tinyurl.com/banepo)

CHARLES EDMUND COYOTE

[27] The Strongman Of Baghdad, Andrew Gilligan, The Spectator.co.uk, 13 November 2004; http://www.antiwar.com/spectator2/spec509.html (SHORTENED URL: http://tinyurl.com/balaki)

[28] The Strongman Of Baghdad, Andrew Gilligan, SPECTOR.CO.UK, 13th November 2004; http://www.spectator.co.uk/print/themagazine/features/12 799/the-strongman-of-baghdad.thtml (SHORTENED URL: http://tinyurl.com/bakali)

[29] American Soldier, General Tommy Franks with Malcolm McConnell; © 2004 by Tommy Franks, Regan Books, an Imprint of HarperCollinsPublishers, p 196.

[30] A Hard Look at Iraq Sanctions, David Cortright, The Nation, November 19, 2001; http://www.alternet.org/story/11933; http://www.alternet.org/authors/david-cortright

[31] Saddam told interrogators of Iran fixation, by Laura Meckler: Associated Press Writer, October 6, 2004, HOMELAND SECURITY POLICY INSTITUTE GROUP; http://www.hspig.org/phpbb/viewtopic.php?f=10&t=1479& start=0&st=0&sk=t&sd=a&sid=3c6e4a9c5b78e5a3993fbfcd 2c457fd4 (SHORTENED URL: http://tinyurl.com/hadaki)

[32] CIA - Iraq's WMD Vol 1, Comprehensive Report of the Special Advisor to the DCI on Iraq's WMD, Desire... Dominance and Deterrence Through WMD, Iran, p 29; http://www.scribd.com/doc/2060248/CIA-Iraqs-WMD-Vol1 (SHORTENED URL: http://tinyurl.com/dokope)

[33] American Soldier, General Tommy Franks with Malcolm McConnell; © 2004 by Tommy Franks, Regan Books, an Imprint of Harper Collins Publishers, p 200.

[34] PRESIDENT GEORGE W. BUSH'S REMARKS TO THE UNITED NATIONS GENERAL ASSEMBLY, 12 September 2002, Addresses by President George W. Bush; http://www.johnstonsarchive.net/terrorism/bushiraqun.html (SHORTENED URL: http://tinyurl.com/dulema)

[35] Human Rights in Iraq, Iraqi Holocaust Files;
http://iraqshoahfiles.blogspot.com/

[36] Saddam Hussein, Wikipedia encyclopedia;
http://en.wikipedia.org/wiki/Saddam_Hussein#cite_note-PIRRR-22#cite_note-PIRRR-22
(SHORTENED URL: http://tinyurl.com/sahusa)

[37] WHITNEY HOUSTON BEST NATIONAL ANTHEM PREFORMANCE, YouTube;
http://www.youtube.com/watch?v=Z1QmeEdFOSc
(SHORTENED URL: http://tinyurl.com/huseto)

[38] Hank Williams Sr - Mind Your Own Business, YouTube;
https://www.youtube.com/watch?v=JSeuDDzjIB8
(SHORTENED URL: http://tinyurl.com/mikano)

[39] Address of Secretary of State George C. Marshall at Harvard University, June 5, 1947;
http://www.oecd.org/document/10/0,3746,en_2649_20118 5_1876938_1_1_1_1,00.html
(SHORTENED URL: http://tinyurl.com/serema)

[40] Speech on conciliation with America (abridged), Edmund Burke, 22 March 1775, From Revolution to Reconstruction Documents, A Hypertext on American History from the colonial period until Modern Times, Department of Humanities Computing, University of Groningen, The Netherlands;
http://odur.let.rug.nl/~usa/D/1751-1775/libertydebate/burk.htm
(SHORTENED URL: http://tinyurl.com/bonuka)

CHARLES EDMUND COYOTE

CHAPTER 9

ONE OF THE GREAT THINGS ABOUT BOOKS

One of the great things about books is, sometimes there are some fantastic pictures.

> George W. Bush, US News & World Report, 3 January 2000

The 1991 Persian Gulf War was a limited conflict in which America and its UN allies fought only to drive Iraq out of Kuwait. Following the stunning collapse of Iraq's military forces, the restraint of the US government toward Saddam – the man that George H.W. Bush had been portraying as *'the new Hitler'* – was not understood. This was particularly true with the world watching televised pictures of Saddam's brutal crackdown on the millions of rebelling Kurds and Shia inside his country. With President Bush elevating Saddam to *'the new Hitler'* in order to build support for the Gulf War, most Americans as well as many citizens in other coalition nations believed their forces should have swept on to Baghdad and eliminated the Iraqi leadership.

George H.W. Bush explained:

> *While we hoped that popular revolt or coup would topple Saddam, neither the US nor the countries of the region wished to see the breakup of the Iraqi state. We were concerned about the long-term balance of power at the head of the Gulf. Trying to eliminate Saddam, extending the ground war into an occupation of Iraq, would have violated our guideline about not changing objectives in midstream, engaging in "mission creep," and would have incurred incalculable human and political costs. Apprehending him was probably impossible. We had been unable to find Noriega in Panama, which we knew inti-*

mately. We would have been forced to occupy Baghdad and, in effect, rule Iraq. The coalition would instantly have collapsed, the Arabs deserting it in anger and other allies pulling out as well. Under those circumstances, furthermore, we had been self-consciously trying to set a pattern for handling aggression in the post-cold war world. Going in and occupying Iraq, thus unilaterally exceeding the U.N.'s mandate, would have destroyed the precedent of international response to aggression we hoped to establish. Had we gone the invasion route, the US could conceivably still be an occupying power in a bitterly hostile land. It would have been a dramatically different – and perhaps barren – outcome.

George H.W. Bush & Brent Scowcroft, "Why We Didn't Remove Saddam", Time, 2 March 1998 [1]

But in George H.W. Bush's home state of Texas another up and coming politician had other ideas. In 1994, George Bush Sr.'s eldest son, George Walker Bush, had been chosen by the Republican Party to be their candidate for Governor of Texas. Facing the popular Governor Ann Richards for the state's highest executive office, George W. Bush's political team, which included Karen Hughes and Karl Rove, aimed their nominee toward a focus on crime reduction, education improvement, and tort reform. Nominee Bush also promised to sign a bill, already vetoed by Governor Richards, which would allow Texans to get permits to carry concealed weapons. Following an outstanding performance in the campaign debates, George W. Bush was elected Governor of Texas with 53 percent of the vote; this was W's first public office.

George W. Bush's first term as governor was defined by bipartisan success, and four years later the once hard-drinking son of a former President won re-election to a second term with 68 percent of the vote. [2] His newly acquired populist fundamentalism and family connections began attracting national, contribution-rich, attention within the Republican Party.

The successful Presidency of Ronald Reagan had moved America to the right on the political spectrum and Bill Clinton, the first Democratic president of the post-Reagan era, found it necessary to govern as a centrist, committing himself even more effectively than the Republicans themselves to such core conservative principles as fiscal responsibility, limited government, and neo-liberal economics. In preparing his own run for the Presidency, George W. Bush portrayed himself to the nation as a *'compassionate conservative'*:

> *I believe in the promise of America – the fundamentally American conviction that each of us can be what we want to be, can achieve what we want to achieve, so long as we are willing to work and earn it. The promise is meant for everyone, not just a few – and as we move into the 21st century, I want the party of Lincoln to be the party that makes sure no one is left behind.*
>
> George W. Bush, March 7, 1999 [3], [4]

Clinton was a popular president in prosperous times, but many Americans felt that Clinton's and British Prime Minister Tony Blair's use of the North Atlantic Treaty Organization to stop the ethnic cleansing of Albanians by nationalist Serbs in the former Yugoslavia represented an excessively interventionist foreign policy. George Bush seemed to agree and told the American people that he wanted to see a more humble foreign policy:

> *Well, I think they ought to look at us as a country that understands freedom where it doesn't matter who you are or how you're raised or where you're from, that you*

can succeed. I don't think they'll look at us with envy. It really depends upon how our nation conducts itself in foreign policy. If we're an arrogant nation, they'll resent us. If we're a humble nation, but strong, they'll welcome us. And it's -- our nation stands alone right now in the world in terms of power, and that's why we have to be humble. And yet project strength in a way that promotes freedom. So I don't think they ought to look at us in any way other than what we are. We're a freedom-loving nation and if we're an arrogant nation they'll view us that way, but if we're a humble nation they'll respect us.

George W. Bush, Second Presidential debate with Al Gore, October 11, 2000 [5]

In numbers large enough to carry him into a contentious battle for the Presidency, America's conservatives stepped up to the ballot box and showed they liked what they were hearing from Governor George W. Bush: *'the promise of America did not have to be exclusive'* and he, unlike his predecessor, was going to be more restrained about committing the nation's military power. [6] From time to time, however, George W. mentioned he had not forgotten that Saddam Hussein had once tried to assassinate his father: [7]

There's no doubt his hatred is mainly directed at us. There's no doubt he can't stand us. After all, this is the guy that tried to kill my dad at one time.

George W. Bush, 26 September 2002 [8]

Were they reasonable, these conservatives, to expect that the promise of America was never intended to be exclusive? Was it possible that America, the one superpower still standing at the end of the Cold War, would willingly deal humbly with other nations? No nation in history, having come to a position of great power, had felt any particular obligation to behave that way. Who were these people who identified them-

CHARLES EDMUND COYOTE

selves as *'conservatives'* and why would they expect that America could be different?

As a way of thinking, Conservatism is not easy to define. *Merriam-Webster's Collegiate Dictionary* calls it a political philosophy based on tradition and social stability, stressing established institutions and preferring gradual, rather than abrupt change. [9] The word comes from a Latin term, *'com servare'*, meaning *'to preserve'* or *'to protect from loss or harm'*. Generally speaking, conservatism supports institutionalized culture and observes a strong orientation toward preserving existing values.

As a political term, the word was first used by the French politician François-René de Chateaubriand in 1819. De Chateaubriand favored the restoration of the French monarchy (*'the ancien régime'*) in the French society and the continuation of the Catholic Church, and described a conservative as *'one who is a partisan of the established social and political order'*. [10] In the Anglo-American tradition, conservatism usually refers to the school of thought advocated by the English statesman Edmund Burke (1729-1797), and by such 20th Century thinkers as Russell Kirk, the latter of whom described conservatism as *'the negation of ideology'*:

> *In essence, the conservative person is simply one who finds the permanent things more pleasing than Chaos and Old Night. (Yet conservatives know, with Burke, that healthy "change is the means of our preservation.") A people's historic continuity of experience, says the conservative, offers a guide to policy far better than the abstract designs of coffee-house philosophers.*
>
> *Russell Kirk, Ten Conservative Principles, 1993* [11]

In an opinion-editorial appearing in *The Wall Street Journal* during the 2005 Harriet Miers' Supreme Court nomination debate, the mainstream conservative commentator, Rush Limbaugh, said of the movement:

> *I love being a conservative. We conservatives are proud of our philosophy. Unlike our liberal friends, who are constantly looking for new words to conceal their true beliefs and are in a perpetual state of reinvention, we conservatives are unapologetic about our ideals. We are confident in our principles and energetic about openly advancing them. We believe in individual liberty, limited government, and capitalism, the rule of law, faith, a color-blind society and national security. We support school choice, enterprise zones, tax cuts, welfare reform, faith-based initiatives, political speech, homeowner rights and the war on terrorism. And at our core we embrace and celebrate the most magnificent governing document ever ratified by any nation – the US Constitution. Along with the Declaration of Independence, which recognizes our God-given natural right to be free, it is the foundation on which our government is built and has enabled us to flourish as a people.*
>
> Rush Limbaugh, The Wall Street Journal, October 17, 2005 [12]

In the United States, conservatives have often been associated with free market liberalism (i.e., a restrained role for government in economic affairs), religious fundamentalism, a strong military and related spending, states' rights, and freedom from oppressive taxation. In earlier decades, conservatives often opposed US involvement in foreign wars and international policy-making organizations such as the League of Nations, the United Nations, and the North Atlantic Treaty Organization.

Conservatives tend to prefer homogeneous communities and are most common in America's south and agricultural heartland and in areas of the west that have lower population densities. The diverse communities common to college towns and urban environments tend to nurture liberal perspectives, less oriented toward upholding existing social beliefs, customs, and institutions.

The 18th century Irish-Anglo statesman, Edmund Burke is considered the philosophical father of Anglo-American conservatism. Burke, a lawyer, author, and influential member of the British House of Commons, was one of the great orators of his time. As a member of the Whig Party, he believed in constitutional monarchism and the rule of law as opposed to the absolute rule of kings and government despotism. He was a supporter of the American Revolution, which he saw as an appropriate response of England's colonists in the New World, trying to maintain their Chartered rights in opposition to the increasingly repressive rule of the English Crown and Prime Minister:

> *If we have equity, wisdom, and justice, it [America] will belong to this country; if we have it not, it will not belong to this country.*
>
> *Edmund Burke, Parliamentary Debate on American taxation* [13]

Burke's based his position on the American rebellion on the fact that when the English established their settlements in the New World, they were granted charters by the English king guaranteeing they and their heirs would continue to have all the liberties and rights of those who remained in the British homeland. The descendants of those original English colonists were taking up arms against the British monarchy not to fight for new liberties, but to preserve the rights that had been theirs and their ancestor's for centuries. Burke maintained that the British government, under the rule of George III, was fighting its own *'English Brethren in the Colonies'*, using German mercenaries to try to take from them the very liberties that belonged to all Englishmen. [14]

> *...Let the colonies always keep the idea of their civil rights associated with your government – they will cling and grapple to you, and no force under heaven will be of power to tear them from their allegiance. But let it be once understood that your government may be one thing and their privileges another, that these two things may exist without any mutual relation – the cement is gone, the cohesion is loosened, and everything hastens to decay and dissolution. As long as you have the wisdom to keep the sovereign authority of this country as the sanctuary of liberty, the sacred temple consecrated to our common faith, wherever the chosen race and sons of England worship freedom, they will turn their faces towards you. The more they multiply, the more friends you will have; the more ardently they love liberty, the more perfect will be their obedience. Slavery they can have anywhere. It is a weed that grows in every soil. They may have it from Spain, they may have it from Prussia. But, until you become lost to all feeling of your true interest and your natural dignity, freedom they can have from none but you. This is the commodity of price, of which you have the monopoly. This is the true Act of Navigation, which binds to you the commerce of the colonies, and through them secures to you the wealth of the world. Deny them this participation of freedom, and you break that sole bond which originally made, and must still preserve, the unity of the empire...*

> *Edmund Burke, 22 March 1775* [15]

On the basis of preserving what the past had proved to be of value, Burke refused to befriend the French Revolution and the radical ideologies by which its leaders sought to transform their society. When, in 1789, the French aristocrat Charles Jean François Depont asked Burke his impressions of their Revolution, the English parliamentarian replied with two letters. His lengthy response, penned in 1790, became *Reflections on the Revolution in France*, and was a strong condemnation of the sweeping social changes advocated by that nation's rootless ideologues. It became one of the most influential works of conservative thought ever published. [16]

Burke perceived that unlike the American Revolution, the French were uprooting the foundations of their own society and instituting in their place social experiments that were disconnected from the complex realities of human behavior. He understood that the abstract ideals of the French revolution failed to recognize the practical realities of the human condition and would therefore bring disaster and not the liberty, equality, and fraternity that the French people sought.

Phrased in the emancipating thought of the Age of Reason, the American Revolution had been fought to maintain the rights the colonists had long enjoyed as subjects of the British king. Many of the leading figures of America's Revolution, such as John Adams, Alexander Hamilton, George Washington and others, agreed with Burke's observations on the French. In the centuries since then, Burke's views have become the core of conservative thought in the English-speaking world.

Burke understood that civilization cannot be composed of individuals having the same distinctions, interests and skills. It also needed those broadly cultured just as much as it needed those diligently skilled, so that it might function well. Similar to Plato in *The Republic*, he argued that any attempts by the multitude to directly govern deprive a nation of the substantial strengths of personal merit, standing in for an enervating mediocrity that tends to erode greatness and moral vitality.

Edmund Burke (1729 – 1797): influential Irish-Anglo politician, orator and political thinker, notable for his strong support for the American Revolution and fierce opposition to the French Revolution

While acknowledging the essential equality of mankind, Burke nevertheless maintained that social egalitarianism was unjust because it relied upon compulsion and would inevitably reduce people to the lowest common denominator, since leveling them up is impossible. Social equality, he held, undermined the natural order of things as nature itself was hierarchical. And, as the novelist Ayn Rand later observed, self-serving elites find it easy to use the pretext of equality as a means to appropriate power and resour-

CHARLES EDMUND COYOTE

ces for themselves, considering the idea to be theoretically just as long as it does not apply to them and their privileges.

Burke was one of the first to point out the difficulty inherent in utopian planning. He argued that naturally evolved customs and institutions are superior to the designs of abstract reason, such as those advanced in the French Revolution of his own day or observed in the Soviet states a century and a half later. People face a nearly impenetrable challenge when trying to grasp the profound ways in which inherited behavior sways thinking to such a degree that objective judgment about society becomes extremely difficult. Yet, so long as intellect remains unequal to the task of fully grasping human nature, freedom remains possible.

Overall, conservatives believe that good government, like good Scotch, develops from aged experience and the rich proving of time. The responsible state extends from the inherent virtues of fundamental social institutions matured by long experience. Tradition drawn from the practical character of multiple generations makes itself the appropriate foundation for social construction, while reason is seldom able to offer more than the mostly untested perspective of a single cohort.

> We are afraid to put men to live and trade each on his own private stock of reason, because we suspect that this stock in each man is small, and that the individuals would do better to avail themselves of the general bank and capital of nations and ages.
>
> Edmund Burke, *Reflections on the Revolution in France,* 1790

CHAPTER 9 REFERENCES

[1] George H.W. Bush and Brent Scowcroft, "Why We Didn't Remove Saddam", Time, 2 March 1998; Full Article at 'Reasons Not to Invade Iraq, by George Bush Sr.', The Memory Hole;
http://www.thememoryhole.org/mil/bushsr-iraq.htm
(SHORTENED URL: http://tinyurl.com/becobe)

[2] George W. Bush A legacy reclaimed, by Mary Leonard, The Boston Globe, 23 January 2000;
http://web.archive.org/web/20071012215629/http://boston.com/news/politics/president/bush/articles/2000/01/23/george_w_bush/
(SHORTENED URL: http://tinyurl.com/lemena)

[3] GEORGE WALKER BUSH (1946 -), Life Before the Presidency; American President, An Online Reference Resource, Miller Center of Public Affairs, University of Virginia;
http://millercenter.org/academic/americanpresident/gwbuh/essays/biography/2
(SHORTENED URL: http://tinyurl.com/wobere)

[4] The Promise of America, Governor George W. Bush, Exploratory Committee Announcement, 7 March 1999;
http://www.4president.org/speeches/georgewbush2000announce.htm
(SHORTENED URL: http://tinyurl.com/romise)

[5] October 11 2000 Debate Transcript, October 11, 2000, The Second Gore-Bush Presidential Debate, COMMISSION ON PRESIDENTIAL DEBATES;
http://www.debates.org/index.php?page=october-11-2000-debate-transcript
(SHORTENED URL: http://tinyurl.com/bakema)

[6] George W Bush's Humble Foreign Policy? LiveLeak.com;
http://www.liveleak.com/view?i=7bd_1195614597
(SHORTENED URL: http://tinyurl.com/hudema)

[7] Bush calls Saddam 'the guy who tried to kill my dad', by John King, CNN.com, 27 September 2002;

CHARLES EDMUND COYOTE

140

http://archives.cnn.com/2002/ALLPOLITICS/09/27/bush.war.talk/
(SHORTENED URL: http://tinyurl.com/gotyca)

[8] Conflicts Shaped Two Presidencies, by Peter Baker, The Washington Post, 31 December 2006;
http://www.washingtonpost.com/wp-dyn/content/article/2006/12/30/AR2006123000663_pf.html
(SHORTENED URL: http://tinyurl.com/zosepe)

[9] Definition of 'Conservative', Merriam-Webster's Collegiate Dictionary, Tenth Edition, copyright © 1999 by Merriam-Webster, Incorporated, Springfield, Massachusetts, U.S.A.; ISBN 0-87779-708-0

[10] The Scary Echo of the Intolerance of the French Revolution in America Today, Carol Hamilton, History News Network, George Mason University; 9 December 2007;
http://hnn.us/articles/43075.html

[11] Ten Conservative Principles, by Russell Kirk, The Russell Kirk Center for Cultural Renewal, Adapted from The Politics of Prudence, ISI Books, 1993 Copyright © 1993;
http://www.kirkcenter.org/index.php/detail/ten-conservative-principles/
(SHORTENED URL: http://tinyurl.com/woruki)

[12] Holding Court, by Rush Limbaugh, The Wall Street Journal, 17 October 2005; AMERICAN CONSERVATISM.

[13] Edmund Burke (1729-1797) Anglo-Irish Statesman & Political Philosopher, flickr.com;
http://www.flickr.com/photos/costi-londra/904323433/
(SHORTENED URL: http://tinyurl.com/edbuke)

[14] Edmund Burke: Biography from Answers.com, Western Philosophy 18th century philosophy;
http://www.answers.com/topic/edmund-burke
(SHORTENED URL: http://tinyurl.com/buselo)

[15] Speech on Conciliation with America, by Edmund Burke, 22 March 1775; Sources of British History, Britannia Historical Documents;
http://www.britannia.com/history/docs/eburke.html

(SHORTENED URL: http://tinyurl.com/codebe)

[16] Reflections on the Revolution in France, by Edmund Burke, 1790;
http://www.constitution.org/eb/rev_fran.htm
(SHORTENED URL: http://tinyurl.com/rafina)

Chapter 10

Why I Do Things

I'm also not very analytical. You know I don't spend a lot of time thinking about myself, about why I do things.

George W. Bush, Aboard Air Force One, 4 June 2003

Attempts, say Conservatives, to impose an ideology on the complex interactions of human culture will almost invariably run afoul of the Law of Unintended Consequences. Few situations provide such dramatic demonstration of the cost of violating this fundamental axiom as the Bush Administration's decision to invade Iraq in 2003. Human societies have deep roots. Dictating reform according to the shallow edicts of a belief system are invitations to disaster, a lesson the Bush administration insisted on learning the hard way.

Conservatives do not reject the evolution that naturally takes place with all things. Allowing change to take place according to its own rules and rhythm makes more certain and less costly the good that individuals or nations often seek to impose violently. The natural unveiling of the good is usually gradual, developing that which is latent into that which is preferred.

We must all obey the great law of change. It is the most powerful law of nature, and the means perhaps of its conservation.

Edmund Burke, 1792 [1]

Thus Conservative norms include a healthy respect for gradual, institutional reform and traditions of support for the Rule of Law, which itself rests on the groundwork of *Stare decisis*, the obligation to include in the present case a strong consideration for the relevant precedents of prior decisions. In the Anglo-American culture, this adherence to the Rule of Law, which actually dates back a thousand years, started to be codified in the 12th Century English Charter of Liberties, and was given a firmer foundation a hundred years later by the Magna Carta.

Due process is central to the Rule of Law. Formally established by the 39th Clause of the Great Charter Magna Carta of 1215 and incorporated in the US Constitution, it came to mean that governments may only exercise authority in accordance with publicly disclosed written codes and law that have been adopted which are enforceable by a well-established process. Democracies are characterized by equality under the law for all citizens, by transparency in government, and by fair and open election of those appointed to govern.

In America, both conservatives and liberals have commonly maintained that the purpose of the state is to administer justice and facilitate individual liberty and wellbeing. Towards those ends, liberals tend to assert that government must restrain an unbalanced accumulation of power and resources in the hands of small numbers of individuals and organizations, while conservatives traditionally allow more leeway to individual prerogative; both sides hold common ground in maintaining that the state exists for the well-being of the individual and not vice-versa.

The 1215 AD signing of the Great Charter (Magna Carta) by the English King John affirmed that even the monarchy will be subject to the sovereignty of the Law. The Magna Carta, in turn, had been preceded in

CHARLES EDMUND COYOTE

1100 AD by the Charter of Liberties – an agreement by which the youngest son of William the Conqueror, King Henry I, had contracted his powers as monarch to be subject to certain limitations on royal power. It was voluntarily signed by King Henry and voluntarily ignored by subsequent monarchs until the legendary days of the nemesis of Robin Hood. At that time King John, younger brother of Richard the Lionhearted, was forced by an uprising of the English nobles and the people of London to accept its terms, like it or not. In signing, King John bound not only himself, but also his future heirs to the throne to uphold the rights and liberties of the Great Charter to all the Free Men in the Kingdom:

> *TO ALL FREE MEN OF OUR KINGDOM we have also granted, for us and our heirs forever, all the liberties written out below, to have and to keep for them and their heirs, of us and our heirs.*
>
> *Text of Magna Carta of 1215* [2]

The Magna Carta represented the first lights of democracy for the English speaking peoples, but the idea that even the heads of state were to be subject to the law did not originate with the English. Islam has an even longer history of opposition to despotism and the precedence of Law, the Sharia, over the arbitrary rule of those who govern. The early caliphates upheld the idea that all members of the Muslim community, including the caliphs and their officials, were subject to the Sharia.

Electing rulers and making decisions by means of the Shura, a form of representative democracy, was of central importance to the Muslim faith. The sovereignty of law in Islamic culture can be further traced back even further into ancient Mesopotamia itself and the first city-states.

> *No free man shall be seized or imprisoned, or stripped of his rights or possessions, or outlawed or exiled, or deprived of his standing in any other way, nor will we proceed with force against him, or send others to do so, except by the lawful judgment of his equals or by the law of the land.*

Text of Magna Carta, Clause 39, modern translation [3]

The most important feature of the English Magna Carta was the Writ of *Habeas Corpus*, an element without which the Rule of Law is meaningless. Without the legal instrument of *Habeas Corpus*, liberty and justice have little defense. Habeas corpus, Clause 39 of the 1215 Magna Carta, requires the quick release of those whom the authorities have imprisoned for reasons not supported by the law of the land. The Writ of Habeas Corpus is an invention of the English people and requires the government to assure that prisoners have the right to appeal unlawful imprisonment. Without this Writ, the executive powers of government can lock away anyone, at any time, without regard to the legally permissible reasons or the accepted customs of society. In its absence, a tyrant can lock away those who offend them for as long as they choose, without regard to genuine wrongdoing, thus making government no longer the servant of the people but their law and master.

> *Our oldest reformation is that of Magna Charta. You will see that Sir Edward Coke, that great oracle of our law, and indeed all the great men who follow him, to Blackstone, are industrious to prove the pedigree of our liberties. They endeavor to prove that the ancient charter, the Magna Charta of King John, was connected with another positive charter from Henry I, and that both the*

CHARLES EDMUND COYOTE

one and the other were nothing more than a reaffirmance of the still more ancient standing law of the kingdom. In the matter of fact, for the greater part these authors appear to be in the right; perhaps not always; but if the lawyers mistake in some particulars, it proves my position still the more strongly, because it demonstrates the powerful prepossession toward antiquity, with which the minds of all our lawyers and legislators, and of all the people whom they wish to influence, have been always filled, and the stationary policy of this kingdom in considering their most sacred rights and franchises as an inheritance.

Edmund Burke, Reflections on the Revolution in France, 1790 [4]

Gradually, the foundations for the Rule of Law were enhanced through the English Civil Wars of 1642-1651, the Glorious Revolution of 1688, and the English Bill of Rights of 1689. These events established the United Kingdom as one of the world's oldest extant democracies, sustaining its construction by the power of ancient tradition and rights linked to the Monarchy itself by the commitment of King John. Long has the human heart yearned to combine the benefits of civilization with freedom! The English people's attempts to express this longing in their language became enshrined in the founding documents and Constitution of the United States.

But where says some is the King of America? I'll tell you Friend, he reigns above, and doth not make havoc of mankind like the Royal of Britain. Yet that we may not appear to be defective even in earthly honors, let a day be solemnly set apart for proclaiming the charter; let it be brought forth placed on the divine law, the word of God; let a crown be placed thereon, by which the world may know, that so far as we approve of monarchy, that in America THE LAW IS KING. For as in absolute govern-

ments the King is law, so in free countries the law ought to be King; and there ought to be no other.

Thomas Paine, Common Sense, January 1776 [5]

The Magna Carta and successive civil wars eventually led to the development of constitutional government, guaranteeing that the social order will be governed by rules created by its citizens. The rule of law – the framework that structures democracy – can only exist if no one is above its reach. Without legal predictability, economic behavior becomes uncertain. Value, never intrinsic but always dependent upon appreciation, becomes ill-defined, leading to a consequent deterioration of markets, economies, and the people's prosperity. The prosperity of a people stands in direct relationship to the adherence of their leaders to the tenants of justice.

When the Rulers neglect their responsibilities, violence rises amongst the People.

Confucius, 6th Century BC

The American Revolution was a reassertion of the Rights which the English Kings had established by Charter in the English colonization of the New World. It was also a blending of those Rights with the Age of Reason's deepening appreciation of human dignity and the notion that government must be instituted to secure human individuation. With the help of the French, the American colonists upheld their English rights. The genius of their Revolution was its prudent combining of the preexisting social order with the sparks of imprisoned lightning, the realpolitik of old-world interest, and some good rifle marksmanship.

All who have ever written on government are unanimous,

CHARLES EDMUND COYOTE

that among a people generally corrupt, liberty cannot long exist.

Edmund Burke, 1777 [6]

The United States became the first nation to codify the centuries old understanding that governments rule by consent of the governed. This Constitution established republican forms of government at the state and federal level – ultimately, though indirectly, responsible to the interests of the people – with their powers being restrained by a well thought-out system of balance and review. The authority of the Federal Executive was subject to the evenhanded power of the Law-Making Congress, with its two chambers, in turn, subject to the Law-Interpreting power of the Judiciary. All these were able to restrain the other: the Power of the Federal government was balanced against the Domestic Rights, Interests, and Powers of the various States, which in turn were held accountable to the people, who in turn were subject to the Rule of Law that they themselves chose.

> *We the People of the United States, in Order to form a more perfect Union, establish Justice, insure domestic Tranquility, provide for the common defense, promote the general Welfare, and secure the Blessings of Liberty to ourselves and our Posterity, do ordain and establish this Constitution for the United States of America.*
>
> *Constitution for the United States of America, Adopted 17 September 1787* [7], [8], [9]

The purpose of this balance of powers was to protect the liberty of the people and the Rule of Law by preventing power from being concentrated in the hands of any one individual. The danger to Republican government posed by the power and expense of standing armies was to be balanced by subjugating military power to civilian authority. The freedom young America possessed to hold militarism in suspicion was largely sustained by oceanic distance and the power, thereon, of the English navy. [10]

> Our Constitution was made only for a moral and religious people. It is wholly inadequate to the government of any other.
>
> John Adams

Over the course of centuries, the State had returned to the point where it was seen to exist in order to reasonably promote individual rights with decreased regard to social rank. To achieve these ends, broad support is given to freedom of speech and thought, to limitations on the power of government, and to the advancement of economic freedom. In the right of individual property, conservatives found one of the most important restraints on the tyranny of the state and the tyranny of poverty.

Fiscal conservatism advocates prudence in government spending, maintaining that government does not have the right to run up huge debts that burden the taxpayer, the economy, and future generations. Throughout history, the state's assumption of massive debt has been the ruin of government and commerce. It was massive debts, primarily war-related, that shackled the Spanish Empire of Philip II and the French 18th Century monarchs, declining their nations from the heights of power. Conservatives, seeking economic and social stability for their countries, have historically asserted that the taxpayers' right to freedom from oppressive taxation is more important than the obligation to pay back oppressive levels of debt irresponsibly assumed by the state. This position is consistent with the notion that government exists to be the servant of the people, not their master.

> It is to the property of the citizen, and not to the demands of the creditor of the state, that the first and original faith of civil society is pledged. The claim of the citizen is prior in time, paramount in title, superior in equity. The fortunes of individuals, whether possessed by acquisition or by descent or in virtue of a participation in the goods of some community, were no part of the creditor's security, expressed or implied... The public, whether represented by a monarch or by a senate, can pledge nothing but the public estate; and it can have no public estate except in what it derives from a just and proportioned imposition upon the citizens at large.
>
> Edmund Burke, Reflections on the Revolution in France, 1790 [11]

The English economist, Adam Smith, developed the principles of economic liberalism, advocating market freedom for the individual. Government responsibility in this endeavor should focus on providing the infrastructure for those markets by building and maintaining the roads, highways, ports and transit systems necessary for their efficient function. Smith, an eccentric 18th century genius, is regarded as one of the most influential economists of all time. His most famous work, An Inquiry into the Nature and Causes of the Wealth of Nations, commonly known as, The Wealth of Nations, is considered the core thesis of modern economics. It was published in 1776, just as the industrial revolution and the United States were both getting started. [12], [13]

The 18th Century's Age of Reason nurtured the idea that if people are free to determine their own destiny – instead of the state determining it for them – society will be more egalitarian, harmonious, and prosperous. The wealth available to humankind was no longer seen as a fixed commodity, but rather a function of individual creativity nurtured by the policies of government. This Classic Liberalism (essentially Conservatism from Edmund Burke through Ronald Reagan) was developed with the Industrial Revolution and the rise of Capitalism. At its core, classic liberalism believes that laissez-faire economics works to bring about the highest social good by being centered on individual self-interest and ownership of the means of production.

So certain were these early libertarians that such an *'Invisible Hand'* underlay the pursuit of enlightened self interest, that Adam Smith began his first book, The Theory of Moral Sentiments, by explaining:

> *How selfish soever man may be supposed, there are evidently some principles in his nature, which interest him in the fortune of others, and render their happiness necessary to him, though he derives nothing from it except the pleasure of seeing it. Of this kind is pity or compassion, the emotion that we feel for the misery of others, when we either see it, or are made to conceive it in a very lively manner. That we often derive sorrow from the sorrow of others, is a matter of fact too obvious to require any instances to prove it; for this sentiment, like all the other original passions of human nature, is by no means confined to the virtuous and humane, though they perhaps may feel it with the most exquisite sensibility. The greatest ruffian, the most hardened violator of the laws of society, is not altogether without it.*

Adam Smith, The Theory of Moral Sentiments, 1759 [14]

Classic liberalism calls itself *'conservatism'* because its modern advocates seek to conserve the general libertarian principles under which the United States was brought into existence. The classical liberalism of Edmund Burke and Adam Smith, commonly called 'Conservatism' in the United States, distinguishes it from the 'New Liberalism' associated with such 20th century political leaders as Woodrow Wilson and Franklin Roosevelt. It is also significantly different from the 'Neo-Conservatism' that was developed since the fall of the Soviet Union, which urges the US government should assume an interventionist role in the affairs of other nations.

Foreign intervention can include both humanitarian and military support. Foreign Interventionists hold that liberal nations should be involved in the affairs of other sovereign states for the purpose of promoting a liberalized world order of free trade, economic autonomy, and the spread of western democratic forms throughout the global community. They argue that relationships between liberal states are usually more peaceful and that democracies seldom go to war with one another. The principles of interventionism gained prominence after World War I with Woodrow Wilson's Fourteen Points. [15]

Most conservative thinkers, from the time of Edmund Burke to the present, have been generally opposed to military interventionism and the massive statism it requires, and have been disinclined to use military force to alter the character of other non-aggressive sovereign states. The republican governments that Anglo-American conservatives generally claim to champion are institutions of limited power whose citizens are inclined to tend to their own business and expect others to do the same. Busy with their own responsibilities, this view of self-government recognizes that the problems of foreign cultures are too frequently made worse by uninvited good intentions and the costly militarism this leads to. The Founding Fathers, in particular, pointed to ancient Rome as an example of how ongoing military expansionism undermines republican government.

The pursuits of Empire and limited government are mutually exclusive. Empires and hegemons not only bully smaller defenseless nations, but they also subject their own hapless citizenry to the purposes of the state and its governing elites, typically cloaking such subjection in the color of patriotic duty. The nation-building interventionists advocate that state power can install the same social institutions that have worked for the dominant power on other vulnerable and dissimilar cultures. Because this cultural hegemony interferes with the organic make-up and traditions of the subjugated culture, it is unstable. Social instability results in social violence necessitating the abandonment of fiscal conservatism, since the effort involved in compelling the unwanted transformation of another society requires extensive military, bureaucratic, and social commitment. This cost diverts significant resources from essential governmental functions in the dominant state such as the provision of efficient infrastructure, governance and justice for its own people.

> Let me comment on that. I'm not so sure the role of the United States is to go around the world and say this is the way it's got to be. We can help. And maybe it's just our difference in government, the way we view government. I want to empower the people. I want to help people help themselves, not have government tell people what to do. I just don't think it's the role of the United States to walk into a country and say, we do it

CHARLES EDMUND COYOTE

this way, so should you. I think we can help. I know we've got to encourage democracy in the marketplaces. But take Russia, for example. We went into Russia, we said here is some IMF money, and it ended up in Viktor Chemomyrdin's pocket, and others, and yet we played like there was reform. The only people that are going to reform Russia are Russia. They're going to have to make the decision themselves. Mr. Putin is going to have to make the decision as to whether or not he wants to adhere to rule of law and normal accounting practices so that if countries and/or entities invest capital, there's a reasonable rate of return, a way to get the money out of the economy. But Russia has to make the decision. We can work with them on security matters, for example, but it's their call to make. So I'm not exactly sure where the vice president is coming from, but I think one way for us to end up being viewed as the ugly American is for us to go around the world saying, we do it this way, so should you. Now, we trust freedom. We know freedom is a powerful, powerful, powerful force, much bigger than the United States of America, as we saw recently in the Balkans. But maybe I misunderstand where you're coming from, Mr. Vice President, but I think the United States must be humble and must be proud and confident of our values, but humble in how we treat nations that are figuring out how to chart their own course.

     George W. Bush, October 11, 2000 [16], [17]

Nation building typically entails military occupation, transitional government, massive investment, and mushrooming bureaucracies, all of which detract from creative wealth building in the modern industrial sense. The typically unstable results lead to more military action and massive expenditure. Throughout history, the failure to exercise prudent respect for these principles has been and continues to be a significant factor in the decline of great nations:

> *It sounds crudely mercantilistic to express it this way, but*

wealth is usually needed to acquire military power, and military power is usually needed to acquire and protect wealth. If, however, too large a proportion of the state's resources is diverted from wealth creation and allocated instead to military purposes, then that is likely to lead to a weakening of national power over the longer term. In the same way, if a state overextends itself strategically – by, say, the conquest of extensive territories or the waging of costly wars – it runs the risk that the potential benefits from external expansion may be outweighed by the great expense of it all – a dilemma which becomes acute if the nation concerned has entered a period of relative economic decline.

Paul Kennedy, The Rise and Fall of the Great Powers, 1987 [18]

CHAPTER 10 REFERENCES

[1] Edmund Burke, Letter to Sir Hercules Langrishe, 1792, ourcivilisation.com;
http://www.ourcivilisation.com/smartboard/shop/burkee/extracts/chap18.htm
(SHORTENED URL: http://tinyurl.com/beheba)

[2] Magna Carta, Grand Lodge of British Columbia and Yukon;
http://www.freemasonry.bcy.ca/texts/magnacarta.html
(SHORTENED URL: http://tinyurl.com/caloba)

[3] The Text of Magna Carta, British Library modern translation;
http://www.fordham.edu:80/halsall/source/magnacarta.html
(SHORTENED URL: http://tinyurl.com/bilano)

[4]

(a) Edmund Burke, Reflections on the Revolution in France, 1790, Library of Economics and Liberty;
http://www.econlib.org/library/LFBooks/Burke/brkSWv2c1.html

(SHORTENED URL: http://tinyurl.com/refelo)

(b)
http://en.wikipedia.org/wiki/Reflections_on_the_Revolution
_in_France
(SHORTENED URL: http://tinyurl.com/relufa)

[5] Thomas Paine, Common Sense, January 1776, Modern History Sourcebook;
http://www.fordham.edu/halsall/mod/paine-common.html
(SHORTENED URL: http://tinyurl.com/pakohi)

[6] Edmund Burke, Letter to the Sheriffs of Bristol, On the Affairs of America, 1777, The Project Gutenberg;
http://www.gutenberg.org/files/15198/15198-h/15198-h.htm#SHERIFFS_OF_THE_CITY_OF_BRISTOL
(SHORTENED URL: http://tinyurl.com/bebona)

[7] The Constitution of the United States of America, US Supreme Court Center;
http://supreme.justia.com/constitution/

[8] The Constitution of the United States, As read by David P. Currie, Edward H. Levi Distinguished Service Professor Emeritus, University of Chicago Law School;
http://www.law.uchicago.edu/constitution#con
(SHORTENED URL: http://tinyurl.com/nokini)

[9] United States Constitution, Primary Documents in American History, The Library of Congress;
http://www.loc.gov/rr/program/bib/ourdocs/Constitution.html
(SHORTENED URL: http://tinyurl.com/mikore)

[10] THE RISE AND FALL OF THE GREAT POWERS, Economic Change and Military Conflict from 1500 to 2000, by Paul Kennedy, Vintage Books, A Division of Random House, New York, Copyright © 1987, p 178.

[11]
(a) Edmund Burke, Reflections on the Revolution in France, 1790; http://www.constitution.org/eb/rev_fran.htm
(SHORTENED URL: http://tinyurl.com/revofa)

(b)
http://en.wikipedia.org/wiki/Reflections_on_the_Revolution_in_France
(SHORTENED URL: http://tinyurl.com/relufa)

[12] An Inquiry into the Nature And Causes of the Wealth of Nations, Adam Smith, 1776, Pennsylvania State University; http://www2.hn.psu.edu/faculty/jmanis/adam-smith/Wealth-Nations.pdf
(SHORTENED URL: http://tinyurl.com/kakahe)

[13] An Inquiry into the Nature and Causes of the Wealth of Nations, Adam Smith, 1776, Library of Economics and Liberty; http://www.econlib.org/library/Smith/smWN.html
(SHORTENED URL: http://tinyurl.com/zakase)

[14] The Theory of the Moral Sentiments, Adam Smith, 1759, ibiblio.org; http://www.ibiblio.org/ml/libri/s/SmithA_MoralSentiments_p.pdf
(SHORTENED URL: http://tinyurl.com/temose)

[15] President Woodrow Wilson's Fourteen points, 8 January 1918, The Avalon Project, Lillian Goldman Law Library, Yale Law Library; http://avalon.law.yale.edu/20th_century/wilson14.asp
(SHORTENED URL: http://tinyurl.com/pefuto)

[16] George W Bush's Humble Foreign Policy? LiveLeak.com; http://www.liveleak.com/view?i=7bd_1195614597
(SHORTENED URL: http://tinyurl.com/bufosa)

[17] October 11 2000 Debate Transcript, October 11, 2000, The Second Gore-Bush Presidential Debate, COMMISSION ON PRESIDENTIAL DEBATES; http://www.debates.org/index.php?page=october-11-2000-debate-transcript
(SHORTENED URL: http://tinyurl.com/serake)

[18] THE RISE AND FALL OF THE GREAT POWERS, Economic Change and Military Conflict from 1500 to 2000, by Paul Kennedy, Vintage Books, A Division of Random

CHARLES EDMUND COYOTE

House, New York, Copyright © 1987, page xvi.

CHAPTER 11
YOU CAN'T GET FOOLED AGAIN

There's an old saying in Tennessee - I know it's in Texas, probably in Tennessee... that says, fool me once, shame on... shame on you. Fool me... you can't get fooled again.

George W. Bush, September 17, 2002

Until the Presidency of George W. Bush, policies of interventionism had been associated with liberal administrations such as those of Democrats Woodrow Wilson, Franklin Roosevelt, and Lyndon Johnson, or with left-centrist politicians such as Prime Minister Tony Blair of the Labor Party in the UK.

The son, George W. Bush, although a natural and charismatic politician, did not have the foreign policy background his father did. Lacking that, he chose to rely on the opinions of Dick Cheney, Donald Rumsfeld, Paul Wolfowitz and other neoconservatives.

It would have been far, far wiser to turn counter-terrorist policy over to the counterterrorist experts such as those who were trying to alert the White House to the looming danger approaching before the September 11 attack. After the attacks, even during the first months of the Afghan War, these experts were re-strained from following through on the opportunities that quickly emerged to finish off Mullah Omar, Osama bin Laden, and Ayman al-Zawahiri. As for Saddam Hussein, with whom al-Qaeda was a shared enemy, the Bush administration was determined to continue Washington's febrile obsession.

I believed going into the war that we were there to help the Iraqi people and find weapons of mass destruction.

CHARLES EDMUND COYOTE

But it quickly became clear that these two reasons for the war were absolutely false. If you mentioned weapons of mass destruction to intelligence officers they would laugh at you. It was not even part of the mission to look for these things. If it was part of the mission I would have known because I was part of the only intelligence company in the north of the country. I thought that maybe we were there to help the Iraqi people, but all I saw when I was there was Iraqis brutalized and their living conditions deteriorate drastically. Iraqis would tell me we were worse than Saddam.

Mike Prysner, US Army Corporal, Iraq War Veteran

That a politician such as George W. Bush would represent himself as a conservative to gain the Presidency and later turn to a fundamentally liberal foreign policy to address the problems and opportunities of the September 11 attacks can be better understood by looking at the perspectives of mainstream media personalities, such as Rush Limbaugh, who exemplified the confusion in his Wall Street Journal op-ed of October 17, 2005:

Unlike our liberal friends, who are constantly looking for new words to conceal their true beliefs and are in a perpetual state of reinvention, we conservatives are unapologetic about our ideals.

Rush Limbaugh, October 17, 2005 [1]

One of the '*new words*' that concealed the true beliefs formulating the Bush Administration's foreign policy is the oxymoronic term '*Neo-conservative*'. A meld of two innately contradictory terms, '*Neo*', (from the Latin word for '*New*') and '*Conservative*', (from the Latin expression for '*Preserving the Old*'), the term illustrates the muddled thinking it represents; yet, because it came in the guise of Republican red, main stream supporters, such as Limbaugh, were deceived by the reinvention.

During the early months of his Administration, George W. Bush was criticized by neo-conservatives for not showing enough support for Israel and for being soft on China during an incident involving a downed US spy plane. [2] His public positions during the early months of his Presidency, however, were little different than the restrained foreign policy he argued for during the 2000 campaign:

> *If we don't have a clear vision of the military, if we don't stop extending our troops all around the world in nation-building missions, then we're going to have a serious problem coming down the road. And I'm going to prevent that.*
>
> *George W. Bush, October 3, 2000* [3]

The Republican Party's campaign platform in the 2000 election called for removing Saddam Hussein from power. Key members of its new administration, including Vice President Dick Cheney and Defense Secretary Donald Rumsfeld, had been open advocates of invading Iraq since 1997. In Cheney's case, this was a reversal of the position he had followed as Secretary of Defense under President George H.W. Bush, by which he had said that invading Iraq would throw American troops into a quagmire. [4] Before his Presidential victory, candidate George W. Bush repeatedly criticized the Clinton-Gore Administration for being too willing to use the US military in interventionist missions. Despite what was said before the election, once in office, only 2 months later, the newly installed Bush administration began secretly moving in the opposite direction.

CHARLES EDMUND COYOTE

Paul O'Neill, Secretary of the Treasury during the first two years of George W. Bush's Presidency, was privy to all meetings of the President's Cabinet and National Security Council. He learned, from the new administration's very first National Security Council meeting on January 30, 2001, that a US invasion of Iraq and the removal of Saddam Hussein were going to be major objectives. [5]

> It was all about finding a way to do it. That was the tone of it. The president saying 'Go find me a way to do this,'... For me, the notion of pre-emption, that the US has the unilateral right to do whatever we decide to do, is a really huge leap.
>
> Paul O'Neill, US Secretary of the Treasury, January 2001 - December 2002 [6]

At the next National Security Council meeting, the occupation of Iraq was discussed and a secret brief titled 'Plan for post-Saddam Iraq' was presented. Based on interviews with others also present at the meetings, Suskind wrote that the planning discussed the portioning out of Iraq's oil wealth and war crimes trials for the Baath Party leadership. A document dated March 5, 2001, titled 'Foreign Suitors for Iraqi Oilfield contracts' includes a map of areas for exploration and discusses contractors and nations interested in Iraqi oil. [7], [8] As reported by Pulitzer prize winning author Ron Suskind:

> The thing that's most surprising, I think, is how emphatically, from the very first, the administration had said 'X' during the campaign, but from the first day was often doing 'Y'. Not just saying 'Y,' but actively moving toward the opposite of what they had said during the election.
>
> Ron Suskind, 11 January 2004 [9]

Secretary O'Neill made some 19,000 documents available to Suskind for his book, 'The Price of Loyalty: George W. Bush, the White House, and the Education of Paul O'Neill', including memoranda to the President, minutes of meetings, and volumes of reports. O'Neill's records reveal Bush to be relatively unconcerned about following much of the agenda on which he had been elected in 2000. O'Neill suspected something unseemly within the administration's power structure and described the President as possibly a pawn of unseen powers, somewhat disengaged and incurious. However O'Neill was not close enough to the inner circle to clearly see what was going on. Secretary O'Neill says that Donald Rumsfeld told him not to get involved with the book. Rumsfeld appeared to be concerned that if the nation began to understand that the President had little interest in domestic issues or understanding of international affairs, his chances of re-election in 2004 would be seriously damaged.

George W. Bush's administration was populated by a group of influential East Coast Intellectuals and political insiders with advanced degrees from prestigious universities. Known as the 'Neoconservatives', their perspective had been developed by influential writers, academics, and publishers who once had subscribed to the ideals of Roosevelt's New Deal. Some even had overtly socialist and Marxist backgrounds but had become disenchanted with the ability of leftist ideologies to develop human potential. [10] These 'new' conservatives saw the protests against the Vietnam War as anti-American, and were shocked by the social meltdown they perceived in the youth counterculture and black power movements of the 1960s. They had come to believe that liberalism had a tendency to degenerate into self-centered hedonism.

> *Finally, there was the realm of culture. If anti-Communism was the ruling passion of the neo-conservatives in foreign affairs, opposition to the counterculture of the 1960's was their ruling passion at home. Indeed, I suspect that revulsion against the counterculture accounted for more converts to neo-conservatism than any other single factor.*
>
> *Norman Podhoretz, March 1996* [11]

Socialist Michael Harrington is often given credit for popularizing the meaning of neo-conservatism, describing the former leftists who comprised its new leadership as *'socialists for Nixon'*. By the late 1970s, writers such as Irving Kristol and Norman Podhoretz were using the term to portray themselves. Kristol argued that neoconservatives could be distinguished from traditional conservatives because they possessed a more forward-looking approach to social issues drawn from their liberal heritage.

Neo-conservatism's former leftists moved through a connection to the Hubert Humphrey/Henry Jackson wing of the Democratic Party to the Republican Party, where they became an amalgam of survivors from the discredited Nixon administration and the former leftists disenchanted with Lyndon Johnson's *'Great Society'*. Those identified with the movement included Ronald Reagan's UN Ambassador Jeane Kirkpatrick, Washington State Senator Henry M. Jackson, publisher Irving Kristol, and writer Norman B. Podhoretz. Many, such as Joe Lieberman and Paul Wolfowitz, had been strong supporters of the 1960's Civil Rights Movement. In many ways, these new conservatives were intellectual elite representing many of the qualities that had always troubled traditional conservatives. They had little in common with the American main stream and little purpose aside from that of formulating policy from the D.C. Beltway, taking well-paid government, think-tank, and university positions from which to formulate statist oriented ideologies.

The counterculture didn't mature as the neocons had foreseen. As American involvement in Vietnam came to an end, much of the hippie and protest movements reintegrated back into the mainstream. Once rebellious youth, they became stockbrokers (Jerry Rubin) or businessmen (Steve Jobs); the Black Power advocates, at least those who survived COINTELPRO, moved on to university professorships (Angela Davis), PhD's (Huey Newton) or the Republican Party (Eldridge Cleaver). The cold and suspicious Soviet bear went into hibernation, and the once omnipresent domestic chaos and international danger faded away like the ominous night of Mussorgsky's Bald Mountain. [12] America's neo-conservative ideologues needed to come up with a new purpose.

The Neo-conservative movement had begun with a focus on domestic policy, criticizing excess in the call for social equality and bringing attention to the unintended consequences of the liberal state. Rather than simply responding to problems as they arose, the neo-conservatives were thinking up new problems for the government to solve, finding new causes in foreign policy and, thanks to their Ivy League degrees and connections, new rationales for good government jobs. Problems once seen inside the United States were now found throughout the world: chaos was everywhere. The solutions would be devised from well-endowed chairs at the think-tanks, university positions, and

CHARLES EDMUND COYOTE

handsome speaker's fees. The US military would have to become strong enough for the US government to dominate the world and the neo-cons intended to dominate the US government. With the neo-liberals endeavoring to export the basis of America's wealth, the neo-conservatives intended to export the basis of its government, democracy, itself.

> *The whole aim of practical politics is to keep the populace alarmed (and hence clamorous to be led to safety) by menacing it with an endless series of hobgoblins, most of them imaginary.*
>
> *H. L. Mencken*

During the 1970s, the neoconservatives had taken up opposition to Détente with the Soviet Union and found therein a champion and a gifted communicator, Ronald Reagan. Their influence on the Carter-Reagan Defense buildups would be profound, with Donald Rumsfeld's Team B creating policy out of an institutionalized distrust of CIA analysis that would continue through the invasion of Iraq 30 years later. Despite the fact that the Soviet Union was beginning to unravel in the late 1970s, Rumsfeld's Team B began promoting expensive military buildups by persuading the President that the Russians were working on military technologies so advanced it was impossible for us to discern their existence. The President was also encouraged to extend the buildup because communist states, such as East Germany, were about to overtake West Germany in economic production. [13] Successful in advancing their careers while Reagan was president, they orchestrated such fiascoes as the Iran-Contra affair. However, they were not appreciated during the administration of ex-CIA chief, George H.W. Bush, who referred to them as *'the crazies in the basement'*. [14]

The coalition that supported Ronald Reagan's Presidency was an alliance of people who shared a strong opposition to communism and the welfare state, and who believed that America was in danger of losing the virtues that made it a great and prosperous nation. That broad alliance included businessmen, constitutionalists, libertarians, militant nationalists, neoconservatives, the religious right, and social conservatives. When the Soviet Union collapsed, the cohesion of that coalition began to unwind.

Out of power during the Clinton years, the neoconservatives took refuge in influential policy centers such as The Heritage Foundation, the federally funded National Endowment for Democracy, and the American Enterprise Institute (AEI). Unlike the traditional conservatives who were enthusiastic about the *'peace dividend'* coming with the end of the Cold War, the neo-cons urged America's leaders to expand America's military power and undertake aggressive foreign policies.

By the late 1980s, a second generation of neoconservatives had begun to rise. They convinced the State department to distance itself from the corrupt administration of Philippine President Ferdinand Marcos, encouraged the removal of Chile's Augusto Pinochet from power, and flummoxed traditional conservatives by getting President Reagan tied up in the Iran-Contra scandal:

> *I'd say it's the god-damned stupidest foreign policy blunder this country's ever made!*
>
> *Senator Barry Goldwater, 1986, quoted by PBS News Anchor Robert MacNeil*

CHARLES EDMUND COYOTE

The neoconservatives had no intention of stopping with that. Ambitious to spread American style democracy and economic values throughout the world, they began to reject US reliance on many of the international organizations and treaties that had been initially advanced by the United States to give a more equitable voice to other peoples. In their worldview, the word 'Democracy' meant the US was preordained to be in charge. Neo-conservatism also had its opaque influences:

> There are different kinds of truths for different kinds of people. There are truths appropriate for children; truths that are appropriate for students; truths that are appropriate for educated adults; and truths that are appropriate for highly educated adults, and the notion that there should be one set of truths available to everyone is a modern democratic fallacy. It doesn't work.
>
> Irving Kristol [15], [16]

Although Kristol, Podhoretz, and those who shared their worldview had come to call themselves 'conservatives', they brought with them the intellectual luggage of a leftist background that believed it was government's duty to provide solutions to problems they – the intellectual elite – decided needed to be solved. The neocons found powerful allies in the rise of the religious right and the two groups began a war for control of the Republican Party. By 1992, traditional conservatism had lost:

> When you say 'radical right' today, I think of these moneymaking ventures by fellows like Pat Robertson and others who are trying to take the Republican Party away from the Republican Party, and make a religious organization out of it. If that ever happens, kiss politics goodbye.

Barry Goldwater, July 1994 [17]

The *'new'* conservatives did not come to the Republican Party in order to learn the values *'old'* conservatives were advocating: Limited Government, the Rule of Law, Fiscal Responsibility, etc. They had no intention of abandoning statism. They believed, despite the mandates of Constitutional federalism, they knew better than the common people what was best, not only for the common people, but also for the other peoples of the world:

> *Viewed in this way, one can say that the historical task and political purpose of neoconservatism would seem to be this: to convert the Republican party, and American conservatism in general, against their respective wills into a new kind of conservative politics suitable to governing a modern democracy.*
>
> *Irving Kristol* [18]

By the middle years of George W. Bush's administration, those calling themselves *'conservatives'* would be supporting an explosive enlargement of the federal government and spending, constitutionally unsupportable warrantless surveillance, a usurpation and arrogant abuse of executive power, global Wilsonianism, and an undefined condition of endless war.

> *Neocons do not feel that kind of alarm or anxiety about the growth of the state in the past century, seeing it as natural, indeed inevitable.*
>
> *Irving Kristol* [19]

The *'new'* conservatives employed fundamentally different tactics than those valued by traditional conservatives who believed in the collective wisdom of American people and endeavored to advance their cause by appealing to fact and logic. The neocon-servatives understood the power of marketing and deftly applied it to the manipulation of the Body Politic. They defined the terms by which the battle for control of the Republican Party was waged and claimed legitimacy for the expanded Federal role they intended to impose:

> *The first overt volley fired on behalf of the neoconservatives in the War for the GOP's soul was an article appearing in National Review on March 16, 1992, entitled "In Pursuit of Anti-Semitism Chapter II." The article was a long, rambling, and utterly dishonest attack on the editorial positions of Joe Sobran and Pat Buchanan occasioned by their reasoned disagreement with American policy toward Israel. Sobran and Buchanan were accused of anti-Semitism, a canard reminiscent of Jesse Jackson's frequent allegations of racism against those who opposed Welfare State social policies. At the time I could not understand the motive for this completely unwarranted hit piece. The article's blatant falseness and unfairness so infuriated me that I cancelled my subscription, one that had been in effect since undergraduate school.*

> *In hindsight, the motive has become obvious. The smear campaign against Sobran and Buchanan was the opening gambit in the process of 'redefining' conservatism. By discrediting the most prominent and effective spokesmen for traditional conservatism, potential impediments to that redefinition would be neutralized. By the way, that many neoconservatives are Jews is true but irrelevant. The neocons use this demographic fact to vaccinate them-selves against opposition by playing the 'anti-Semitic' card whenever their policy preferences are challenged. The tactic is intellectually dishonest and illogical but it has certainly been effective.*

> *An Ordinary Man, Tipping Point, April 5, 2008* [20]

There were other influences as well. One frequently cited

for the highly educated, is the scholar Leo Strauss. An emigrant from Nazi Germany, Strauss held a Political Science Professorship at the University of Chicago from 1949-1969. Like Plato in ancient times, Strauss believed that *'Noble Lies'* were essential to maintain a stable society because they gave purpose to the lives of the mass of people that would otherwise be consumed by the moral relativism and self-indulgence. Strauss believed *'The Wise'*, those who could be comfortable with the truth, must keep their motives secret and take control of the government in a world in which *'deception is the norm in political life'.* [21]

CHAPTER 11 REFERENCES

[1] Holding Court, by Rush Limbaugh, The Wall Street Journal, 17 October 2005; AMERICAN CONSERVATISM - WSJ.com

[2] Wikipedia article on Neoconservatism; 2.6.1 Administration of George W. Bush;
http://en.wikipedia.org/wiki/Neoconservatism
(SHORTENED URL: http://tinyurl.com/kexova)

[3] George W. Bush, First Presidential Debate, 2000 US Presidential Debate - October 3, Wikisource;
http://en.wikisource.org/wiki/2000 U.S. Presidential Debate - October 3
(SHORTENED URL: http://tinyurl.com/bureba)

[4] Cheney Warns of Iraq Quagmire, American Enterprise Institute 1994 Video & Transcript; Mother Jones Blog;
http://www.motherjones.com/mojoblog/archives/2007/08/5151 cheney warns of.html
(SHORTENED URL: http://tinyurl.com/birelo)

[5] Bush Sought 'Way' To Invade Iraq?, O'Neill Tells '60 Minutes' Iraq Was 'Topic A' 8 Months before 9-11, by

Rebecca Leung, 11 January 2004;
http://www.cbsnews.com/stories/2004/01/09/60minutes/main592330.shtml
(SHORTENED URL: http://tinyurl.com/releno)

[6] Bush Sought 'Way' To Invade Iraq?, O'Neill Tells '60 Minutes' Iraq Was 'Topic A' 8 Months before 9-11, by Rebecca Leung, 11 January 2004;
http://www.cbsnews.com/stories/2004/01/09/60minutes/main592330.shtml
(SHORTENED URL: http://tinyurl.com/releno)

[7] Bush Sought 'Way' To Invade Iraq?, O'Neill Tells '60 Minutes' Iraq Was 'Topic A' 8 Months before 9-11, by Rebecca Leung, January 11, 2004;
http://www.cbsnews.com/stories/2004/01/09/60minutes/main592330.shtml
(SHORTENED URL: http://tinyurl.com/releno)

[8] Maps and Charts of Iraqi Oil Fields, as of March 5, 2001; Documents turned over by the US Department of Commerce under a March 5, 2002 court order resulting from a Freedom of Information Act lawsuit filed by Judicial Watch concerning the activities of the Cheney Energy Task Force;
http://www.judicialwatch.org/bulletins/maps-and-charts-of-iraqi-oil-fields/
(SHORTENED URL: http://tinyurl.com/rarako)

[9] Inside the Bush White House: Transcript of Former Treasury Secretary Paul O'Neill's Interview, CBS, 60 Minutes, 11 January 2004, Centre for Research on Globalisation;
http://globalresearch.ca/articles/CBS401A.html
(SHORTENED URL: http://tinyurl.com/hiteho)

[10] Neoconservatism: A Eulogy, by Norman Podhoretz, March 1996, Commentary, commentarymagazine.com;
http://www.commentarymagazine.com/viewarticle.cfm/neoconservatism--a-eulogy-8533
(SHORTENED URL: http://tinyurl.com/weleno)

[11] Neoconservatism: A Eulogy, by Norman Podhoretz,

March 1996, Commentary, commentarymagazine.com;
http://www.commentarymagazine.com/viewarticle.cfm/neo
conservatism--a-eulogy-8533
(SHORTENED URL: http://tinyurl.com/bomesa)

[12] Mussorgsky-Berezovsky: Night on Bald Mountain;
Fantasia, YouTube;
http://www.youtube.com/watch?v=gMmfaaiWMEs
(SHORTENED URL: http://tinyurl.com/hellona)

[13] Ex-Aide Calls CIA Under Casey and Gates Corrupt and
Slanted, by Paul F. Horvitz, The New York Times, 2 October
1991;
http://www.nytimes.com/1991/10/02/news/02iht-
cia .html
(SHORTENED URL: http://tinyurl.com/helaka)

[14] THEY KNEW THEY WERE RIGHT, The Rise of The
Neocons, by Jacob Heilbrunn; Book Review by Ted Widmer
for The Washington Post, February 3, 2008;
http://www.washingtonpost.com/wp-
dyn/content/article/2008/01/31/AR2008013103920 pf.html
(SHORTENED URL: http://tinyurl.com/reneka)

[15] Who Killed the Republican Party?, Tipping Point, April
5, 2008;
http://tippingpoint-watchman.blogspot.com/2008/04/who-
killed-republican-party.html
(SHORTENED URL: http://tinyurl.com/kerepa)

[16] Noble lie, Wikipedia Encyclopedia, 14 April 2009;
http://en.wikipedia.org/wiki/Noble lie
(SHORTENED URL: http://tinyurl.com/vobalu)

[17] Barry Goldwater's Left Turn, by Lloyd Grove,
Washington Post, July 28, 1994, Washingtonpost.com;
http://www.washingtonpost.com/wp-
srv/politics/daily/may98/goldwater072894.htm
(SHORTENED URL: http://tinyurl.com/bagole)

[18] The Neoconservative Persuasion, by Irving Kristol, The
Weekly Standard, August 25, 2003;
http://www.weeklystandard.com/Content/Public/Articles/00

0/000/003/000tzmlw.asp
(SHORTENED URL: http://tinyurl.com/sikopi)

[19] The Neoconservative Persuasion, by Irving Kristol, The Weekly Standard, August 25, 2003;
http://www.weeklystandard.com/Content/Public/Articles/00
0/000/003/000tzmlw.asp
(SHORTENED URL: http://tinyurl.com/sikopi)

[20] Who Killed the Republican Party? Tipping Point, April 5, 2008;
http://tippingpoint-watchman.blogspot.com/2008/04/who-killed-republican-party.html
(SHORTENED URL: http://tinyurl.com/kerepa)

[21] Leo Strauss and the World of Intelligence, by Gary J. Schmitt and Abram N. Shulsky, 1999;
http://turcopolier.typepad.com/sic_semper_tyrannis/files/leo_strauss_and_the_world_of_intelligence.pdf
(SHORTENED URL: http://tinyurl.com/letege)

CHAPTER 12
DID I SAY THOSE WORDS?

I think - tide turning - see, as I remember - I was raised in the desert, but tides kind of - it's easy to see a tide turn - did I say those words?

George W. Bush, Washington, D.C., June 14, 2006

The question of how truthful statesmen can be and still govern effectively has been debated since the dawn of civilization. Leo Strauss believed that institutional myths are essential. Although Anglo-American conservatism and the liberal traditions from which it sprang stress individual liberty and reasonable self-determination, Strauss believed there should be more focus on human excellence and virtue. He questioned the ability of such goals to coexist with individual self-determination. He maintained that the freedoms common to Western democracies led the individual to reject social mores and authority.

Prominent officials who studied under Professor Strauss include Dr. Abram Shulsky, a Director at the Pentagon's Office of Special Plans; Dr. Gary Schmitt, a co-founder of the influential Project for the New American Century (PNAC); and Dr. Paul Wolfowitz, former Deputy Secretary of Defense and one of the chief architects of the Iraq War. [1] Others influenced by Strauss have included Irving Kristol, '*the godfather of neo-conservatism*'; Harvard University Professor of Government, Harvey C. Mansfield, Ph.D.; and The *Weekly Standard's* founder and Editor, William Kristol, Ph.D.

Leo Strauss left his position at Berlin's Academy of Jewish

CHARLES EDMUND COYOTE

Research for work in Paris, France on a Rockefeller Fellowship in 1932. With the rise of Nazism in his native Germany, he never returned. But even that did not sever his support for right-wing politics. In a 1933 letter, which was written one month after Adolf Hitler implemented the first anti-Jewish legislation, Strauss defended right-wing politics. He criticized the Nazis from that perspective, noting that he would rather live in repressed isolation than lend his support to such ideas as the inalienability of human rights:

> *Strauss wrote to Löwith [German scholar Karl Löwith] in May 1933, five months after Hitler's appointment as Chancellor and a month after implementation of the first anti-Jewish legislation, that 'Just because Germany has turned to the right and has expelled us,' meaning Jews, 'it simply does not follow that the principles of the right are therefore to be rejected. To the contrary, only on the basis of principles of the right – fascist, authoritarian, imperial – is it possible in a dignified manner, without the ridiculous and pitiful appeal to 'the inalienable rights of man' to protest against the 'mean nonentity,' the mean nonentity being the Nazi party. In other words, he is attacking the Nazis from the right in this letter. He wrote that he had been reading Caesar's Commentaries, and valued Virgil's judgment that, 'under imperial rule the subjected are spared and the proud are subdued.' And he concluded, 'there is no reason to crawl to the cross, even to the cross of liberalism, as long as anywhere in the world the spark glimmers of Roman thinking. And moreover, better than any cross is the ghetto.'*
>
> *Nicholas Xenos, Spring 2004* [2]

Despite the lip serve paid to Reaganite *'moral clarity'*, neoconservative ideologies were seeking to co-opt power for the national government. This ideology was profoundly different from that advocated by the 40th President who tended to exemplify overbearing government as a problem and not an answer. Reagan's policies often exemplified Theodore Roosevelt's dictum to *"Speak softly and carry a Big Stick"*. Roosevelt, though demonstrating great executive ability and perception, seldom exemplified the habit of speaking softly.

Ronald Reagan almost always avoided the use of direct force; the sum of his use of American military power was a 2-day action in 1983 against the 600-man militia defending the island of Granada, and the 1986 bombing of Libya. About such neoconservatives as Norman Podhoretz and Elliot Abrams, Reagan once told Kenneth Duberstein, his chief of staff:

> *Those sons of bitches won't be happy until we have 25,000 troops in Managua, and I'm not going to do it.*
>
> *Ronald Reagan* [3], [4]

The neoconservative notion that the common man is unequal to the task of self-government would have been an abomination to the Reagan Revolution.

> *If we lose freedom here, there is no place to escape to. This is the last stand on Earth. And this idea that government is beholden to the people, that it has no other source of power except to sovereign people, is still the newest and most unique idea in all the long history of man's relation to man. This is the issue of this election. Whether we believe in our capacity for self-government or whether we abandon the American revolution and confess that a little intellectual elite in a far-distant capital can plan our lives for us better than we can plan them ourselves.*
>
> *Ronald Reagan, Stump Speech for the 1964 Goldwater Campaign* [5]

Nor was the newly conservative Reagan of the 1960s alone

CHARLES EDMUND COYOTE

in holding to that understanding:

> *The world is very different now. For man holds in his mortal hands the power to abolish all forms of human poverty and all forms of human life. And yet the same revolutionary beliefs for which our forebears fought are still at issue around the globe – the belief that the rights of man come not from the generosity of the state but from the hand of God.*
>
> John F. Kennedy, January 20, 1961 [6]

Such words lend little support to the 'noble lies' of government elites. Napoleon was once asked: *'Sir, have you ever given thought to the 3 million people that have been killed by your wars?'*; *'I made their boring lives more interesting,'* was his response, ignoring the reality that most are too busy with work, family, community and their own hopes and dreams, having little room left for the luxury of boredom.

The neoconservatives – almost none of whom have any record of military service – criticized both George H. W. Bush, a war hero, and Bill Clinton for curbing military expenditures at the end of the Cold War. They also criticized Ronald Reagan for his reluctance to use American military power in pursuit of the American interests as they perceived them. [7] The power vacuum created by the collapse of the Soviet Union left the United States standing at the heights of world power, giving this country, the neocons said, a ten-year window of opportunity to remake the world in its own image.

Twenty years before, the leaders of what became the neoconservative movement were similarly concerned about the Democratic Party's plans to scale back the size of the American military following the Vietnam War.

They had other interests they wanted the American people to look after:

> Senator McGovern is very sincere when he says that he will try to cut the military budget by 30%. And this is to drive a knife in the heart of Israel... Jews don't like big military budgets. But it is now an interest of the Jews to have a large and powerful military establishment in the United States... American Jews who care about the survival of the state of Israel have to say, no, we don't want to cut the military budget, it is important to keep that military budget big, so that we can defend Israel.
>
> *Irving Kristol, 1973* [8]

Although the US Constitution had created the federal government for the benefit of the American people, the neocons felt the US needed to be tied in with the ancient religious wars and ethnic conflicts of other peoples on other continents. They chose to ignore the Bill of Rights and joined with those on the religious right who believed constitution or not, the United States, as a country, had a *'Christian'* obligation to support Israel. Despite that fact that the neocons projects would place an immense burden on the blood and wealth of the American people, they were making powerful converts.

One of the most formidable was former Secretary of Defense, Richard Bruce 'Dick' Cheney. A consummate Washington insider, Cheney had presided over much of the massive US military downsizing that came with the end of the Cold War. Despite strong pressure from Congress, his approach was fiscally conservative. He advocated limiting the size of unnecessary government, and reducing the Defense Departments' size and budget by slashing no longer needed weapons systems and bases, and by dropping the number of military personnel from about 2.2 million in 1989 to 1.8 million by 1993.

As a part of George H. W. Bush's cabinet, Cheney had defended the President's decision not to extend the first Gulf War beyond its UN mandate to go on to Baghdad after Saddam:

> *But we made a very conscious decision not to proceed for several reasons...*
>
> *...If you get into the business of committing US forces on the ground in Iraq to occupy the place, my guess is I'd probably still have people there today, instead of having been able to bring them home. We would have been in a situation, once we went into Bagdad, where we would have engaged in the kind of street by street, house to house fighting in an urban setting that would have been dramatically different from what we were able to do in the Gulf and Kuwait, in the desert, where our precision guided munitions and our long range artillery and tanks were so devastating against those Iraqi forces. You would have been fighting in a built-up urban area, large civilian population, and much heavier prospects of casualties...*
>
> *...Everybody, of course, was tremendously impressed with the fact that we were able to prevail at such a low cost, given the predictions with respect to casualties in major modern warfare. But for the 146 Americans who were killed in action, and for their families, it was not a cheap or a low cost conflict. Bottom line question for me was how many additional American lives is Saddam Hussein worth? The answer: not very damn many. I think the President got it right both times: both when he decided to use military force to defeat Saddam Hussein's aggression, but also when he made, what I think was a very wise decision, to stop military operations when we did.*
>
> *Dick Cheney, September 1992* [9], [10], [11]

In 1997, a neoconservative think tank, the Project for

the New American Century (PNAC), was founded by William Kristol, son of Irving Kristol, and Robert Kagan, a bestselling foreign policy commentator. The PNAC would become the intellectual center of the drive to a second war with Iraq. Its directors included Chairman William Kristol, Robert Kagan, Bruce Jackson, Mark Gerson and Randy Scheunemann. The PNAC began promoting a radical departure from the more reserved foreign policies that had prospered the American nation since the days of its Founding Fathers. These traditions of restraint had been well articulated by George Washington at the end of his Presidency. Washington, along with co-authors James Madison and Alexander Hamilton, composed 'Washington's Farewell Address' as the First President's parting counsel to the new nation:

> Observe good faith and justice towards all nations; cultivate peace and harmony with all. Religion and morality enjoin this conduct; and can it be, that good policy does not equally enjoin it – It will be worthy of a free, enlightened, and at no distant period, a great nation, to give to mankind the magnanimous and too novel example of a people always guided by an exalted justice and benevolence. Who can doubt that, in the course of time and things, the fruits of such a plan would richly repay any temporary advantages which might be lost by a steady adherence to it? Can it be that Providence has not connected the permanent felicity of a nation with its virtue? The experiment, at least, is recommended by every sentiment which ennobles human nature. Alas! is it rendered impossible by its vices?

Washington's Farewell Address 1796 [12]

Now, 200 years later, The Project for the New American Century proclaimed that 'American leadership is good both for America and for the world' and advocated military strength and energetic diplomacy as the

CHARLES EDMUND COYOTE

key to the still young nation's world leadership and *'to shape a new century favorable to American principles and interests'*: [13]

Project for the New American Century
Statement of Principles
June 3, 1997

American foreign and defense policy is adrift. Conservatives have criticized the incoherent policies of the Clinton Administration. They have also resisted isolationist impulses from within their own ranks. But conservatives have not confidently advanced a strategic vision of America's role in the world. They have not set forth guiding principles for American foreign policy. They have allowed differences over tactics to obscure potential agreement on strategic objectives. And they have not fought for a defense budget that would maintain American security and advance American interests in the new century.

We aim to change this. We aim to make the case and rally support for American global leadership.

As the 20th century draws to a close, the United States stands as the world's preeminent power. Having led the West to victory in the Cold War, America faces an opportunity and a challenge: Does the United States have the vision to build upon the achievements of past decades? Does the United States have the resolve to shape a new century favorable to American principles and interests?

We are in danger of squandering the opportunity and failing the challenge. We are living off the capital – both the military investments and the foreign policy achievements – built up by past administrations. Cuts in foreign affairs and defense spending, inattention to the tools of statecraft, and inconstant leadership are making it increasingly difficult to sustain American influence around the world. And the promise of short-term commercial benefits threatens to override strategic considerations. As a consequence, we are jeopardizing the nation's ability to meet present threats and to deal with potentially greater challenges that lie ahead.

We seem to have forgotten the essential elements of the Reagan Administration's success: a military that is strong and ready to meet both present and future challenges; a foreign policy that boldly and purposefully promotes American principles abroad; and national leadership that accepts the United States' global responsibilities.

Of course, the United States must be prudent in how it exercises its power. But we cannot safely avoid the responsibilities of global leadership or the costs that are associated with its exercise. America has a vital role in maintaining peace and security in Europe, Asia, and the Middle East. If we shirk our responsibilities, we invite challenges to our fundamental interests. The history of the 20th century should have taught us that it is important to shape circumstances before crises emerge, and to meet threats before they become dire. The history of this century should have taught us to embrace the cause of American leadership.

Our aim is to remind Americans of these lessons and to draw their consequences for today. Here are four consequences:

• We need to increase defense spending significantly if we are to carry out our global responsibilities today and modernize our armed forces for the future;

• We need to strengthen our ties to democratic allies and to challenge regimes hostile to our interests and values;

• We need to promote the cause of political and economic freedom abroad;

• We need to accept responsibility for America's unique role in preserving and extending an international order friendly to our security, our prosperity, and our principles.

Such a Reaganite policy of military strength and moral clarity may not be fashionable today. But it is necessary if the United States is to build on the successes of this past century and to ensure our security and our greatness in the next.

CHARLES EDMUND COYOTE

Elliott Abrams - Gary Bauer - William J. Bennett

Jeb Bush - Dick Cheney - Eliot A. Cohen - Midge Decter

Paula Dobriansky - Steve Forbes - Aaron Friedberg

Francis Fukuyama - Frank Gaffney - Fred C. Ikle

Donald Kagan - Zalmay Khalilzad - I. Lewis Libby

Norman Podhoretz - Dan Quayle - Peter W. Rodman

Stephen P. Rosen - Henry S. Rowen - Donald Rumsfeld

Vin Weber - George Weigel - Paul Wolfowitz

On January 26, 1998, Project for the New American Century members (including Richard Armitage, John Bolton, Zalmay Khalilzad, Richard Perle, Donald Rumsfeld, Vin Weber and Paul Wolfowitz) posted an open letter on the PNAC website to President Bill Clinton, calling for his administration to undertake a military ground operation to remove Saddam Hussein and the threat they perceived he posed to the United States. [14] Flouting the Rule of Law their posting continued:

> *In any case, American policy cannot continue to be crippled by a misguided insistence on unanimity in the UN Security Council.*
>
> *Project for the New American Century, Letter to President Clinton on Iraq* [15]

UNSCOM (the United Nations Special Commission on Iraq) is an organization created to verify Iraqi compliance with UN policies concerning its weapons of mass destruction. Executive Chairman Richard Butler was optimistic about reaching a successful conclusion to their work of verifying Saddam's compliance with the UN mandates. But, according to Eric Fournier, a French diplomat formerly assigned as advisor to Chairman Butler, the US State Department called Butler to let him know they would not be happy if the disarmament issue were to be concluded at that time. [16]

Former UNSCOM member and senior weapons inspector, Scott Ritter, said later that Richard Butler and his staff were gathering intelligence unrelated to the issue of prohibited WMDs, but useful in the event of future military attacks. [17], [18], [19] According to Ritter, the UNSCOM team he was in charge of was secretly trying to provoke Iraq into non-compliance so that the US military would have an excuse to attack. [20] Iraq had long been balking at cooperating with UNSCOM because Tariq Aziz, the country's Deputy Prime Minister, complained that UNSCOM officials were acting as spies for the United States. [21] Aziz's claims were later confirmed by Weapons Inspector, Scott Ritter, as well as others who had been on the UNSCOM team. [22]

On January 13, 1998, Iraq announced it was withdrawing its cooperation with the UN inspection team, claiming it did not trust those in the group having US or UK citizenship. [23] Throughout most of 1998, the UN Security Council and the Revolutionary Command Council of Iraq were in contention. The UN asserted that Iraq's actions were in violation of the relevant resolutions but Iraq maintained that officials within UNSCOM were using those resolutions to pursue their own agendas. [24] In his book, *Saddam Defiant*, published in 2000, former UNSCOM Chairman Richard Butler says Saddam Hussein did not expel the weapons inspectors from Iraq in 1998, as George W. Bush would later allege. Rather, according to Butler, it was US Ambassador Peter Burleigh, acting on instructions from Washington, who suggested Butler should pull his team from Iraq to protect them from the forthcoming US and British airstrikes. [25], [26]

Regime change for Iraq became the official policy of the United States on October 31, 1998, with President Clinton signing into law *H.R. 4655 – the Iraq Liberation Act of 1998*, which was enacted following the withdrawal of the U.N. weapons inspectors. The initiative was a marked departure from the terms of UN Security Council Resolution 687 of April 1991, which had been established to deal with the elimination of Iraq's WMDs, their missile delivery systems, and its repayment of international debts and reparations. [27] The Iraq Liberation Act provided up to $97 million in broadcasting, humanitarian, and military assistance to *'Iraqi individuals, groups, or both, opposed to the Saddam Hussein regime and committed to democratic values'* and declared:

> It should be the policy of the United States to support efforts to remove the regime headed by Saddam Hussein from power in Iraq and to promote the emergence of a democratic government to replace that regime.
>
> *Iraq Liberation Act of 1998* [28]

One month after the passage of the *"Iraq Liberation Act,"* the US and UK launched Operation Desert Fox – a four-day attack on Iraq with an arsenal of military bombers and cruise missiles. Even though its official goal was to degrade Iraq's ability to produce and use weapons of mass destruction, America's national security directors were also seeking to undermine Saddam Hussein's hold on power. [29] US Special Forces were placed on the ground in northern Iraq to protect Kurdish settlements. During the four-day assault, more Cruise missiles were fired on Iraq than were unleashed during the entirety of the 42-day bombing campaign of the 1991 Gulf War.

The operation was conducted without UN support and the relevance of enforcement of the UN mandates was a matter of dispute. [30] US and UK intelligence analysts selecting the targets have since stated they did not have a high degree of confidence the operation was actually hitting WMD sites. [31]

> *I'm sure No.10 wanted it to be a success and I'm sure the MoD wanted it to be a success, but wanting does not make it so. After Dessert Fox, I actually sent a note round to all the analysts involved congratulating them on standing firm in the face of, in some cases, individual pressure to say things that they knew weren't true.*
>
> John Morrison, UK Intelligence and Security Committee Investigator, November 7 2004 [32]

Desert Fox was an iteration of what became a decades-long war on Iraq. Politicians on both sides of the Atlantic sought to boast their public standing by using the appeal of a comfortable video-game war to degrade an unpopular tyrant, often unsure of the real value of the decisions being made and pressuring their own intelligence communities. [33] Following *'Operation Desert Fox'*, Russia, France, and the People's Republic of China called for lifting Iraq's eight-year oil embargo and the dismissal of UNSCOM and its chairman, Richard Butler. In Egypt, an Islamic group called upon jihadists to carry out attacks against the United States in retaliation for the more than 1,000 Iraqis killed by the attacks.

According to Charles A. Duelfer, a former deputy chairman of the UN Special Commission on Iraq, the Iraqi ambassador to the UN told him after the bombing:

> If we had known that was all you would do, we would have ended the inspections long ago.
>
> Charles A. Duelfer, Iraq Survey Group 2004-2005 [34]

The 2000 Republican Party Platform called for 'full implementation' of the Iraq Liberation Act and the removal of Saddam Hussein. The election of George W. Bush as President quietly put the highest levels of the US government on an active policy of 'regime change' for the Middle Eastern nation with key positions in the new administration given to Washington insiders that were advocates of invading Iraq, such as Dick Cheney, Donald Rumsfeld, and Paul Wolfowitz. According to Secretary of the Treasury, Paul O'Neill, the war on Iraq was planned from the first meeting of the Bush administration's National Security Council.

> You can fool some of the people all the time, and those are the ones you want to concentrate on.
>
> George W. Bush, Gridiron Club Dinner, March 2001 [35]

During its first eight months, the public face of Bush's presidency remained conservative and low-key. The President spent a large portion of his time on vacation, mostly at his ranch in Crawford, Texas. But after the Twin Tower, Pentagon, and Pennsylvania attacks, his policies assumed the neo-conservative agenda, as Project for the New American Century members and sympathizers saw their opportunity to take the shocked nation in the direction of remaking the Middle East. The fear, anger, and patriotism that unites a citizenry behind their government, gave the PNAC the

'Pearl Harbor' moment they had seen as necessary for the agenda they had developed already a few years before.

CHAPTER 12 REFERENCES

[1] Profile: Abram Shulsky, History Commons;
http://www.historycommons.org/entity.jsp?entity=abram_s hulsky
(SHORTENED URL: http://tinyurl.com/hisuki)

[2] Leo Strauss and the Rhetoric of the War on Terror, by Nicholas Xenos, Logos, a journal of modern society & culture, Spring 2004;
http://www.logosjournal.com/xenos.htm
(SHORTENED URL: http://tinyurl.com/zenoma)

[3] The Myth of Ronald Reagan's Foreign Policy, Classic Liberal, 6 July 2010;
http://the-classic-liberal.com/myth-ronald-reagan-foreign-policy/
(SHORTENED URL: http://tinyurl.com/hyroto)

[4] What Would Reagan Really Do? by Andrew Romano, Newsweek 9 July 2010;
http://www.newsweek.com/2010/07/09/what-would-reagan-really-do.html
(SHORTENED URL: http://tinyurl.com/regado)

[5] A Time for Change, by Ronald Wilson Reagan, October 1964;
http://www.dailyrepublican.com/rwr_archive_speech1964.html
(SHORTENED URL: http://tinyurl.com/rebica)

[6] Inaugural Address, John F. Kennedy, 20 January 1961;
http://www.jfklibrary.org/Asset-Viewer/BqXIEM9F4024ntFl7SVAjA.aspx?gclid=COj89rzDiLkC FcN_QgoddnwAIA
(SHORTENED URL: http://tinyurl.com/baroke)

CHARLES EDMUND COYOTE

[7] *Think Again; Ronald Reagan, by Peter Beinart, Foreign Policy, July August 2010;*
http://www.foreignpolicy.com/articles/2010/06/07/think_ag ain_ronald_reagan?page=full
(SHORTENED URL: http://tinyurl.com/pebefo)

[8] *30 Years Ago, Neocons Were More Candid About Their Israel-Centered Views, Mondoweiss, May 23, 2007;*
http://mondoweiss.net/2007/05/30_years_ago_ne.html
(SHORTENED URL: http://tinyurl.com/zisevi)

[9] *Cheney on Invading Iraq, 14 September 1992, YouTube;*
http://www.youtube.com/watch?v=pT7Ik_X1HU0&feature=f vw
(SHORTENED URL: http://tinyurl.com/heneva)

[10] *Cheney in 1994 on Iraq, YouTube;*
http://www.youtube.com/watch?v=YENbElb5- xY&feature=related
(SHORTENED URL: http://tinyurl.com/henevo)

[11] *Has Dick Cheney Lost His Mind?, The Young Turks, 28 September 2007, YouTube;*
http://www.youtube.com/watch?v=a7kkx9domJo&feature=f vw
(SHORTENED URL: http://tinyurl.com/rikesi)

[12] *Washington's Farewell Address 1796; Avalon Project, Yale Law School, Lillian Goldman Law Library;*
http://avalon.law.yale.edu/18th_century/washing.asp
(SHORTENED URL: http://tinyurl.com/farawe)

[13] *Statement of Principles, Project for the New American Century, 3 June 1997;*
http://www.newamericancentury.org/statementofprinciples. htm
(SHORTENED URL: http://tinyurl.com/tateme)

[14] *Letter to President Clinton on Iraq, Project for the New American Century;*
http://www.newamericancentury.org/iraqclintonletter.htm
(SHORTENED URL: http://tinyurl.com/lereji)

IRAQ WAR 2003

[15] *Letter to President Clinton on Iraq, Project for the New American Century;*
http://www.newamericancentury.org/iraqclintonletter.htm
(SHORTENED URL: http://tinyurl.com/lereji)

[16] *Frontier Rugs, Review of the Carpet Wars by Christopher Kremmer; Reality, one bite at a time; Siddharth Varadarajan, September 30, 2002;*
http://svaradarajan.blogspot.com/2002/09/frontier-rugs-review-of-carpet-wars-by.html
(SHORTENED URL: http://tinyurl.com/rorevi)

[17] *The coup that wasn't, The Guardian, 27 September 2005;*
http://www.guardian.co.uk/world/2005/sep/28/iraq.military
(SHORTENED URL: http://tinyurl.com/cowaga)

[18] *Iraq Confidential, by Scott Ritter, 2005, I.B. Tauris Publishers;*
http://books.google.com/books?id=saPBlBJPKggC&printsec=frontcover#v=onepage&q&f=false
(SHORTENED URL: http://tinyurl.com/varemu)

[19] *Iraq Confidential: The Untold Story, C-Span Video Library, 19 October 2005;*
http://www.c-spanvideo.org/program/189494-1
(SHORTENED URL: http://tinyurl.com/valiru)

[20] *Bombing of Iraq (December 1998), Wikipedia encyclopedia, 20 June 2009;*
http://en.wikipedia.org/wiki/Operation_Desert_Fox#Accusations_of_US_interference_in_the_UN_inspection_process
(SHORTENED URL: http://tinyurl.com/bowidi)

[21] *Iraq applauds spy claims, BBC News, 7 January 1999.*

[22] *INSPECTOR A US SPY, Mirror.co.uk, 1 July 2009;*
http://web.archive.org/web/20030225093525/http://www.mirror.co.uk/news/allnews/page.cfm?objectid=12304324&method=full&siteid=50143
(SHORTENED URL: http://tinyurl.com/petomi)

[23] *US silence on new Iraq spying allegations, BBC News*

World: Middle East, January 7, 1999;
http://news.bbc.co.uk/2/hi/middle_east/250808.stm
(SHORTENED URL: http://tinyurl.com/sinena)

[24] UNSCOM: CHRONOLOGY OF MAIN EVENTS, UNITED
NATIONS SPECIAL COMMISSION, 1999;
http://www.un.org/Depts/unscom/Chronology/chronologyfr
ame.htm
(SHORTENED URL: http://tinyurl.com/conolo)

[25] Richard Butler (diplomat), Wikipedia encyclopedia, 1
July 2009;
http://en.wikipedia.org/wiki/Richard_Butler_(diplomat)
(SHORTENED URL: http://tinyurl.com/wedema)

[26] Annan, Iraq sign weapons-inspection deal, CNN World
News, February 23, 1998;
http://www.cnn.com/WORLD/9802/23/iraq.deal.update.4a
m/index.html
(SHORTENED URL: http://tinyurl.com/rawede)

[27] Resolution 687: Iraq-Kuwait, 3 April 1991, United
Nations SECURITY COUNCIL RESOLUTION;
http://www.fas.org/news/un/iraq/sres/sres0687.htm
(SHORTENED URL: http://tinyurl.com/reluti)

[28] SEC.3.SENSE OF THE CONGRESS REGARDING UNITED
STATES POLICY TOWARD IRAQ, Iraq Liberation Act of 1998;
http://www.iraqwatch.org/government/US/Legislation/ILA.h
tm
(SHORTENED URL: http://tinyurl.com/wogove)

[29] The Difference Was In The Details, by William M.
Arkin, The Washington Post, January 17, 1999;
http://www.washingtonpost.com/wp-
srv/inatl/longterm/iraq/analysis.htm
(SHORTENED URL: http://tinyurl.com/wapode)

[30] A failure of intelligence, BBC - Panorama, November
7, 2004;
http://news.bbc.co.uk/nol/shared/spl/hi/programmes/panor
ama/transcripts/afailureofintelligence.txt
(SHORTENED URL: http://tinyurl.com/fatepa)

*[31] The Difference Was in the Details, by William M. Arkin,
The Washington Post, January 17, 1999;
http://www.washingtonpost.com/wp-
srv/inatl/longterm/iraq/analysis.htm
(SHORTENED URL: http://tinyurl.com/wapode)*

*[32] A failure of intelligence, BBC - Panorama, November
7, 2004;
http://news.bbc.co.uk/nol/shared/spl/hi/programmes/panor
ama/transcripts/afailureofintelligence.txt
(SHORTENED URL: http://tinyurl.com/fatepa)*

*[33] Dr Brian Jones "confused" by Prime Minister's
evidence to Hutton, BBC - Press Office, November 7, 2004;
http://www.bbc.co.uk/pressoffice/pressreleases/stories/200
4/07_july/11/panorama.shtml
(SHORTENED URL: http://tinyurl.com/jofume)*

*[34] Bombing of Iraq (December 1998), Wikipedia
encyclopedia, 20 June 2009;
http://en.wikipedia.org/wiki/Operation_Desert_Fox#Criticis
m_of_the_extent_of_the_operation
(SHORTENED URL: http://tinyurl.com/gowedi)*

*[35] Bush mocks Bush, BBC News, 25 March, 2001;
http://news.bbc.co.uk/2/hi/americas/1241240.stm
(SHORTENED URL: http://tinyurl.com/tumuno)*

CHARLES EDMUND COYOTE

CHAPTER 13

I AM NOT PART OF THE PROBLEM

I am not part of the problem. I am a Republican.
  George W. Bush

In 1999, Mickey Herskowitz, a longtime sports writer for the Houston Chronicle and Bush family acquaintance, struck a deal with George W. Bush to interview the governor and ghost-write his autobiography. The book they began working on would eventually be called, *A Charge to Keep: My Journey to the White House*. As part of the process, Herskowitz was given full access to Governor Bush, meeting with him some 20 times, from May through July 1999, to collect his views in preparation for the manuscript.

By July that summer, Herskowitz had completed 6 chapters and was on track to finish the project. Suddenly, he was pulled off of the job and replaced by Karen Hughes, a long-time Bush associate. The Bush team was concerned that the garrulous governor was talking too much, particularly about his troubled early years and business failings. They wanted the book to represent him as fit for the responsibilities of the President of the United States. [1] Hughes claimed publicly that Herskowitz, a successful author of more than 30 books, had *'habits that interfered with his writing and had missed deadlines'*. Privately, the Bush organization was determined to keep the embarrassments out of the record as much as possible. Herskowitz was too good at getting at the facts. Karen Hughes would finish the book and see it published that same year.

The title of George W. Bush's campaign biography, *A*

Charge to Keep, is associated with a short story illustration by William Henry Dethlef Koerner, an early Twentieth Century artist who specialized in paintings of the American West. Koerner's illustration, itself called *A Charge to Keep*, shows three determined horsemen dashing madly up a rugged, forested hillside. The depiction is a favorite of George W. Bush's. It had been loaned to him shortly after his 1995 inauguration as governor of Texas by his childhood friend, Joseph I. O'Neill III. Joseph 'Spider' O'Neill said the lead cowboy in the painting reminded him of Bush, and the governor happily accepted the characterization.

> *I thought I would share with you a recent bit of Texas history which epitomizes our mission. When you come into my office, please take a look at the beautiful painting of a horseman determinedly charging up what appears to be a steep and rough trail. This is us.*
>
> *Governor George W. Bush, memo to staff* [2]

When he became President, George W. Bush took the painting with him to Washington, where it occupied a prominent place in any personal tour he gave Oval Office visitors during his eight years in the White House. [3]

> *I love the painting because it speaks to serving a cause that is greater than yourself. The picture reminds me every day that my most important job is to unite our country and provide leadership to overcome America's toughest challenges.*
>
> *George W. Bush, 2004 fundraising letter* [4]

Bush identified with the heroic struggle he saw in the painting. To him it represented the resolute determination of the nineteenth century circuit riding

CHARLES EDMUND COYOTE

preachers as they spread Methodism across the Allegheny region of frontier America. He maintained that the painting's title was *"based upon a religious hymn... about serving God,"* a song written by Charles Wesley called *A Charge to Keep I Have.* [5]

Longtime Presidential advisor and director of the Center for Public Leadership at Harvard's John F. Kennedy School of Government, David Gergen, spoke of the President's fondness for the painting:

> *Bush's personal identification with the painting, which now hangs in the Oval Office, reveals a good deal about his sense of himself as a political leader – who he thinks he is, the role he plays, and the centrality of his religious faith... His followers today tend to see in Bush what he sees in the painting: a brave, daring leader riding fearlessly into the unknown, striking out against unseen enemies, pulling his team behind him, seeking, in the words of Wesley's hymn, "to do my Master's will." They see him as a straight shooter and a straight talker.*
>
> *David Gergen, professor of public service at Harvard's John F. Kennedy School of Government and director of its Center for Public Leadership, Fall 2003* [6]

The original was commissioned in 1916 by *The Saturday Evening Post*. William H.D. Koerner, the artist given the job, was a German immigrant who had studied at New York's Howard Pyle School of Art to become a successful illustrator for popular magazines in early twentieth century America. Earlier, in 1912, *The Saturday Evening Post* had also chosen Koerner to illustrate Zane Grey's famous story *'Riders of the Purple Sage'.* [7]

Both W.H.D. Koerner and his daughter, Ruth, in later interviews explained that the inspiration for Koerner's work came from the painter's willingness to become engrossed in the stories for which they were used:

> I try to draw the man the author describes... I con-
> centrate on the character until it comes alive and I can
> see him in my mind's eye.
>
>> William Henry Dethlef Koerner, 'Yes We Read the
>> Story', interview for The Saturday Evening Post; 25
>> June 1932 [8]

The painting would be used for other short stories, including, in 1918, one entitled, 'A Charge to Keep'. In *Country Gentleman* magazine, it supported a story about a timberland inheritance and the responsibility that came with it to keep property safe from the robber barons who wanted to exploit it for its lumber. The character that William Koerner saw in his mind's eye, however, was the horseman barely riding out front in the 1916 *Saturday Evening Post* narrative called 'The Slipper Tongue'.

As with so many other positions embraced by George W. Bush, it might have been better if he been a little less sure of his own point of view and a little more inclined toward healthy curiosity and reflective deliberation in the decision making process. The horseman he was so certain depicted a resolute preacher 'determinedly charging up what appears to be a steep and rough trail' was actually an illustration of a smooth-talking horse thief on the run, risking the well-being, even the life, of the mount he galloped up the rugged slopes in an attempt to flee justice closing from behind.

The former President's perspective on the painting exemplifies the decision making style that characterized his leadership of the nation. 'This is us,' he proudly proclaimed and tied his own autobiography to that of a

CHARLES EDMUND COYOTE

slippery tongued horse thief fleeing from justice. The illustration captioned in the original *'Slipper Tongue'* story was *'Had His Start Been Fifteen Minutes Longer He Would Not Have Been Caught'.*

Had His Start Been Fifteen Minutes Longer
He Would Not Have Been Caught
W.H.D. Koerner, The Slipper Tongue, 1916

Writing for Harper's Magazine on the President's relationship with the painting, attorney Scott Horton observed:

> *Bush has consistently exhibited what psychologists call the 'Tolstoy syndrome.' That is, he is completely convinced he knows what things are, so he shuts down all avenues of inquiry about them and disregards the information that is offered to him. This is the hallmark of a tragically bad executive. But in this case, it couldn't be more precious.*

The president of the United States has identified closely with a man he sees as a mythic, heroic figure. In fact that man is a wily criminal one step out in front of justice.

Scott Horton, Esq.; Harper's Magazine, January 24, 2008 [9]

When you come into my office, please take a look at the beautiful painting of a horseman determinedly charging up what appears to be a steep and rough trail. This is us.

George W. Bush

As President, George W. Bush would remark about his biography, *"Some say it's a novel,"* but Mickey Herskowitz' earlier work on the book offers some insight into the Presidency of George W. Bush that Karen Hughes turned aside. Referring to his interviews for the book, Herskowitz later said:

He thought of himself as a superior, more modern politician than his father and [the elder Bush's close adviser and friend] Jim Baker. He told me, '[My father] could have done anything [during the Gulf War]. He could have invaded Switzerland. If I had that political capital, I would have taken Iraq.'

Mickey Herskowitz, November 1, 2004 [10]

In November 2004 Herskowitz sat down for a tape recorded interview with investigative journalist Russ Baker to talk about the 1999 discussions with Governor George W. Bush. Herskowitz said Bush believed the key to a successful presidency lies through having a small war began with some justification and quickly brought to a triumphant conclusion. He had seen this with his own father, who had reached an astonishing 90 percent approval rating with the American people as a result of leading the country through the dramatic success of the 1991 Persian Gulf War. Herskowitz said Bush's advisers were captivated by the following British Prime Minister Margaret Thatcher gained from her success with the 1982 Falklands War. He felt his dad had made no use of the favorable approval ratings he gained from the popular 1991 Gulf War. Should he have the chance, he intended to take full advantage of the *'political capital'* thus obtained to secure passage of his legislative agenda, the centerpiece of which would be the privatization of Social Security. [11]

> *They were just absolutely blown away, just enthralled by the scenes of the troops coming back, of the boats, people throwing flowers at [Margaret Thatcher] and her getting these standing ovations in Parliament and making these magnificent speeches.*

Mickey Herskowitz, Russ Baker Interview, 2004 [12]

W's advisors had told him that Jimmy Carter's political downfall came because of his failure to wage a war. Unlike his father, however, George W. Bush had no experience of war and looked at it instead through the lens of a politician, as a means of acquiring 'political capital'. Even for reasons vital to the defense of the American people, George W. Bush seemed little inclined to consider the impact the war would have on nations and on those who participate, their families and the innocent.

> He said to me: 'One of the keys to being seen as a great leader is to be seen as a commander-in-chief. ' And he said, 'My father had all this political capital built up when he drove the Iraqis out of Kuwait and he wasted it.' He said, 'If I have a chance to invade, if I had that much capital, I'm not going to waste it. I'm going to get everything passed that I want to get passed and I'm going to have a successful presidency.'
>
> Mickey Herskowitz, 2004 [13]

In the Herskowitz interview we can foresee the motivations of the White House staff in arranging the May 1, 2003 photo-op of President Bush's jet landing in full military flight jacket on the USS Abraham Lincoln. The purpose was to make a televised address to announce 'Mission Accomplished' and the end of major combat operations in Iraq. Herskowitz says Bush was frustrated over his life as a relative under-achiever in comparison to his accomplished father and believed that he could emerge from that shadow on the merits of his own military triumph. [14]

History affords endless examples of leaders that sought to prove their prowess by military conquest. However, the technology of modern war and the sensibilities of modern democracies have somewhat reduced the opportunities for those individuals to find expression. Those who experience modern war often become less inclined to rush into it. Those who played

CHARLES EDMUND COYOTE

202

prominent roles in the second Bush administration – with few exceptions – had no experience of its dark realities.

In 2004, a book entitled *Bush on the Couch: Inside the Mind of a President* was published. Written by psychoanalyst Justin A. Frank, M.D., it offered an in-depth perspective on the psyche of the forty-third President, making use of the vast public record of behavior, biographical information, and statements available on George W. Bush. Dr. Frank is a practicing psychiatrist with more than thirty years' experience, and a clinical professor in the Department of Psychiatry at George Washington University Medical School in Washington D.C. [15] The psychological profile of the former Chief Executive he developed is along the lines of the psychoanalytic assessments of other world leaders routinely undertaken by the Central Intelligence Agency. The book became a bestseller and an object of controversy.

Management experts have long understood that the behavior of an organization, to a large degree, reflects the personality of its top executives. [16], [17] The portrait presented in *Bush on the Couch* is troubling, but its themes parallel many of the troubling themes that developed during the Bush administration. In science, the utility of a theory is directly proportional to the range of phenomena it explains.

A great deal of Bush on the Couch is taken up with providing sufficient fundamentals of the clinical process to permit the lay reader to grasp the gravity of George W. Bush's psychological problems. The book is a devastating psychological dossier on the 43rd President, and a compassionate profile of a human being in need of care.

Jeffrey Steinberg, Executive Intelligence Review, August 20, 2004 [18]

According to Dr. Frank, George W. Bush has displayed signs of mental health issues throughout most of his life that allowed him to be functional, but poorly suited to the responsibilities of leading the world's most powerful democratic nation. Dr. Frank found indications of sadistic traits in the former President, noting that he feels entitled to live unencumbered by constraints that apply to ordinary people. [19] He points out the former President's aversion to introspection and tendency to deny responsibility, describing him as suffering from megalomania, the need to defy authority, and probably incapable of genuine compassion.

> *As you can possibly see, I have an injury myself – not here at the hospital, but in combat with a cedar. I eventually won. The cedar gave me a little scratch. As a matter of fact, the Colonel asked if I needed first aid when she first saw me. I was able to avoid any major surgical operations here, but thanks for your compassion, Colonel.*
>
> > *George W. Bush, after visiting amputee veterans at the Amputee Care Center of Brooke Army Medical Center, San Antonio, Texas, January 1, 2006*

Dr. Frank maintains that the research he did on President Bush – and later on President Obama – is similar to the psychological assessments of world leaders routinely developed by the CIA's Center for Analysis of Personality and Political Behavior (the unit of applied psychoanalysis within the Central Intelligence Agency established by Dr. Jerrold Post, a colleague of Dr. Frank's at George Washington University). [20]

> *If one of my patients frequently said one thing and did*

CHARLES EDMUND COYOTE

another, I would want to know why. If I found that he often used words that hid their true meaning and affected a persona that obscured the nature of his actions, I would grow more concerned. If he presented an inflexible worldview characterized by an over-simplified distinction between right and wrong, good and evil, allies and enemies, I would question his ability to grasp reality. And if his actions revealed an un-acknowledged – even sadistic – indifference to human suffering, wrapped in pious claims of compassion, I would worry about the safety of the people whose lives he touched.

For the past three years, I have observed with increa-sing alarm the inconsistencies and denials of such an individual. But he is not one of my patients. He is our president.

Justin Frank, M.D., Bush on the Couch – Inside the Mind of the President [21]

Public figures, with the important exception of not having an emotional interaction with a therapist, often present more material for analysis than the patients only seen within the limits of the clinical setting. By virtue of being intensely in the public eye, the Presi-dent of the United States offers hundreds of hours of video footage as well as reams of biographical infor-mation on himself, his associates, and almost every member of his family – an abundance of material for the trained analyst. In characterizing President Bush, Dr. Frank had access to considerably more data than he normally would with a more conventional patient.

In *Bush on the Couch*, Dr. Frank argues that at an early age George W. Bush was left distressed by the loss of a sister to cancer. There are few things as devastating to a family as the loss of a child. Yet, according to Dr. Frank, young George W's father remained unavailable, busy with his own career and his mother stern and unresponsive. As a result the future leader of the country did not learn to manage anxiety well.

In *Bush on the Couch*, Dr. Frank describes a President still suffering from psychological disorders that include Attention Deficit Hyperactivity Disorder (ADHD), a diminished capacity to distinguish between reality and fantasy, an omnipotence complex, paranoia, sadism, a mild form of Tourettes Syndrome, and untreated alcoholism. His parent's failure to provide the necessary adult involvement that could have enabled him to grow through the distress likely led to the former President's long history of alcohol and probable drug abuse which, in turn, may have induced brain damage for which he should be tested. His *'diminished ability to manage anxiety'* has led to a tendency to demand total loyalty, speak sarcastically, and act as a bully when circumstances permit.

> *George W. was six years old at the beginning of the tragic episode that he has said yielded his first vivid childhood memories – the illness and death of his sister. In the spring of 1953, young Robin was diagnosed with leukemia, which set into motion a series of extended East Coast trips by parents and child in the ultimately fruitless pursuit of treatment. Critically, however, young George W. was never informed of the reason for the sudden absences; unaware that his sister was ill, he was simply told not to play with the girl, to whom he had grown quite close, on her occasional visits home. Robin died in New York in October 1953; her parents spent the next day golfing in Rye, attending a small memorial service the following day before flying back to Texas. George learned of his sister's illness only after her death, when his parents returned to Texas, where the family remained while the child's body was buried in a Connecticut family plot. There was no funeral.*
>
> *Justin Frank, M.D., Bush on the Couch – Inside the*

CHARLES EDMUND COYOTE

Mind of the President [22]

Dr. Frank found *Bush on the Couch: Inside the Mind of a President* was well received by those who read it, but was not widely appreciated within the psychiatric community or by Republicans. The latter dismissed it, even though few actually read it. Psychoanalysts and psychiatrists tend not to be familiar with applied psychoanalysis, he says, or inclined to feel it should only be applied to foreign leaders, even though Dr. Jerrold Post, founder of The CIA's Center for the Analysis of Personality and Political Behavior, has also used it in application to Bill Clinton. [23]

It is unfortunate that Republicans generally choose to avoid reading Dr. Frank. By the time President Bush had finished his two terms, he had damaged the country's conservative movement and facilitated the Democratic Party's regaining of power. Much of that might have been different if the Republicans had been more willing to understand where they were being lead.

> *I would love to find who they are [Republicans interested in the book], and if I could find Republican groups, I would be very interested in talking with them, because I do think there's an audience for this. I think that they are very concerned about a couple of things: One is the deficit spending; two is really pre-emptive war. And three, I think some of them, especially the ones that are not very deeply religious, are concerned with this kind of mission quality that he has, and his deep connection to Jesus. I think that all of those three things are really very deeply disturbing to Republicans who come from a different – and then the arrogance, which a lot of people have commented on. Senator Byrd's new book is great. He talks about the arrogance of Bush, and how lots of Republicans that he knows, colleagues, are quite alarmed.*
>
> *Justin Frank, M.D., 2004* [24]

Dr. Frank credits George W. with a higher level of intelligence than most of the nation was willing to concede by the middle of his second term. He does not believe Vice President Cheney was secretly running the Presidency. He believes that George W. Bush was the *'decider'* he claimed to be, but gave Cheney the job of thinking through those decisions. That thinking-through would have been anxiety-producing for Bush. This view is compatible with the one presented by Cheney, who poured considerable effort into enhancing the President's powers, regarding – as he stated himself – the Office of the President as that of a king. According to Dr. Frank, Bush knew what he wanted to do, but avoided the work of thinking it through because it made him too anxious. Frank believes the core of George W's functioning lies in defending himself against anxiety.

> *Yes, it has to do with the fact that he was never able to mourn, and when you don't mourn, you can't integrate your inner life. What happens is that, as I write in the book, sorrow is the vitamin of growth, and until you face who you are and what you've lost, you really can't organize your mind, and so what happens is when you're the first born, and the next one dies, you're left with a lot of unworked-out hostility, anger, guilt, that maybe your wishes killed them. You have lots of magical thinking, and if you don't have a family that helps you gather those things together, you can be in a lot of trouble.*

> *So then you have to manage your feelings yourself. And one of the ways people do manage them when they are that age, is they have friends to talk to; but he doesn't seem to have had anybody to talk too much. But they also read, and pay attention to things, so they learn about human beings from reading about other people, if their parents aren't responsive to them. But he really has such a hard time reading, that it's like swimming with weights. I mean, it's just too much for him. So he*

CHARLES EDMUND COYOTE

didn't have that avenue either, so he became sometimes cruel to people, with animals, which is one way of managing your aggression, and then to drink in order to manage his anxiety, and he became a very heavy drinker, that's very clear, till he was 40, at least.

Justin Frank, M.D., 2004 [25]

Dr. Frank believes the press was afraid to ask President Bush the tough questions because there was an unspoken understanding that dealing with Bush meant walking on egg shells with unknown consequences if he became upset.

The only way [to really break through, and get through to him] would be for somebody to actually directly confront him in a clear way, to bring him out, so you would really see the bully, and you would also see the fear.

So Cheney is very powerful, and Cheney is really a destructive guy, but I don't think that Bush needs him as much as we like to think he does. That is one of the strengths of Bush. Bush is an amazing person at ducking blame and ducking responsibility, so he's even got a lot of people who oppose him thinking it's all Cheney's fault. And through this secret way, it's a way of getting off the hook yet again.

Dr. Justin Frank, 2004 [26]

Dr. Frank includes a chapter in *Bush on the Couch* that discusses why Americans chose him as their leader and tolerated counterproductive and profligate policies supported by misrepresentation, domestic spying, and the use of torture in ways that undermined our national security and enriched friends and associates. [27]

Considerable insight into the Bush Administration's departure from traditional American values can be gained from Dr. Frank's profile. By the time George Bush had left office, most of America recognized that something had gone wrong and that the great American ship of state was beginning to act as though it had struck an iceberg and was taking on water quickly.

What, then, is to be said of the 22 percent of American that continued to approve of George W. Bush's Presidency at the end of his two terms – the lowest in history for the office? Were these Americans working too hard to pay attention, too easily mislead by talk-radio sophists, too fond of tax cuts and deficit spending or just inclined to remain with the usual default of the Republican perspective? Or could it be that too many of that 22 percent were of a mindset that allows them to assume the fortunate combinations of chance, choice, and historical struggle for the greater good that made America is something that can be taken for granted?

The fate of the Roman Republic some 2,000 years ago stands as a reminder that those who do not wish to be bound to conditions must strive to understand them. George W. Bush's administration was populated by individuals who believed the United States was *'the indispensable nation'* and claimed for it the special attire of *'American Exceptionalism'* – the freedom to live free from the constraints that apply to ordinary nations. They failed to understand that a nation loses such a distinction by the degree to which it acts as if that distinction confers special privilege. [28] The Art of holding Power cannot be separated from the cultivation of wisdom. The grace of seeing that exceptionalism lies only in the quiet genius of all things.

> *Beware the leader who bangs the drums of war in order to whip the citizenry into a patriotic fervor, for patriotism is indeed a double-edged sword. It both*

CHARLES EDMUND COYOTE

emboldens the blood, just as it narrows the mind. And when the drums of war have reached a fever pitch and the blood boils with hate and the mind has closed, the leader will have no need in seizing the rights of the citizenry. Rather, the citizenry, infused with fear and blinded by patriotism, will offer up all of their rights unto the leader and gladly so. How do I know? For this is what I have done. And I am Caesar.

Attributed to Julius Caesar

CHAPTER 13 REFERENCES

[1] Excerpt from 'The Bush Tragedy', by Jacob Weisberg, The New York Times, February 1, 2008; http://www.nytimes.com/2008/02/01/books/chapters/1st-chapter-bush-tragedy.html?_r=2&pagewanted=12 (SHORTENED URL: http://tinyurl.com/bugedy)

[2]
(a) The Illustrated President, by Scott Horton, HARPER'S MAGAZINE, January 24, 2008; http://www.harpers.org/archive/2008/01/hbc-90002237 (SHORTENED URL: http://tinyurl.com/rehotu)
(b) http://harpers.org/author/ScottHorton/

[3] The BILD Interview; 45 Minutes with Bush, by Kai Diekmann, Counterpunch, May 5, 2006; http://www.counterpunch.org/diekmann05112006.html (SHORTENED URL: http://tinyurl.com/joteka)

[4] Good referencing for the Koerner painting and its relationship to Bush; The Illustrated President, by Scott Horton, January 24, 2008; http://www.churchofvirus.org/bbs/Printpage.php?board=33;threadid=42086 (SHORTENED URL: http://tinyurl.com/gokone)

[5] A CHARGE TO KEEP I HAVE, Words by Charles Wesley, Short Hymns on Select Pass ages of Holy Scripture, 1762; http://www.cyberhymnal.org/htm/c/h/chargkeep.htm

(SHORTENED URL: http://tinyurl.com/kewese)

[6] Horseshit! Bush and the Christian Cowboy, by Jonathan Hutson, TALK TO ACTION, May 12, 2006; http://www.talk2action.org/story/2006/5/12/7393/57216 (SHORTENED URL: http://tinyurl.com/hokojo)

[7] From Norman Rockwell to Abu Ghraib, by Sidney Blumenthal, Salon.com, April 26, 2007; http://www.salon.com/2007/04/26/torture_policy/ (SHORTENED URL: http://tinyurl.com/robusi)

[8] Horseshit! Bush and the Christian Cowboy, by Jonathan Hutson, TALK TO ACTION, May 12, 2006; http://www.talk2action.org/story/2006/5/12/7393/57216 (SHORTENED URL: http://tinyurl.com/taketi)

[9] The Illustrated President, by Scott Horton, HARPER'S MAGAZINE, January 24, 2008; http://www.harpers.org/archive/2008/01/hbc-90002237 (SHORTENED URL: http://tinyurl.com/hihopa)

[10] 1999: George W. Bush Hints at Invading Iraq in Future Presidency, History Commons; http://www.historycommons.org/context.jsp?item=complete_timeline_of_the_2003_invasion_of_iraq_2874#complete_timeline_of_the_2003_invasion_of_iraq_2874 (SHORTENED URL: http://tinyurl.com/bufote)

[11] Writer says Bush talked about war in 1999, by Kim Cobb, Copyright 2004 Houston Chronicle, November 1, 2004; http://www.chron.com/news/houston-texas/article/Writer-says-Bush-talked-about-war-in-1999-1975031.php (SHORTENED URL: http://tinyurl.com/sakipi)

[12] Two Years Before 9/11, Candidate Bush was Already Talking Privately About Attacking Iraq, According to His Former Ghost Writer; by Russ Baker, 26 October 2004 (GNN.tv), Common Dreams NEWS CENTER; http://www.commondreams.org/headlines04/1028-01.htm (SHORTENED URL: http://tinyurl.com/katalo)

[13] October 11 2000 Debate Transcript, October 11, 2000,

CHARLES EDMUND COYOTE

The Second Gore-Bush Presidential Debate, COMMISSION ON PRESIDENTIAL DEBATES;
http://www.debates.org/index.php?page=october-11-2000-debate-transcript
(SHORTENED URL: http://tinyurl.com/kerano)

[14] Two Years Before 9/11, Candidate Bush was Already Talking Privately About Attacking Iraq, According to His Former Ghost Writer; Interview of Mickey Herskowitz by Russ Baker, Published October 28, 2004 by GNN.tv, Common Dreams NEWS CENTER;
http://www.commondreams.org/headlines04/1028-01.htm
(SHORTENED URL: http://tinyurl.com/ronona)

[15] Justin A. Frank, M.D. Biography, Harper Collins Publishers;
http://www.harpercollins.com/authors/28048/Justin_A_Frank_MD/index.aspx
(SHORTENED URL: http://tinyurl.com/hacopa)

[16] The Leadership Challenge - Why Great Leaders Don't Take Yes for an Answer, by Michael A. Roberto, ©2006, GovLeaders.org;
http://govleaders.org/no_yes_men_print.htm
(SHORTENED URL: http://tinyurl.com/lemoda)

[17] The Dark Side of Discretion, by Robert B. Kaiser and Robert Hogan, Copyright© 2006 Hogan Assessment Systems, Inc;
http://www.hoganassessments.com/_hoganweb/documents/dark%20side%20of%20discretion.pdf
(SHORTENED URL: http://tinyurl.com/hogana)

[18] The Ugly Truth About G.W. Bush, BOOK REVIEW by Jeffrey Steinberg, Executive Intelligence Review, August 20, 2004;
http://www.larouchepub.com/other/2004/book_reviews/3133bush_on_couch.html
(SHORTENED URL: http://tinyurl.com/herumi)

[19] Justin Frank: Inside the Mind of President Bush, FORA.tv;
http://fora.tv/2008/01/19/Justin_Frank_Inside_the_Mind_of

  President Bush
(SHORTENED URL: http://tinyurl.com/samida)

[20] Psychological Portraits of George W. Bush, George Washington University / Elliot School of International Affairs, 25 October 2004;
http://www.c-spanvideo.org/program/166586-1
(SHORTENED URL: http://tinyurl.com/sapoge)

[21] The Ugly Truth About G.W. Bush, BOOK REVIEW: Bush on the Couch - Inside the Mind of the President by Justin A. Frank, M.D., New York: Harper Collins Publishers, 2004, Executive Intelligence Review, August 20, 2004;
http://larouchepub.com/other/2004/book_reviews/3133bush_on_couch.html
(SHORTENED URL: http://tinyurl.com/rubusi)

[22] The Ugly Truth About G.W. Bush, BOOK REVIEW by Jeffrey Steinberg, Executive Intelligence Review, August 20, 2004;
http://www.larouchepub.com/other/2004/book_reviews/3133bush_on_couch.html
(SHORTENED URL: http://tinyurl.com/herumi)

[23] The Psychological Assessment of Political Leaders: With Profiles of Saddam Hussein and Bill Clinton, Jerrold M. Post, 2005, University of Michigan Press;
http://www.amazon.com/The-Psychological-Assessment-Political-Leaders/dp/0472068385/ref=pd_sim_b_1/185-3074738-4302253
(SHORTENED URL: http://tinyurl.com/potisa)

[24] INTERVIEW: DR. JUSTIN FRANK, George Bush: 'A Puppet Who Chose His Puppeteers', Executive Intelligence Review, August 20, 2004;
http://larouchepub.com/other/interviews/2004/3133dr_justin_frank.html
(SHORTENED URL: http://tinyurl.com/jaremu)

[25] INTERVIEW: DR. JUSTIN FRANK, George Bush: 'A Puppet Who Chose His Puppeteers', Executive Intelligence Review, August 20, 2004;

http://larouchepub.com/other/interviews/2004/3133dr_justi n_frank.html
(SHORTENED URL: http://tinyurl.com/jaremu)

[26] INTERVIEW: DR. JUSTIN FRANK, George Bush: 'A Puppet Who Chose His Puppeteers', Executive Intelligence Review, August 20, 2004;
http://larouchepub.com/other/interviews/2004/3133dr_justi n_frank.html
(SHORTENED URL: http://tinyurl.com/japaku)

[27] GEORGE W. BUSH versus the US CONSTITUTION, THE DOWNING STREET MEMOS AND DECEPTION, MANIPULATION, TORTURE, RETRIBUTION, AND COVERUPS IN THE IRAQ WAR AND ILLEGAL DOMESTIC SPYING; Compiled at the Direction of Representative John Conyers, EDITED by ANITA MILLER, © 2006, p 58.

[28] Only in America, Economist.com, 24 April 2008;
http://www.economist.com/world/unitedstates/PrinterFriend ly.cfm?story_id=11089896
(SHORTENED URL: http://tinyurl.com/pomali)

CHAPTER 14
OUR COUNTRY'S INTERESTS

It's in our country's interests to find those who would do harm to us and get them out of harm's way.

George W. Bush, Washington, D.C., 28 April 2005

Those who wanted the US to flex its muscle internationally knew they would have to wait for a *'galvanizing event'*, such as the Pearl Harbor attacks had been a couple of generations before. Unless the American people were behind them, they would be unable to take significant action on their plans to remake the Middle East. They did not have to wait that long.

As the National Coordinator for Counter-terrorism, Richard Clarke was the US government's top counter-terrorism official in the White House under President Clinton and during the first two years of the Bush administration. On 25 January 2001, Clarke sent a memo to Condoleezza Rice, the new National Security Advisor, and to her deputy, Stephen Hadley, requesting that a Cabinet-level meeting be scheduled to discuss the gathering al-Qaeda storm clouds. [1] Clarke wanted to make sure the new administration understood that al Qaeda constituted a clear and present danger to the people of the United States. Dr. Rice responded to Clarke's request by deferring it to a meeting of the deputies of the relevant security agencies to be held later. She also downgraded Clarke's position, removing it from the President's cabinet, but keeping it in the White House.

When the meeting of the deputies was finally held in April 2001, Richard Clarke put a plan on the table

CHARLES EDMUND COYOTE

designed to pressure bin Laden and the Taliban by targeting al Qaeda's leadership with unmanned MQ-1 Predator flights and by supporting Afghanistan's Northern Alliance. Deputy Secretary of Defense Paul Wolfowitz was not interested:

> *I began saying, 'We have to deal with bin Laden; we have to deal with al Qaeda.'*
>
> *Paul Wolfowitz, the Deputy Secretary of Defense, said 'No, no, no. We don't have to deal with al Qaeda. Why are we talking about that little guy? We have to talk about Iraqi terrorism against the United States.'*
>
> *And I said, 'Paul, there hasn't been any Iraqi terrorism against the United States in eight years!' And I turned to the deputy director of the CIA and said, 'Isn't that right?'*
>
> *And he said, 'Yeah, that's right. There is no Iraqi terrorism against the United States.'*
>
> > Richard Clarke, former Chief Counter-Terrorism Adviser to the US National Security Council, 21 March 2004 [2]

Clarke tried to communicate the need to focus on al-Qaeda, *"because it and it alone poses an immediate and serious threat to the US,"* but the warnings fell on Wolfowitz's ideologically preoccupied ears. [3] The new Bush administration wanted to pick up where the old Bush administration had left off, regardless of the foreign policy concerns that may have developed in the intervening eight years.

Warnings about a gathering terrorist tempest continued to mount through the spring and summer of 2001. These included a two page memo from NSC member Lieutenant General, Donald Kerrick, to Deputy National Security Advisor, Stephen Hadley, reiterating the need to focus on al-Qaeda because, *"We are going to be struck again".* General Kerrick also encountered little interest in the subject on the part of the new administration:

> *They never responded. It was not high on their priority list. I was never invited to one meeting. They never asked me to do anything. They were not focusing. They didn't see terrorism as the big mega issue that the Clinton administration saw it as. They were gambling nothing would happen.*
>
> *Lieutenant General Donald Kerrick* [4]

By June 2001, Khalid Sheikh Mohammed, a Kuwaiti-born militant, was being tied by US intelligence *"to terrorist plans to use aircraft as weapons, and to terrorist activity in the United States".* [5] Finding him, however, was given low priority. They focused primarily on his past activities. That same month, German intelligence warned the US that Middle Eastern terrorists were *"planning to hijack commercial aircraft to use as weapons to attack important symbols of American and Israeli culture."* The following month, Egypt had informed the CIA that 20 al-Qaeda Operatives had slipped into the US and were taking flight training. [6] Jordan soon followed, informing the administration that al Qaeda was planning to use aircraft to carry out a major attack on American soil. [7]

On 10 July 2001, the CIA's counterterrorism chief, Cofer Black, and Richard Blee, the officer in charge of Alec Station (the Agency's bin Laden unit), met with the Director of Central Intelligence, George Tenet, to discuss the communications intercepts and intelligence pouring into the agency on the looming al-Qaeda threat. Director Black felt the large volume of information coming in indicated a compelling probability that al-Qaeda was about to attack. George Tenet later said the information *"literally made my hair stand on end"*, and requested an immediate meeting at the White House. En route to the White House, Tenet made a phone call from his car to National Security Advisor Condoleezza Rice to request a conference. [8] At the White House, Blee outlined the situation to Rice, Stephen Hadley, and Richard Clarke, telling them point blank, *"There will be a significant terrorist attack in the coming weeks or months!"* [9]

The intelligence presented included a mid-June statement by bin Laden to his Afghan trainees that there would be an attack on the US in the near future. Blee predicted attacks would be *'spectacular'*, calculated to inflict mass casualties, and would possibly constitute a *'stunning turn of events'* involving multiple simultaneous strikes within the US. [10] The intelligence chiefs said their agency was trying to disrupt al-Qaeda's plans by spreading rumors they had been exposed, but emphasized the pressing need to go on the offensive. Blee said bin Laden's threats were public knowledge in the Middle East and would lead to a loss of face for the terrorist leader if they were not followed through.

Cofer Black stressed that the danger had grown into a major foreign policy issue requiring immediate action. [11] Richard Clarke agreed with the seriousness. Earlier, Tenet had told Clarke:

> It's my sixth sense, but I feel it coming. This is going to be the big one.
>
> George Tenet, Director of Central Intelligence, June 2001 [12]

Cofer Black made a direct request to Dr. Rice for the funding to undertake urgent measures against al-Qaeda and for a Presidential authorization to kill bin Laden. Both requests were both denied. [13] Rice directed that Defense Secretary Rumsfeld and Attorney General Ashcroft be given the same briefing she had just received, and promised that a high-level meeting on al-Qaeda would be scheduled later. [14] Apart from that, CIA Director Tenet felt they had made little impression on Dr. Rice and left believing there would be no immediate response to the looming danger. [15] The Agency's feelings of urgency were not conveyed to the President, and Attorney General Ashcroft said he did not want to hear about it. The administration chose, for the time being, to remain dormant on the issue.

> *Adults should not have a system like this.*
> George Tenet, Director of Central Intelligence [16]

Shortly after the White House meeting, Rumsfeld and Ashcroft were given the same strong warning that al-Qaeda was preparing to attack. [17] Journalist Andrew Cockburn reported that Secretary Rumsfeld's reaction to the report was *'one of vehement dismissal'*. John Ashcroft later claimed he was never given the briefing, saying it was *"disappointing"* he had not been informed. [18] When the US State Department later confirmed the brief had been given to both officials, Ashcroft then made the claim that he only remembered the July 5 2001 CIA briefing relating to al-Qaeda's preparations for attacks outside the United States. [19]

In July FBI agents in Arizona wrote a memorandum warning about suspicious activities involving Middle

Eastern men taking flight lessons in the Phoenix area. Their memo specifically mentions Osama bin Laden and possible associations to terrorist activities. [20]

In mid-July, acting FBI Director Thomas Pickard tried again to brief Attorney General Ashcroft about the high al-Qaeda threat. Pickard testified to the 9/11 commission that Ashcroft told him then he did not want to hear anything more about it. [21] On 26 July 2001, CBS News reported that Attorney General Ashcroft had begun flying by private jet instead of the usual commercial flights on which he had previously flown. When asked about the change, the Attorney General claimed he knew nothing and gave little explanation apart from citing an FBI *'enhanced threat assessment'*. [22]

In the midst of a month-long vacation at his Texas ranch, President Bush received a Presidential Daily Briefing (PDB) from the CIA entitled *"Bin Ladin Determined To Strike in US"*. [23] Hand delivered to the President, on August 6, 2001, the document spelled out that Bin Laden was planning to exploit his operatives' access to the US to *'bring the fighting to America'*. Anti-terrorism officials in Washington were alarmed at the increasing flood of information pointing to imminent attacks. They had sent the hand delivered PDB to the ranch in the hope that an alarmed President would order federal security agencies into action to uncover the exact nature of the growing threat. Bush, who had spent more than 40 percent of the first seven months in office on vacation, seemed irritated at the interruption and told the briefer *"Alright, you've covered your ass now,"* and went fishing. [24]

Despite the document's title, *"Bin Ladin Determined To Strike in US"*, when 9/11 Commission Member Richard Ben-Veniste asked National Security Advisor Condoleezza Rice about the August 6 PDB, she testified under oath:

> *...It did not warn of attacks inside the United States. It was historical information based on old reporting. There was no new threat information. And it did not, in fact, warn of any coming attacks inside the United States.*
>
> > Condoleezza Rice, testimony to the National Commission on Terrorist Attacks Upon the United States, 8 April 2004 [25]

That same month, warnings also came in from France and Israel. Russian President Vladimir Putin ordered his own intelligence service to warn the US government *"in the strongest possible terms"* of impending terrorist attacks on American airports and government buildings. [26]

> *George Tenet was saying to the White House, saying to the president – because he briefed him every morning – a major al Qaeda attack is going to happen against the United States somewhere in the world in the weeks and months ahead. He said that in June, July, August [of 2001].*
>
> > Richard Clarke, former White House counterterrorism adviser, March 21, 2004 [27]

When the attacks came that Tuesday in September, Richard Clarke remained at station in the White House's West Wing Situation Room manning the government's response:

> *I kept thinking of the words from 'Apocalypse Now,' the whispered words of Marlon Brando, when he thought about Vietnam. 'The horror. The horror.' Because we knew what was going on in New York. We knew about*

the bodies flying out of the windows. People falling through the air. We knew that Osama bin Laden had succeeded in bringing horror to the streets of America.

Richard Clarke, former White House counterterrorism adviser, 21 March 2004 [28], [29], [30], [31], [32], [33], [34], [35]

Despite the attack on the Pentagon itself, Defense Secretary Donald Rumsfeld remained in his office and prepared to lead a counterattack against Iraq:

Rumsfeld was saying that we needed to bomb Iraq. And we all said ...no, no. Al-Qaeda is in Afghanistan. We need to bomb Afghanistan. And Rumsfeld said there aren't any good targets in Afghanistan. And there are lots of good targets in Iraq. I said, 'Well, there are lots of good targets in lots of places, but Iraq had nothing to do with it.'

Richard Clarke, CBS 60 Minutes Interview, 21 March 2004 [36]

The National Security Council's chief counter-terrorism advisor, Richard Clarke, the Director of Central Intelligence, George Tenet, as well as the FBI told the Administration there simply was no connection between al-Qaeda and Saddam Hussein:

I said, 'Mr. President. We've done this before. We have been looking at this. We looked at it with an open mind. There's no connection.'

He came back at me and said, 'Iraq! Saddam! Find out if there's a connection.' And in a very intimidating way. I mean that we should come back with that answer. We wrote a report.

It was a serious look. We got together all the FBI experts, all the CIA experts. We wrote the report. We sent the report out to CIA and found FBI and said, 'Will you sign this report?' They all cleared the report. And we sent it up to the president and it got bounced by the

National Security Advisor or Deputy. It got bounced and sent back saying, 'Wrong answer... Do it again'.

Richard Clarke, National Security Counter-terrorism Director 1993-2003, 21 March 2004 [37]

In the weeks that followed 9/11, more than 90 countries teamed up with the US to take on terrorist organizations. With no urging on the part of the United States government, the North Atlantic Treaty Organization met and declared that al-Qaeda's attacks on American soil were considered to be attacks on all the nations holding NATO membership. It was the first time the organization's Article V mutual Defense Clause had ever been invoked.

Citing the ANZUS Treaty (Australia, New Zealand, and United States Security Treaty), Australia affirmed that the attacks upon America would also be treated the same as attacks upon Australia itself. Russia, finding common cause with the US in its own fight against Islamic terrorism, generously made available to the US old Soviet military bases in Central Asia, as well as the large stock of Afghan intelligence it had collected during its 1980s conflict in Afghanistan. The Islamic Republic of Iran helped the US build a relationship with Afghanistan's Northern Alliance and made its sovereign airspace available for US over flights. Throughout Iran, the youth held rallies and prayer vigils in support of America. Retired Lieutenant General William Odom, the former director of President Reagan's National Security Agency, noted:

We never have had so much international support in our history.

General William Odom, March 8, 2006 [38]

Within weeks, a few hundred American and British intelligence and special agents, in combination with the Northern Alliance and US airpower, had driven the Taliban government from power and were poised on the slopes of Tora Bora to finish off al-Qaeda's leaders. [39] Suddenly, the Bush administration seemed to lose focus as it turned its attention to Iraq. The opportunity for closure in the *War on Terror* that came so quickly was disregarded as Osama bin Laden, wounded in body and spirit, slipped off to the safety of northern Pakistan. [40]

The fires in the rubble of the World Trade Center were still smoldering. [41], [42], [43] Nationally, anger and uncertainty still remained, but a degree of satisfaction was taken in the speedy collapse of the Taliban's government. Al-Qaeda's narrow escape would be withheld from public knowledge for years. [44] In Washington, the idea that a strapping, broad-shouldered United States that roused powerfully to flex its hypermuscles could now remake the vast and ancient cultures of the Middle East with ease was beginning to boil over.

On January 29, 2002, President Bush gave his first State of the Union Address since the routing of the Taliban and al-Qaeda. The speech was generally a well-written affirmation of American values assembled by neoconservative David Frum. It declared that the United States had the terrorist leaders on the run and smoothed over the fact they had been allowed to do so. It also advanced the incoherent notion that Saddam Hussein had begun scheming with his hated enemies in Iran to make life difficult for America and that, somehow, Iraq (the historic Arab bulwark against Iran), Iran, and North Korea had teamed up in an *axis of evil* to pose *a grave and growing danger* to the

United States and its allies. The price of this con-fabulation would prove to be immense.

Great nations persevere and then prevail. They do not jump from one unfinished task to another.

Al Gore, 23 September 2002 [45]

CHAPTER 14 REFERENCES

[1] *Memorandum for Condoleezza Rice, From: Richard A. Clarke, Subject: Presidential Policy Initiative/Review - The Al-Qida Network;*
http://www2.gwu.edu/~nsarchiv/NSAEBB/NSAEBB147/clarke%20memo.pdf
(SHORTENED URL: http://tinyurl.com/vonako)

[2] *Clarke's Take On Terror, by Rebecca Leung, CBS, 21 March 2004;*
http://www.cbsnews.com/stories/2004/03/19/60minutes/main607356.shtml
(SHORTENED URL: http://tinyurl.com/takoro)

[3] *Paul Wolfowitz's fatal weakness, by Juan Cole, 14 May 2007, salon.com;*
http://www.salon.com/opinion/feature/2007/05/14/wolfowitz/index.html
(SHORTENED URL: http://tinyurl.com/salobo)

[4] *Profile: Brian Sheridan, History Commons;*
http://www.historycommons.org/entity.jsp?entity=brian_sheridan
(SHORTENED URL: http://tinyurl.com/bedele)

[5] *Panel details intelligence slip on terror suspect, by John Diamond, USA TODAY;*
http://www.usatoday.com/news/washington/2002-12-11-intell-panel-report_x.htm
(SHORTENED URL: http://tinyurl.com/xepela)

[6] *Context of 'Late July 2001: Egypt Warns CIA of 20 Al-*

Qaeda Operatives in US; Four Training to Fly; CIA Is Not Interested', History Commons; http://www.historycommons.org/context.jsp?item=a0701eg ypt#a0701egypt
(SHORTENED URL: http://tinyurl.com/somala)

[7] Late Summer 2001: Jordan Warns US that Aircraft Will Be Used in Major Attack Inside the US, History Commons; http://www.historycommons.org/context.jsp?item=alatesu mmer01jordan
(SHORTENED URL: http://tinyurl.com/garama)

[8] Two Months Before 9/11, an Urgent Warning to Rice, The Washington Post, 1 October 2006; http://www.washingtonpost.com/wp-dyn/content/article/2006/09/30/AR2006093000282.html
(SHORTENED URL: http://tinyurl.com/gerata)

[9] July 10, 2001: CIA Director Gives Urgent Warning to White House of Imminent, Multiple, Simultaneous Al-Qaeda Attacks, Possibly within US; History Commons: Context of 'July 10, 2001: CIA Director Tenet Briefed about Al-Qaeda; Urgent White House Meeting Results';
http://www.historycommons.org/context.jsp?item=a071001 tenetwarnsrice#a071001tenetwarnsrice
(SHORTENED URL: http://tinyurl.com/veteba)

[10] July 10, 2001: CIA Director Gives Urgent Warning to White House of Imminent, Multiple, Simultaneous Al-Qaeda Attacks, Possibly within US; History Commons: Context of 'July 10, 2001: CIA Director Tenet Briefed about Al-Qaeda; Urgent White House Meeting Results';
http://www.historycommons.org/context.jsp?item=a071001 tenetwarnsrice#a071001tenetwarnsrice
(SHORTENED URL: http://tinyurl.com/hireka)

[11] Two Months Before 9/11, an Urgent Warning to Rice, The Washington Post, 1 October 2006; http://www.washingtonpost.com/wp-dyn/content/article/2006/09/30/AR2006093000282_pf.html
(SHORTENED URL: http://tinyurl.com/biresi)

[12] Two Months Before 9/11, an Urgent Warning to Rice,

The Washington Post, 1 October 2006;
http://www.washingtonpost.com/wp-
dyn/content/article/2006/09/30/AR2006093000282 pf.html
(SHORTENED URL: http://tinyurl.com/biresi)

[13] July 10, 2001: Urgent CIA Request for Funds to
Immediately Deal with Bin Laden Is Denied, History
Commons;
http://www.historycommons.org/context.jsp?item=a071001
blackrequest#a071001blackrequest
(SHORTENED URL: http://tinyurl.com/sirefa)

[14] July 11-17, 2001: Rumsfeld and Ashcroft Receive
Urgent Al-Qaeda Warning Recently Given to White House,
History Commons;
http://www.historycommons.org/context.jsp?item=a071001
tenetwarnsrice#a071101rumsfeldashcroft
(SHORTENED URL: http://tinyurl.com/rugeni)

[15] July 10, 2001: CIA Director Gives Urgent Warning to
White House of Imminent, Multiple, Simultaneous Al-Qaeda
Attacks, Possibly within US, History Commons;
http://www.historycommons.org/context.jsp?item=a071001
tenetwarnsrice#a071001tenetwarnsrice
(SHORTENED URL: http://tinyurl.com/veteba)

[16] Two Months Before 9/11, an Urgent Warning to Rice,
The Washington Post, 1 October 2006;
http://www.washingtonpost.com/wp-
dyn/content/article/2006/09/30/AR2006093000282 pf.html
(SHORTENED URL: http://tinyurl.com/biresi)

[17] July 11-17, 2001: Rumsfeld and Ashcroft Receive
Urgent Al-Qaeda Warning Recently Given to White House,
History Commons;
http://www.historycommons.org/context.jsp?item=a071101
rumsfeldashcroft#a071101rumsfeldashcroft
(SHORTENED URL: http://tinyurl.com/rugeni)

[18] July 11-17, 2001: Rumsfeld and Ashcroft Receive
Urgent Al-Qaeda Warning Recently Given to White House,
History Commons;
http://www.historycommons.org/context.jsp?item=a071101

rumsfeldashcroft#a071101rumsfeldashcroft
(SHORTENED URL: http://tinyurl.com/rugeni)

[19]
(a) 8. "The System Was Blinking Red"; 8.1 The Summer of Threat, pp 258 -259;
http://www.gpoaccess.gov/911/pdf/sec8.pdf.
(SHORTENED URL: http://tinyurl.com/sybire)
(b) The 9-11 Commission Report, Final Report of the National Commission on Terrorist Attacks Upon the United States, Official Government Edition;
http://www.gpoaccess.gov/911/

[20] The Phoenix Memo and Related Investigations, History Commons;
http://www.historycommons.org/timeline.jsp?timeline=complete_911_timeline&projects_and_programs=phoenixMemo
(SHORTENED URL: http://tinyurl.com/homelo)

[21] Did Ashcroft ignore terrorism warnings before 9/11, by Lisa Myers, NBC 22 June 2004;
http://www.msnbc.msn.com/id/5271234/
(SHORTENED URL: http://tinyurl.com/tenifo)

[22] Ashcroft Flying High, CBS News, 26 July 2001;
http://www.cbsnews.com/stories/2001/07/26/national/main303601.shtml
(SHORTENED URL: http://tinyurl.com/lehamo)

[23] Bin Laden Determined To Strike in US, Presidential Daily Briefing On bin Laden, August 6, 2001, Declassified and Approved for Release 10 April 2004, The National Security Archive, George Washington University;
http://www.gwu.edu/~nsarchiv/NSAEBB/NSAEBB116/pdb8-6-2001.pdf
(SHORTENED URL: http://tinyurl.com/kadako)

[24] The Shadow War, In a Surprising New Light, by Barton Gellman, The Washington Post, 20 June 2006;
http://www.washingtonpost.com/wp-dyn/content/article/2006/06/19/AR2006061901211.html
(SHORTENED URL: http://tinyurl.com/dosuba)

[25] Excerpts from April 8, 2004 Testimony of Dr. Condoleezza Rice Before the 9/11 Commission Pertaining to The President's Daily Brief of August 6, 2001, The National Security Archive, George Washington University; http://www.gwu.edu/~nsarchiv/NSAEBB/NSAEBB116/testimony.htm
(SHORTENED URL: http://tinyurl.com/setedo)

[26] Clues Alerted White House to Potential Attacks, by Carl Cameron, Fox News, 17 May 2002; http://www.foxnews.com/story/0,2933,53065,00.html
(SHORTENED URL: http://tinyurl.com/lugera)

[27] Clarke's Take On Terror, CBS 60 Minutes Interview, by Rebecca Leung, March 21, 2004; http://www.cbsnews.com/stories/2004/03/19/60minutes/main607356.shtml
(SHORTENED URL: http://tinyurl.com/takoro)

[28] Clarke's Take On Terror, CBS 60 Minutes Interview, by Rebecca Leung, March 21, 2004; http://www.cbsnews.com/stories/2004/03/19/60minutes/main607356.shtml
(SHORTENED URL: http://tinyurl.com/takoro)

[29] INSIDE 9/11: ZERO HOUR (PART 1 of 4), You Tube; http://www.youtube.com/watch?v=M-B6c6xxXug&feature=related
(SHORTENED URL: http://tinyurl.com/tureto)

[30] Part 4 of 10 - Inside The Twin Towers.wmv, You Tube, Aired on September 3, 2006 on The Discovery Channel 2007, Narrated by Terrence Stamp; http://www.youtube.com/watch?v=iac6J4gITa0&feature=related
(SHORTENED URL: http://tinyurl.com/patowe)

[31] INSIDE 9/11: ZERO HOUR (PART 2 of 4), You Tube; http://www.youtube.com/watch?v=-kVg9iaDdE0&feature=related
(SHORTENED URL: http://tinyurl.com/patowa)

[32] 911 Call in World Trade Center, while tower collapse;

http://www.youtube.com/watch?v=RLW0jKKRXMo
(SHORTENED URL: http://tinyurl.com/polate)

[33] INSIDE 9/11: ZERO HOUR (PART 3 of 4), You Tube;
http://www.youtube.com/watch?v=a-
3ZOEXxdYg&feature=related
(SHORTENED URL: http://tinyurl.com/patotu)

[34] Part 09 of 10 - Inside The Twin Towers, You Tube,
Aired on September 3, 2006 on The Discovery Channel
2007, Narrated by Terrence Stamp;
http://www.youtube.com/watch?v=pDOtWD1Lx6Q&feature
=related
(SHORTENED URL: http://tinyurl.com/retema)

[35] When the World Stopped Turning: A 9/11 tribute,
Music by Alan Jackson;
http://www.youtube.com/watch?v=AW8puRqE4Sc
(SHORTENED URL: http://tinyurl.com/tewoso)

[36] Clarke's Take On Terror, CBS 60 Minutes Interview, by
Rebecca Leung, 21 March 2004;
http://www.cbsnews.com/stories/2004/03/19/60minutes/m
ain607356.shtml
(SHORTENED URL: http://tinyurl.com/terele)

[37] Clarke's Take On Terror, CBS 60 Minutes Interview, by
Rebecca Leung March 21, 2004;
http://www.cbsnews.com/stories/2004/03/19/60minutes/m
ain607356.shtml
(SHORTENED URL: http://tinyurl.com/takoro)

[38] General Condemnation, byGeorge Kenny, IN THESE
TIMES, March 8, 2006;
http://www.inthesetimes.com/main/article/2522/
(SHORTENED URL: http://tinyurl.com/gecoke)

[39] Airpower in Afghanistan, by Rebecca Grant, A Mitchell
Institute Special Report, 2009 Air Force Association;
http://higherlogicdownload.s3.amazonaws.com/AFA/6379b7
47-7730-4f82-9b45-
a1c80d6c8fdb/UploadedImages/Mitchell%20Publications/Air
power%20in%20Afghanistan.pdf

IRAQ WAR 2003

(SHORTENED URL: _http://tinyurl.com/remara_)

[40] The Osama bin Laden I Know, An Oral History of al Qaeda's Leader, by Peter L. Bergen; © 2006, Free Press, a Division of Simon & Schuster, Inc., pp 369-371.

[41] WTC Fires All But Defeated, CBSNEWS, 19 December 2001;
http://www.cbsnews.com/stories/2001/12/19/archive/main 321907.shtml
{Page No Longer Found} Go to:
http://careandwashingofthebrain.blogspot.com/2013/02/91 1-unseen-footage-tower-7-blasted-into.html
(SHORTENED URL: _http://tinyurl.com/potaga_)

[42] Collapse of the World Trade Center, eNotes (100 & 101);
_http://www.enotes.com/topic/Collapse_of_the_World_Trade _Center#cite_note-103_
(SHORTENED URL: _http://tinyurl.com/tasosa_)

[43] WTC Fire Extinguished, People's Daily Online, 20 December 2001;
_http://english.people.com.cn/200112/20/eng20011220_871 19.shtml_
(SHORTENED URL: _http://tinyurl.com/figupe_)

[44] The Osama bin Laden I Know, An Oral History of al Qaeda's Leader, by Peter L. Bergen; © 2006, Free Press, a Division of Simon & Schuster, Inc., pp 331-336.

[45] Former Vice President Al Gore Iraq and the War on Terrorism, Commonwealth Club of California San Francisco, California September 23, 2002;
http://www.gwu.edu/~action/2004/gore/gore092302sp.htm l
(SHORTENED URL: _http://tinyurl.com/reqate_)

CHAPTER 15

WE KNOW THEY'RE THERE

When I was coming up it was a dangerous world and we knew exactly who the 'they' were. It was us versus them and it was clear who 'them' was. Today, we're not sure who the 'they' are, but we know they're there.

George W. Bush, campaign 2000

The shift of focus away from the 9/11 attackers gave al-Qaeda the breathing room it needed to survive. It also began the attrition of the new and the usual friends that had lined up to support America after the attacks. The world understood the need to take on the *'grave and growing danger'* of al-Qaeda, but it had little interest in chasing Mesopotamian phantasies.

They didn't sign up for that, and they weren't even asked. And then the president marches on, acting as if Europeans were fools because they didn't sign up for the war, as if they were out of place to question whether they should even be consulted.

General William Odom, former Director of the NSA under President Ronald Reagan, 8 March 2006 [1]

With his *'Axis of Evil'* State of the Union Speech, the President prepared the United States, and any other nation that could be persuaded or bought, to be taken in a direction no American leader had tried to take them before. [2] Informally known as *'The Bush Doctrine'*, this new direction represented in the concluding years of America's *'unipolar moment'* an extension of trends that had been developing in US foreign policy since the Second World War. It represented a profound drift from the generally conservative traditions that had guided American foreign policy since *'Wash-*

ington's Farewell Address' (a document that had recognized America would become a Great Power, but cautioned against the abuse of that likely good fortune). [3]

A nation has the right to respond preemptively to a clear and present danger. The Bush administration's, though, new view was that the United States should use its great military power to take anticipatory action against even vague possibilities of danger. In practical application, it meant that rather than concentrating on the clear and present danger already existing in al-Qaeda, new enemies would be gratuitously pursued if they even seemed to present a one percent chance of threat. [4]

In 2006, the US Supreme Court reminded the nation that participation in a *'common plan to wage aggressive war'* is a war crime. [5] However, the signatories to the Project for the New American Century had been given so many key positions in the administration of George W. Bush that the mood of the nation and the supportive press following 9/11 afforded PNAC and their associates an opportunity to transform their geopolitical projects into Presidential Doctrine.

> *International Law? I better call my lawyer; he didn't bring that up to me.*
>
> George W. Bush, December 12, 2003

Ignoring the advice of experts ranging from the CIA's bin Laden station [6] to Brent Scowcroft (national security advisor to President George H.W. Bush), the neoconservative Bush administration carelessly prepared to hand al-Qaeda almost exactly what it had been trying to incite: an unwarranted, full-scale military invasion of an oil-rich Muslim nation. [7] George W. Bush was determined to hand al-Qaeda the means to revitalize itself as a defender of the Islamic homelands: [8], [9]

> Osama bin Laden had been saying for years, 'America wants to invade an Arab country and occupy it, an oil-rich Arab country.' He had been saying this. This is part of his propaganda.
>
> So what did we do after 9/11? We invade an oil-rich and occupy an oil-rich Arab country which was doing nothing to threaten us. In other words, we stepped right into bin Laden's propaganda. And the result of that is that al Qaeda and organizations like it, offshoots of it, second-generation al Qaeda have been greatly strengthened.
>
> Richard Clarke, former White House counter-terrorism adviser, 21 March 2004 [10]

Publically the Bush administration maintained it was not a foregone conclusion that military action would be taken against Iraq. In October 2002, the President said:

> The stated policy of the United States is regime change. However, if Hussein were to meet all the conditions of the United Nations, the conditions that I have described very clearly in terms that everybody can understand, that in itself will signal the regime has changed.
>
> George W. Bush, 21 October 2002 [11]

But the US began energetically pushing the UN to confront the 'grave and gathering danger' it asserted Saddam Hussein presented to the International Community. President Bush, in partnership with British Prime Minister Tony Blair, was trying to get a single resolution from the UN Security Council. The proposed resolution would both demand Iraq demonstrate it no longer had any Weapons of Mass Destruction programs and authorize the use of force if Iraqi leadership was not willing to submit. The President also required that Saddam Hussein end his support of terrorism and persecution of non-Sunni ethnic groups inside Iraq. The other three permanent members of the Security Council, China, France and Russia, sought two separate resolutions on the issue: the first to reauthorize a strong WMD inspections regime for Iraq, and a second to spell out the consequences its leadership would face if they failed to comply.

In December 2002, the Chief of Iraqi Intelligence, General Tahir Jalil Habbush al-Tikriti, indirectly contacted Vincent Cannistraro, former Chief of Operations and Analysis for the CIA's Counterterrorist Center. His purpose was to ask him to inform the US Government that Saddam Hussein was willing to satisfy all the administration's concerns regarding his alleged al-Qaeda links and possession of WMDs. At the same time, the Iraqis also tried to reach the US Government through the governments of Egypt, France, Germany, Russia and Syria, in order to discuss the allegations. Nothing would come of all these attempts to resolve the issue.

Meanwhile Bush and Blair contained to pursue their quarry:

> BUSH: *Saddam Hussein is not disarming. He is a danger to the world. He must disarm. And that's why I have constantly said, and the prime minister has constantly said, this issue will come to a head in a matter of weeks, not months.*

> BLAIR: *[W]hen we went down the United [Nations] route, we passed Resolution 1441, and I think it really repays reading that, because we said very clearly that Saddam had what we said was a final opportunity to*

disarm, and that he had to cooperate fully in every respect with the U.N. weapons inspectors.

As Dr. Blix said in his report to the Security Council earlier this week, he's not doing that. And therefore, what is important is that the international community comes together again and makes it absolutely clear that this is unacceptable.

BUSH: I want to remind you, I was the guy who went to the United Nations in the first place. I said, 'Why don't we come together as a world to resolve this issue once and for all? Why doesn't the United Nations stand up as a body and show the world that it's got the capacity to keep the peace?'

This needs to be resolved quickly. Should the United Nations decide to pass a second resolution, it'd be welcome if it is yet another signal that we're intent upon disarming Saddam Hussein.

But 1441 gives us the authority to move without any second resolution. And Saddam Hussein must understand that if he does not disarm, for the sake of peace, we, along with others, will go disarm Saddam Hussein.

BUSH: Well, all due modesty, I thought I did a pretty good job myself of making it clear that he's not disarming and why he should disarm.

Secretary Powell will make a strong case about the danger of an armed Saddam Hussein. He will make it clear that Saddam Hussein is fooling the world -- or trying to fool the world. He will make it clear that Saddam is a menace to peace in his own neighborhood. And he will also talk about al Qaeda links, links that really do portend a danger for America and for Great Britain; anybody else who loves freedom.

> *President George W. Bush and Prime Minister Tony Blair, Excerpts of 31 January 2003 Washington D.C. Joint News Conference* [12]

That same month, the Syrian Government expressed to Mohammed Nassif, a businessman with high level

US Defense contacts, the frustration it was having in trying to contact the US government on Iraq's behalf. A Lebanese-American with contacts to the neoconservatives, Imad al-Hage, was finally successful in relaying to Richard Perle a message from Hassan al-Obeidi, Iraqi Intelligence Chief of Foreign Operations. The message questioned why Baghdad was being targeted and invited Washington to send FBI agents into Iraq to determine for themselves there were no WMDs in the country. [13]

In late February 2003, al-Hage had met with General Habbush and Tariq Aziz, Iraq's Deputy Prime Minister, and received an invitation for the US to send up to 5,000 inspectors into the country to search for WMDs. [14] The offer also included priority of access for American oil companies to Iraqi oil and the pledge of full support for any plan the US might advance in the Arab-Israeli peace process. In March, Perle told al-Hage that Washington was not interested in further discussion and the message he should carry to his Iraqi contacts was: *'Tell them that we will see them in Baghdad.'*

> *When he [Saddam Hussein] chose to deny inspectors, when he chose not to disclose, then I had the difficult decision to make to remove him.*
>
> > *George W. Bush, March 21, 2005, (145 U.N. inspectors were in Iraq in December 2002 and in January 2003, just before the March 20, 2003 American-led invasion)* [15]

While the world talked about the issues, in the summer of 2002, the US and UK governments stepped up their targeting of Iraqi defenses and in September that year (six months before the war's official beginning) Special

CHARLES EDMUND COYOTE

Forces teams infiltrated the country. Iraqi air defenses were targeted in the *'no-fly zones'* that reached north (from the 36th parallel to the Turkish border) and south (from a latitudinal line 20 miles south of Baghdad to the Kuwait border) about two thirds of the country. These No-fly zones had been established by the Americans, British, and French to protect Iraq's northern Kurds and southern Shiites during civil unrest following the 1991 Persian Gulf War.

The 1991 Gulf War victors cited UN Security Council Resolution 688 as their authority for the No-fly zones, even though the resolution contains no clear authorization to do so. [16] Once the 1991 domestic turmoil calmed down, the American and British forces continued to use the No-fly zones, a means of continually degrading Iraq's military capabilities in the north and south. The French withdrew from the No-fly operations in 1998. American and British aircraft continued to arbitrarily maintain the Zones, receiving almost daily anti-aircraft fire from Iraqi forces from the time of the Operation Desert Fox bombings in December 1998 until the 2003 Invasion. During the same period, American and British air forces carried out weekly retributions against Iraqi anti-aircraft and other military targets. Former Secretary-General of the UN, Boutros Boutros-Ghali hesitantly called the No-fly zones *'illegal'*. [17]

> *The issue of no fly zones was not raised and therefore not debated: not a word. They offer no legitimacy to countries sending their aircraft to attack Iraq. They are illegal.*
>
> *Dr Boutros Boutros-Ghali, former Secretary-General of the United Nations, February 2003* [18]

The enduring No-Fly campaign received little attention from the Anglo-American press. During 1999, alone, more than 1,800 bombs were dropped on Iraq and the growing shortage of targets in the Northern and Southern Zones was becoming pronounced. In 1999, The Wall Street Journal quoted one US official as saying:

> We're down to the last outhouse. There are still some things left, but not many.
>
> Citation by John Pilger, A People Betrayed, 23 February 2003 [19]

The Americans and British had even taken to attacking harmless sheepherders. An assault investigated by UN Assistant Secretary-General, Hans C. von Sponeck, found that a family in the Kurdish north had lost their grandfather, father, four siblings, and 105 sheep when a coalition aircraft dive-bombed them as they were tending their flock. Dozens of similar attacks on civilians were documented by the United Nations Security Section. [20] As with Denis Halliday before him, von Sponeck could no longer stomach his job as UN Humanitarian Coordinator for Iraq heading all UN operations in the country, including the Oil-for-Food program. Resigning in February 2000, von Sponeck and Halliday subsequently spoke out against the sanctions regime accusing it of violating the Geneva Conventions and international law. [21]

In the spring of 2002, US and UK aircraft began bombing the remaining command structure in the southern part of Iraq. By September 2002, tonnage dropped had increased from 7-14 tons per month during May-August to over 54 tons. On September 5, 2002, more than 100 aircraft attacked the main air defense site in western Iraq, so that coalition Special

Forces would be able to enter the country undetected from Jordan. [22] As war had not been declared or authorized by the US Congress, the bombing and Special Ops campaigns, carried out to degrade Iraq's remaining defenses in preparation for major conflict, were done in secret. Because international law does not recognize *'regime change'* as a legitimate reason to attack another country, the Bush and Blair governments were also hoping thereby to provoke Saddam into reprisals that could be used to justify the American hostilities.

At a July 2002 meeting of Tony Blair's ministers, a secret paper was presented in which the US laid out two alternative war plans for war on Iraq. One option described a pre-invasion build-up of 250,000 troops in Kuwait, after which coalition aircraft would mount an air war followed by a full-scale ground offensive similar to the strategy of 1991 Persian Gulf War. The second plan used a *'running start'* in which a continuous air campaign, justified by an initial Iraqi misstep, would be undertaken in conjunction with the insertion of special operations forces to support indigenous Iraqi opposition groups. These would be joined by regular troops as they arrived in theater. The eventual operation evolved into a hybrid of the two, in which the air war would commence as soon as the Iraqis provided a *'casus belli'*.

> *The same document [the July 2002 briefing paper for Tony Blair's ministers] also stated bluntly that 'regime change per se is not a proper basis for military action under international law' and it was therefore 'necessary to create the conditions in which we could legally support military action'.*
>
> *America had none of these problems. It was Washington's*

view that it could decide for itself whether Saddam was in breach of his obligations to let in weapons inspectors. With British officials holding Blair back, insisting that without UN backing an invasion would be illegal, it would have been extremely convenient for Bush and Rumsfeld if Saddam had retaliated against the bombing offensive, thus giving London and Washington the chance to cry, 'He started it!'

Michael Smith, The Sunday Times, 30 May 2005 [23]

As it became clear that even the May through September 2002 bombings were not going to provoke Saddam into providing the *'casus belli'*, the coalition attacked anyway, dropping 17.7 tons of ordinance in October 2002, 33.6 tons in November, and 53.2 tons in December. [24] Though only Congress has the power to authorize war under the US constitution, the air strikes and covert war were well under way by October 11, 2002.

In the interests of securing Congressional authorization, a few days before the October 10th and 11th votes for the *Authorization for Use of Military Force Against Iraq Resolution of 2002*, the White House called the US Senate into an unusual closed session. [25] During that meeting, members of the administration told the Senate that Saddam Hussein had developed the ability to attack the Eastern seaboard of the US with biological and chemical WMDs by means of Unmanned Aerial Drones (UAVs) launched from ships positioned off the coast. [26] The 75 Senators in attendance seemed to have been impressed that Saddam had somehow managed to overcome the technical difficulties involved in mounting the 1,805 foot runway required by his two out-of-date L-29 Czech trainer jet drones on one of the littoral craft that

CHARLES EDMUND COYOTE

comprised Iraq's navy. The entire Iraqi navy consisted of a 1,850-ton FFT BOGOMOL Class patrol ship, a 126 ft long I Class PTG, and 150 other miscellaneous speed boats. [27] The 1,805 foot-long flight deck required by the two drones – the only unmanned aerial vehicles in Iraq's possession – would make whatever ship used it the largest warship ever built, dwarfing the US Navy's Super carriers by more than 600 feet. [28]

What remains unknown, however, was whether the Bush administration explained how Saddam's newly monstrous warships would remain unseen as they snuck past the US 5th Fleet stationed in the Persian Gulf, sailed around the Arabian peninsula and up the single-lane Suez Canal, past the US 6th Fleet as it prowled the Mediterranean to escape out the Straits of Gibraltar and across the broad and rough Atlantic to take on America's defenseless Eastern seaboard. Neither does it appear that anything was said about how these tiny boats with the horrifically outsized flight decks would be fueled on their outlandishly difficult journey... or whether the $1 Trillion/year appropriated to the US military was being spent wisely in light of the Bush administration's certainty that the US Navy, Air Force, and National Guard were about to be badly out-foxed by a couple of Iraqi speedboats. [29]

In less pressing circumstances a reasonable individual might ask what kind of hyperactive executive amygdala could come up with such paranoid delusions and should they really be trusted with the strategic responsibilities of a great nation. But, given the underwhelming character of the under-threatening peril, there was nothing the 'The Greatest Deliberative Body in the World' could do but stick its finger to the

political winds, hold its nose and abandon its responsibilities. [30]

Saddam – the Bush administration wanted the US Senate
to know – was rapidly morphing into a superman.

*The obscure we see eventually. The completely obvious,
it seems, takes longer.*

Edward R. Murrow

CHAPTER 15 REFERENCES

*[1] General Condemnation, by George Kenny, IN THESE
TIMES, March 8, 2006;*
http://www.inthesetimes.com/main/article/2522/
(SHORTENED URL: http://tinyurl.com/gekoke)

*[2] Coalition of the billing - or unwilling? by Laura McClure,
Salon.com, 12 March 2003;*
*http://dir.salon.com/story/news/feature/2003/03/12/foreig
n_aid/print.html*
(SHORTENED URL: http://tinyurl.com/fahano)

*[3] Washington's Farewell Address, 1796; The Avalon
Project of the Yale University Law School, Lillian Goldman
Law Library;*
http://avalon.law.yale.edu/18th_century/washing.asp
(SHORTENED URL: http://tinyurl.com/wafahe)

*[4] Who's Counting: Cheney's One Percent Doctrine, by
John Allen Paulos, July 2, 2006, ABC NEWS;*
http://abcnews.go.com/Technology/story?id=2120605
(SHORTENED URL: http://tinyurl.com/wohene)

*[5] HAMDAN v. RUMSFELD, SECRETARY OF DEFENSE, ET
AL., CERTIORARI TO THE UNITED STATES COURT OF
APPEALS FOR THE DISTRICT OF COLUMBIA CIRCUIT,
Argued March 28, 2006 - Decided June 29, 2006, SUPREME
COURT OF THE UNITED STATES, p 46;*
http://www.hamdanvrumsfeld.com/05-184.pdf

(SHORTENED URL: http://tinyurl.com/harase)

[6] *Frontline: Bush's War, PBS;*
http://www.pbs.org/wgbh/pages/frontline/bushswar/
(SHORTENED URL: http://tinyurl.com/robupa)

[7] *Don't Attack Saddam, It would undermine our antiterror efforts; BRENT SCOWCROFT, The Wall Street Journal, 15 August 2002.*

[8] *The Power of Nightmares, Adam Curtis, Internet Archive;*
http://archive.org/details/ThePowerOfNightmares-Episode1BabyItsColdOutside
(SHORTENED URL: http://tinyurl.com/ponime)

[9] *The Power of Nightmares Part 3: The Shadows in the Cave, by Adam Curtis;*
http://dotsub.com/view/53b8e7df-fa03-4e44-a47a-c27f70f276f5
(SHORTENED URL: http://tinyurl.com/ponima)

[10] *Clarke's Take On Terror, CBS 60 Minutes Interview, March 21, 2004;*
http://www.cbsnews.com/stories/2004/03/19/60minutes/main607356.shtml
(SHORTENED URL: http://tinyurl.com/tamoro)

[11] *Saddam can keep rule if he complies: Bush, Daily Times, 23 October 2002;*
http://www.dailytimes.com.pk/default.asp?page=story_23-10-2002_pg4_1
(SHORTENED URL: http://tinyurl.com/sabuda)

[12] *Bush, Blair: Time running out for Saddam, CNN.com, 31 January 2003;*
http://www.cnn.com/2003/US/01/31/sprj.irq.bush.blair.topics/
(SHORTENED URL: http://tinyurl.com/tirasa)

[13] *"They Were All Non-Starters" The Thwarted Iraqi Peace Proposals, by Gary Leupp, Counterpunch, 10 November 2003, edited by Alexander Cockburn and Jeffrey St. Clair;*

http://www.counterpunch.org/2003/11/10/edited-by-alexander-cockburn-and-jeffrey-st-clair/print
(SHORTENED URL: http://tinyurl.com/somapa)

[14] *Failed Iraqi peace initiatives, EconomicExpert.com;*
http://www.economicexpert.com/a/Failed:Iraqi:peace:initiatives.htm
(SHORTENED URL: http://tinyurl.com/farani)

[15] *May I Quote You, Mr. President? A selection of 50 quotes from President George W. Bush, by Prof. Rodrigue Tremblay, Center for Research on Globilization, www.globalresearch.ca;*
http://www.globalresearch.ca/index.php?context=va&aid=3907
(SHORTENED URL: http://tinyurl.com/masile)

[16] *RESOLUTION 688 (1991), Adopted by the Security Council at its 2982nd meeting on 5 April 1991, United Nations S/RES/0688 (1991) 5 April 1991;*
http://www.fas.org/news/un/iraq/sres/sres0688.htm
(SHORTENED URL: http://tinyurl.com/reluse)

[17] *A People Betrayed, John Pilger, ZNET, 23 February 2003; http://www.zmag.org/znet/viewArticle/10911*
(SHORTENED URL: http://tinyurl.com/perelo)

[18] *A People Betrayed, John Pilger, ZNET, 23 February 2003; http://www.zmag.org/znet/viewArticle/10911*
(SHORTENED URL: http://tinyurl.com/perelo)

[19] *A People Betrayed, John Pilger, ZNET, 23 February 2003; http://www.zmag.org/znet/viewArticle/10911*
(SHORTENED URL: http://tinyurl.com/perelo)

[20] *AIRSTRIKES IN IRAQ, 28 DECEMBER 1998 - 31 MAY 1999, PREPARED BY UN SECURITY SECTION - UNOHCI - BAGHDAD;*
http://www.casi.org.uk/info/undocs/airstrikes1.html
(SHORTENED URL: http://tinyurl.com/recela)

[21] *The hostage nation, Hans von Sponeck and Denis Halliday, The Guardian, 28 November 2001;*

CHARLES EDMUND COYOTE

*http://www.guardian.co.uk/world/2001/nov/29/iraq.comme
nt*
(SHORTENED URL: http://tinyurl.com/honaha)

*[22] The unofficial war: U.S., Britain led massive secret
bombing campaign before Iraq war was declared, Larisa
Alexandrova and John Byrne, Copyright © 2004-05 Raw
Story Media, 27 June 2005;
http://rawstory.com/news/2005/The_unofficial_war_U.S._a
nd_Britain_led_massive_air_campaign_before_Iraq_war_be
_0627.html*
(SHORTENED URL: http://tinyurl.com/horali)

*[23] The war before the war, Michael Smith, defense writer
for The Sunday Times, New Statesman, 30 May 2005;
http://www.newstatesman.com/node/150737*
(SHORTENED URL: http://tinyurl.com/varabo)

*[24] Michael Smith, Michael Smith (newspaper reporter),
Wikipedia Encyclopedia;
https://en.wikipedia.org/wiki/Michael_Smith_(newspaper_re
porter)*
(SHORTENED URL: http://tinyurl.com/vimiro)

*[25] NEW INFORMATION ON IRAQ'S POSSESSION OF
WEAPONS OF MASS DESTRUCTION, Senator Bill Nelson,
Congressional Record: January 28, 2004 (Senate) p S311-
S312;
http://www.fas.org/irp/congress/2004_cr/s012804b.html*
(SHORTENED URL: http://tinyurl.com/secoge)

*[26] IRAQ SCRAPS "NEW" DRONE, Defense Tech, 11 March
2003;
http://defensetech.org/2003/03/11/iraq-scraps-new-drone/*
(SHORTENED URL: http://tinyurl.com/refeta)

*[27] Saddam's Navy, GlobalSecurity.org,
http://www.globalsecurity.org/military/world/iraq/navy.htm*
(SHORTENED URL: http://tinyurl.com/sereva)

*[28] Senators were told Iraqi weapons could hit U.S., by
John McCarthy, Florida Today, 16 December 2003,
GlobalSecurity.org;*

IRAQ WAR 2003

http://www.globalsecurity.org/org/news/2003/031216-iraqi-weapons.htm
(SHORTENED URL: http://tinyurl.com/vatoki)

[29] SENATOR: WHITE HOUSE WARNED OF IRAQ UAV ATTACK, Defense Tech, 16 December 2003;
http://defensetech.org/2003/12/16/senator-white-house-warned-of-iraq-uav-attack/
(SHORTENED URL: http://tinyurl.com/verete)

[30] Fast Fun in Saddam's Avenger, The Times, 6 March 1999;
http://www.yakuk.com/times_6-3-99.asp
(SHORTENED URL: http://tinyurl.com/fafuve)

CHAPTER 16

YOU DISARM OR WE WILL

I was proud the other day when both Republicans and Democrats stood with me in the Rose Garden to announce their support for a clear statement of purpose: you disarm, or we will.

George W Bush, Speaking on Saddam Hussein, Manchester, New Hampshire, October 5, 2002

Common sense and putting the interests of the country higher than a focus on the next election still held place amongst some in Congress:

I believe in this beautiful country. I have studied its roots and gloried in the wisdom of its magnificent Constitution. I have marveled at the wisdom of its founders and framers. Generation after generation of Americans has understood the lofty ideals that underlie our great republic. I have been inspired by the story of their sacrifice and their strength.

But, today, I weep for my country. I have watched the events of recent months with a heavy, heavy heart. No more is the image of America one of strong yet benevolent peacekeeper. The image of America has changed. Around the globe, our friends mistrust us, our word is disputed, our intentions are questioned.

Instead of reasoning with those with whom we disagree, we demand obedience or threaten recrimination. Instead of isolating Saddam Hussein, we seem to have isolated ourselves. We proclaim a new doctrine of pre-emption which is understood by few and feared by many. We say that the United States has the right to turn its firepower on any corner of the globe which might be suspect in the war on terrorism.

We assert that right without the sanction of any international body. As a result, the world has become a much more dangerous place.

We flaunt our superpower status with arrogance. We treat UN Security Council members like ingrates who offend our princely dignity by lifting their heads from the carpet. Valuable alliances are split.

After war has ended, the United States will have to rebuild much more than the country of Iraq. We will have to rebuild America's image around the globe.

The case this administration tries to make to justify its fixation with war is tainted by charges of falsified documents and circumstantial evidence. We cannot convince the world of the necessity of this war for one simple reason. This is a war of choice.

There is no credible information to connect Saddam Hussein to 9/11. The Twin Towers fell because a worldwide terrorist group, al-Qaeda, with cells in over 60 nations, struck at our wealth and our influence by turning our own planes into missiles, one of which would likely have slammed into the dome of this beautiful Capitol except for the brave sacrifice of the passengers on board.

The brutality seen on 11 September and in other terrorist attacks we have witnessed around the globe are the violent and desperate efforts by extremists to stop the daily encroachment of Western values upon their cultures. That is what we fight. It is a force not confined to borders. It is a shadowy entity with many faces, many names and many addresses.

But this administration has directed all of the anger, fear and grief which emerged from the ashes of the Twin Towers and the twisted metal of the Pentagon towards a tangible villain, one we can see and hate and attack. And villain he is. But he is the wrong villain. And this is the wrong war. We will probably drive Saddam Hussein from power. But the zeal of our friends to assist our global war on terrorism may have already taken flight.

The general unease surrounding this war is not just due to 'orange alert'. There is a pervasive sense of rush and risk and too many questions unanswered. How long will

CHARLES EDMUND COYOTE

we be in Iraq? What will be the cost? What is the ultimate mission? How great is the danger at home?

What is happening to this country? When did we become a nation which ignores and berates our friends? When did we decide to risk undermining international order by adopting a radical and doctrinaire approach to using our awesome military might? How can we abandon diplomatic efforts when the turmoil in the world cries out for diplomacy?

Why can this President not seem to see that America's true power lies not in its will to intimidate, but in its ability to inspire?

I along with millions of Americans will pray for the safety of our troops, for the innocent civilians in Iraq, and for the security of our homeland. May God continue to bless the United States of America in the troubled days ahead, and may we somehow recapture the vision which for the present eludes us.

> *US Senator Robert Byrd of West Virginia, 19 March 2003* [1]

Senator Byrd spoke to a largely empty chamber. The other Senators, for the most part, had apparently decided there was little point in trying to shine the light of reason on the senseless stampede to war.

On November 13, 2002, Saddam Hussein had accepted U.N. Security Council Resolution 1441, giving his regime its *'final opportunity to comply with its disarmament obligations'.* [2] Under the direction of the United Nations Monitoring, Verification and Inspection Commission (UNMOVIC), its Chairman Hans Blix, and the International Atomic Energy Agency (IAEA) led by Director-General Mohamed El Baradei, inspectors returned to Iraq to begin their search for the non-existent Weapons of Mass Destruction. The inspectors had exited the nation 4 years ago in 1998 at the request of A. Peter Burleigh, the acting US Ambassador to the UN. Burleigh was concerned for their safety as the US-UK coalition prepared for the massive bombings of Operation Desert Fox. [3]

Although the US President and the Prime Minister of Great Britain maintained that Saddam Hussein was deceiving the world and preparing to unleash hidden WMDs against both their countries, UN weapons inspectors were stating:

> *In my 27 January update to the Council, I said that it seemed from our experience that Iraq had decided in principle to provide cooperation on process, most importantly prompt access to all sites and assistance to UNMOVIC in the establishment of the necessary infrastructure. This impression remains, and we note that access to sites has so far been without problems, including those that had never been declared or inspected, as well as to Presidential sites and private residences.*
>
> *Hans Blix, 1st Executive Chairman of the United Nations Monitoring, Verification and Inspection Commission, 14 February 2003* [4]

Shortly before the invasion, the director of the IAEA team formally declared:

> *After three months of intrusive inspections, we have to date found no evidence or plausible indication of the revival of a nuclear weapons programme in Iraq.*
>
> *Dr. Mohamed ElBaradei, Director General of the International Atomic Energy Agency (IAEA), 7 March 2003* [5]

Seymour Hersh, the investigative reporter who won a Pulitzer Prize for exposing the My Lai cover-up, described the perception that Saddam had WMDs as an *'urban myth'* and *'mass hysteria'*. [6]

CHARLES EDMUND COYOTE

And furthermore, the CIA knew this, the British intelligence knew this, Israeli intelligence knew this, German intelligence, the whole world knew this. They weren't going to say that Iraq was disarmed because nobody could say that, but they definitely knew that the Iraqi capability regarding WMD had been reduced to as near to zero as you could bring it, and that Iraq represented a threat to no one when it came to weapons of mass destruction.

Scott Ritter, former UN Weapons Inspector [7]

Speaking to the UN Security Council, French Foreign Minister Dominique de Villepin urged that the inspectors be allowed to finish their work before military intervention. His speech to the UNSC was loudly applauded by those who opposed the premature invasion and is quoted in its entirety below. The Bush administration, mainstream media, and right-wing America had no interest in listening to the French. Had they done so, al-Qaeda would not have been able to gain a foothold in Iraq. In addition, Iran would not have become a regional hegemon, and well over a million Iraqi's would still be alive. America also would not have thrown away the lives of thousands of its soldiers and trillions of tax-payer dollars to achieve such ends.

Address on Iraq, by Dominique de Villepin, French Minister of Foreign Affairs, at the UN Security Council
New-York, February 14, 2003

Mr. President,

Mr. Secretary-General,

Ministers,

Ambassadors, I would like to thank Mr. Blix and Mr. ElBaradei for the information they have just given us on the continuing inspections in Iraq. I would like to express to them again France's confidence and complete support in their mission.

You know the value that France has placed on the unity of the Security Council from the outset of the Iraq crisis. This unity rests on two fundamental elements at this time:

We are pursuing together the objective of effectively disarming Iraq. We have an obligation to achieve results. Let us not cast doubt on our common commitment to this goal. We shoulder collectively this onerous responsibility which must leave no room for ulterior motives or assumptions. Let us be clear: Not one of us feels the least indulgence towards Saddam Hussein and the Iraqi regime.

In unanimously adopting resolution 1441, we collectively expressed our agreement with the two-stage approach proposed by France: the choice of disarmament through inspections and, should this strategy fail, consideration by the Security Council of all the options, including the recourse to force. It was clearly in the event the inspections failed and only in that scenario that a second resolution could be justified.

The question today is simple: Do we consider in good conscience that disarmament via inspections is now leading us to a dead-end? Or do we consider that the possibilities regarding inspections presented in resolution 1441 have still not been fully explored?

In response to this question, France has two convictions:

The first is that the option of inspections has not been taken to the end and that it can provide an effective response to the imperative of disarming Iraq;

The second is that the use of force would be so fraught with risks for people, for the region and for international stability that it should only be envisioned as a last resort.

So what have we just learned from the report by Mr. Blix and Mr. ElBaradei? That the inspections are producing results. Of course, each of us wants more, and we will continue together to put pressure on Baghdad to obtain more. But the inspections are producing results.

CHARLES EDMUND COYOTE

In their previous reports to the Security Council on January 27, the executive chairman of UNMOVIC and the director-general of the IAEA had identified in detail areas in which progress was expected. Significant gains have been made on several of these points:

In the chemical and biological areas, the Iraqis have provided the inspectors with new documentation. They have also announced the establishment of commissions of inquiry led by former officials of weapons programs, in accordance with Mr. Blix's requests;

In the ballistic domain, the information provided by Iraq has also enabled the inspectors to make progress. We know exactly the real capabilities of the Al-Samoud missile. The unauthorized programs must now be dismantled, in accordance with Mr. Blix's conclusions;

In the nuclear domain, useful information was given to the IAEA on important points discussed by Mr. ElBaradei on January 27: the acquisition of magnets that could be used for enriching uranium and the list of contacts between Iraq and the country likely to have provided it with uranium.

We all realize that the success of the inspections presupposes that we obtain Iraq's full and complete cooperation. France has consistently demanded this.

Real progress is beginning to be apparent:

Iraq has agreed to aerial reconnaissance over its territory;

It has allowed Iraqi scientists to be questioned by the inspectors without witnesses;

A bill barring all activities linked to weapons of mass destruction programs is in the process of being adopted, in accordance with a long-standing request of the inspectors;

Iraq is to provide a detailed list of experts who witnessed the destruction of military programs in 1991.

France naturally expects these commitments to be durably verified. Beyond that, we must maintain strong pressure on Iraq so that it goes further in its cooperation.

Progress like this strengthens us in our conviction that in-

spections can be effective.

But we must not shut our eyes to the amount of work that still remains; questions still have to be cleared up, verifications made, and installations and equipment probably still have to be destroyed.

To do this, we must give the inspections every chance of succeeding:

I submitted proposals to the Council on February 5;

Since then we have detailed them in a working document addressed to Mr. Blix and M. ElBaradei and distributed to Council members.

What is the spirit of these proposals?

They are practical, concrete proposals that can be implemented quickly and are designed to enhance the efficiency of inspection operations.

They fall within the framework of resolution 1441 and consequently do not require a new resolution.

They must support the efforts of Mr. Blix and Mr. ElBaradei:

The latter are naturally the best placed to tell us which ones they wish to adopt for the maximum effectiveness of their work.

In their report they have already made useful and operational comments. France has already announced that it had additional resources available to Mr. Blix and Mr. ElBaradei, beginning with its Mirage IV reconnaissance aircraft.

Now, yes, I do hear the critics:

There are those who think that the inspections, in their principle, cannot be the least effective. But I recall that this is the very foundation of resolution 1441 and that the inspections are producing results. One may judge them inadequate but they are there.

There are those who believe that continuing the inspection process is a sort of delaying tactic to prevent military intervention. That naturally raises the question of the time allowed Iraq. This brings us to the core of the debates. At

CHARLES EDMUND COYOTE

stake is our credibility, and our sense of responsibility. Let us have the courage to see things as they are.

There are two options:

The option of war might seem a priori to be the swiftest. But let us not forget that having won the war, one has to build peace. Let us not delude ourselves; this will be long and difficult because it will be necessary to preserve Iraq's unity and restore stability in a lasting way in a country and region harshly affected by the intrusion of force.

Faced with such perspectives, there is an alternative in the inspections which allow us to move forward day by day with the effective and peaceful disarmament of Iraq. In the end is that choice not the most sure and most rapid?

No one can assert today that the path of war will be shorter than that of the inspections. No one can claim either that it might lead to a safer, more just and more stable world. For war is always the sanction of failure. Would this be our sole recourse in the face of the many challenges at this time?

So let us allow the United Nations inspectors the time they need for their mission to succeed. But let us together be vigilant and ask Mr. Blix and Mr. ElBaradei to report regularly to the Council. France, for its part, proposes another meeting on March 14 at ministerial level to assess the situation. We will then be able to judge the progress that has been made and what remains to be done.

Given this context, the use of force is not justified at this time. There is an alternative to war: disarming Iraq via inspections. Furthermore, premature recourse to the military option would be fraught with risks:

The authority of our action is based today on the unity of the international community. Premature military intervention would bring this unity into question, and that would detract from its legitimacy and, in the long run, its effectiveness.

Such intervention could have incalculable consequences for the stability of this scarred and fragile region. It would compound the sense of injustice, increase tensions and risk paving the way to other conflicts.

We all share the same priority – that of fighting terrorism mercilessly. This fight requires total determination. Since the tragedy of September 11 this has been one of the highest priorities facing our peoples. And France, which was struck hard by this terrible scourge several times, is wholly mobilized in this fight which concerns us all and which we must pursue together. That was the sense of the Security Council meeting held on January 20, at France's initiative.

Ten days ago, the US Secretary of State, Mr. Powell, reported the alleged links between al-Qaeda and the regime in Baghdad. Given the present state of our research and intelligence, in liaison with our allies, nothing allows us to establish such links. On the other hand, we must assess the impact that disputed military action would have on this plan. Would not such intervention be liable to exacerbate the divisions between societies, cultures and peoples, divisions that nurture terrorism?

France has said all along: We do not exclude the possibility that force may have to be used one day if the inspectors' reports concluded that it was impossible to continue the inspections. The Council would then have to take a decision, and its members would have to meet all their responsibilities. In such an eventuality, I want to recall here the questions I emphasized at our last debate on February 4 which we must answer:

To what extent do the nature and extent of the threat justify the immediate recourse to force?

How do we ensure that the considerable risks of such intervention can actually be kept under control?

In any case, in such an eventuality, it is indeed the unity of the international community that would guarantee its effectiveness. Similarly, it is the United Nations that will be tomorrow at the center of the peace to be built whatever happens.

Mr. President, to those who are wondering in anguish when and how we are going to cede to war, I would like to tell them that nothing, at any time, in this Security Council, will be done in haste, misunderstanding, suspicion or fear.

CHARLES EDMUND COYOTE

In this temple of the United Nations, we are the guardians of an ideal, the guardians of a conscience. The onerous responsibility and immense honor we have must lead us to give priority to disarmament in peace.

This message comes to you today from an old country, France, from a continent like mine, Europe, that has known wars, occupation and barbarity. A country that does not forget and knows everything it owes to the freedom-fighters who came from America and elsewhere. And yet has never ceased to stand upright in the face of history and before mankind. Faithful to its values, it wishes resolutely to act with all the members of the international community. It believes in our ability to build together a better world.

Dominique de Villepin, French Minister of Foreign Affairs, Address on Iraq at the UN Security Council, 14 February 2003 [8], [9]

CHAPTER 16 REFERENCES

[1] Why I weep for my country, by US Senator Robert Byrd of West Virginia, 19 March 2003 (excerpts of speech), The Observer, 23 March 2003; http://www.guardian.co.uk/world/2003/mar/23/usa.iraq2/print (SHORTENED URL: http://tinyurl.com/hywiti)

[2] Security Council resolution 1441 (2002) The situation between Iraq and Kuwait, Security Council Resolutions; http://www.al-bab.com/arab/docs/iraq/unscr1441.htm (SHORTENED URL: http://tinyurl.com/secolu)

[3] Inspectors voluntarily ended their mission because of the threat of military action by the United States and its allies; Rumsfeld's flight of fancy on Iraq, by Glenn Kessler, The Washington Post, 9 February 2011; http://voices.washingtonpost.com/fact-checker/2011/02/rumsfelds_flight_of_fancy_on_i.html (SHORTENED URL: http://tinyurl.com/felama)

[4] Briefing of the Security Council, 14 February 2003: An update on inspections, Selected Security Council Briefings,

Documents, UNMOVIC - United Nations Monitoring,
Verification and Inspection Commission;
http://www.unmovic.org/

[5] The Status of Nuclear Inspections in Iraq: An Update,
by IAEA Director General Dr. Mohamed ElBaradei,
Statement to the United Nations Security Council, 7 March
2003; IAEA.org News Center;
http://www.iaea.org/NewsCenter/Statements/2003/ebsp20
03n006.shtml
(SHORTENED URL: http://tinyurl.com/tatunu)

[6] Scott Ritter and Seymour Hersh: Iraq Confidential, The
Nation, 14 November 2005;
http://www.thenation.com/article/scott-ritter-and-seymour-
hersh-iraq-confidential
(SHORTENED URL: http://tinyurl.com/risehe)

[7] Scott Ritter and Seymour Hersh: Iraq Confidential, The
Nation, 14 November 2005;
http://www.thenation.com/article/scott-ritter-and-seymour-
hersh-iraq-confidential
(SHORTENED URL: http://tinyurl.com/risehe)

[8] French address on Iraq at the UN Security Council
Address on Iraq, by Dominique de Villepin, French Minister
of Foreign Affairs, 14 February 2003;
http://en.wikisource.org/wiki/French_address_on_Iraq_at_t
he_UN_Security_Council
(SHORTENED URL: http://tinyurl.com/wifede)

[9] Newshour with Jim Lehrer Transcript: DOMINIQUE
GALOUZEAU DE VILLEPIN, 14 February 2003, Public
Broadcasting System, Online News Hour;
http://www.pbs.org/newshour/bb/middle_east/iraq/france_
2-14.html
(SHORTENED URL: http://tinyurl.com/herado)

CHAPTER 17

THE WAR ON TERROR INVOLVES SADDAM HUSSEIN BECAUSE

The war on terror involves Saddam Hussein because of the nature of Saddam Hussein, the history of Saddam Hussein, and his willingness to terrorize himself.

>   *George W. Bush, Grand Rapids Michigan, January 29, 2003*

Worldwide protests against the impending invasion took place on February 15, the day after Villepin's address to the Security Council. In Rome, Italy, three million people participated in the largest anti-war gathering ever. During the first 4 months of 2003, an estimated 36 million people across the globe marched to protest the impending conflict.

The invasion was opposed by many of America's traditional allies, including Canada, France and Germany, on the grounds that there was no evidence of WMDs in Iraq. NATO member Turkey, risking $26 billion in potential future aid from the United States, would not allow an invasion of Iraq to be conducted from its territory. [1]

In the US, the unresolved trauma of 9/11 led the Fourth Estate to largely abandon its responsibilities of monitoring the government. The domestic drums were beaten loudly for the broad definition the Bush administration intended to give to the *'War on Terror'*, whether or not it made sense to punish Iraq for al-Qaeda's offenses.

The Bush administration's belated concerns over the suffering of Iraq's citizens, as it tried to rally support for the war, were not upheld by those who had been monitoring the situation for years. *Human Rights Watch* pointed out that the incidents that had taken place constituted no excuse to attack decades later:

> *Such interventions should be reserved for stopping an imminent or ongoing slaughter. They shouldn't be used belatedly to address atrocities that were ignored in the past.*
>
> Kenneth Roth, executive director Human Rights Watch, Annual Report, 26 January 2004 [2]

As it became clear that the UN wanted further inspections before it would authorize war on Iraq, the US and the UK determined to invade regardless of the opinion of the international community. [3] Robin Cook, the leader of the British House of Commons, resigned in protest against his government's imminent participation in the attack. UN Secretary-General, Kofi Annan, ever constrained by the need to appease the US government, eventually spoke:

> *BBC News: So you don't think there was legal authority for the war?*
>
> *Secretary-General Kofi Annan: I have stated clearly that it was not in conformity with the Security Council – with the UN Charter.*
>
> *BBC News: It was illegal?*
>
> *Secretary-General Kofi Annan: Yes, if you wish.*
>
> *BBC News: It was illegal?*
>
> *Secretary-General Kofi Annan: Yes, I have indicated it is not in conformity with the UN Charter, from our point of view and from the Charter point of view it was illegal.*
>
> U.N. Secretary-General Kofi Annan, 16 September 2004 [4]

CHARLES EDMUND COYOTE

What discolored Franco-American relations was the antagonism between the diplomatic approach, sought by the majority of the Security Council, and the route to military intervention pursued by the US and Britain. During the fall and winter of 2002-2003, the Bush administration dominated the political winds and Rupert Murdoch's *New York Post* and *The Sun*, as well as right-wing talk radio, led the mass outcry against France's failure to fall in line. French President Jacques Chirac was called *'a worm'* and Murdoch's publications declared the French people were turning their backs on the sacrifice American GIs had made for their nation during World War II.

Although the French pointed out that the popular *'French Fried'* style of preparing potatoes probably originated in Belgium, the US House of Representatives, under the authority of the Committee on House Administration, declared that henceforth those French fries served in the three House of Representatives cafeterias would be known as *'Freedom Fries'*. [5] *'French Toast'* was similarly named.

Representative Walter Jones Jr. from North Carolina, one of the leaders of the briefly popular *'Freedom Fries'* movement, came to regret his participation in the name change as he began to learn that the Bush administration had been selectively feeding intelligence to Congress to prod it into supporting the war. [6] Before the invasion, however, the mainstream media promoted the invasion of Iraq with leading articles and reports. Even venerable publishing institutions, such as *The New York Times*, were featuring descriptions of Saddam Hussein's (non-existent) efforts to build WMDs and military systems as revenge against American interests. The substantial doubts that were also surfacing, even those from the CIA and members of Congress, were buried in small articles well hidden from the leading stories. In particular, a high percentage of viewers of Rupert Murdoch's Fox Television network, which frequently cited *'conclusive evidence'* of Saddam Hussein's involvement in the 9/11 attack, were found to be wildly misinformed about the circumstances leading to the 2003 Invasion, when compared to the viewers of other networks, such as the Public Broadcasting Service. [7]

Even 5 years later, in a 2008 poll conducted by FactCheck.org, 48 percent of Americans believed that Saddam Hussein was involved in the September 11 attacks. Once voters have accepted a deception, they tend to prefer it over evidence to the contrary.

> *If a nation expects to be ignorant and free, in a state of civilization, it expects what never was and never will be.*
>
> Thomas Jefferson

By March 2003, the United States, the United Kingdom, Australia, Spain, Denmark, and Poland had assembled 248,000, 46,000, 2,000 1,300, 500, and 194 troops respectively along the Kuwaiti border, and were ready to send them into Iraq. In the north, 70,000 Kurdish Peshmerga, along with CIA Special Activities Division teams and the US Army's 10th Special Forces Group, were already preparing the way for thousands of US paratroopers from the 173rd Airborne Brigade to join them and strike south from the 36th parallel. [8], [9] At the start of the invasion, CENTCOM had 467,000 US military personnel in the Persian Gulf Theater. [10]

CHARLES EDMUND COYOTE

On 17 March 2003, President Bush went on national television and announced that Saddam Hussein and his two sons, Qusay and Uday, had 48 hours to surrender control of Iraq and leave the country. [11], [12] Two days later, an air attack led by two F-117 Nighthawks dropped 4 satellite-guided 2,000-pound GBU-27 Bunker Buster bombs. They were accompanied by 40 Tomahawk cruise missiles launched by submarines and destroyers striking at al-Dora Farms Presidential compound on the southwest outskirts of Baghdad. However, this was an unsuccessful attempt to kill Hussein. [13], [14] Saddam was not there. Three of the Tomahawk missiles hit a residential area nearby where they killed the person who was the primary source of the misinformation about Saddam Hussein's presence at Dora Farms. Fourteen others were wounded, including nine women and a child. [15] The first blood of Iraq War of 2003 had been shed.

On March 20, the President returned to national television to announce the start of the war. Inside Baghdad, prepositioned commandos from the CIA's Special Activities Division called in air strikes. [16] Military units waiting in Kuwait began their 'running start' across the border, racing in to take control of Iraq's giant oil fields before any significant destruction of wells and facilities could take place.

The next day a massive 'Shock and Awe' bombardment of Iraq's military and governmental targets opened in an attempt to destroy the leadership's command structure and morale. [17] Homes, offices, and palaces belonging to Saddam Hussein and his family, as well as members of the Ba'ath Party's inner circle, were prioritized for destruction. From Saddam International Airport, through the offices and barracks of the security organizations, to the ministries and VIP housing near the Tigris River in Baghdad, a rain of bombs and missiles shredded the regime. [18] Across the country, heavy bombing threw the defending military into disarray, preventing – with the exception of the irregular Fedayeen – almost all serious resistance to the coalition army advancing from the south. [19], [20]

By the 23rd of March, the invaders were at Nasiriyah, more than 100 miles from the Kuwaiti border. There, heavy fighting took place for the control of three important bridges crossing the Euphrates River. [21] The US Army's Third Infantry Division had already defeated Iraqi forces at nearby Talil Airfield two days before. Then they bypassed the city, leaving the Marines to enter Nasiriyah. [22] By the 23rd of March, the Third Infantry had penetrated 320 miles in its race toward Baghdad. Facilitated by Iraq's modern highways the 3rd Infantry was moving through enemy territory faster than any other military division in the history of warfare. [23]

During the months preceding the war, an undercover American officer had sold Iraqi intelligence phony 'top secret' plans developed by CENTCOM to intentionally mislead. The misinformation persuaded Iraq's leadership that the main Coalition armies would strike from Turkey and Jordan. The trick worked. While the main invasion force raced in from the south, Saddam kept 13 divisions in the country's north and west to block armies that never came. [24]

On the 25th of March, as the 3rd Infantry closed in on Karbala, about 60 miles Southwest of Baghdad, a severe sandstorm arose. This halted the advance of the mechanized columns and suspended helicopter support.

CHARLES EDMUND COYOTE

On the ground, visibility was down to 100 feet. [25] The Iraqi generals seized on the opportunity to reinforce the Republican Guard divisions preparing to defend Baghdad. As the monstrous storm blasted across the desert, the paramilitary Saddam Fedayeen struck at the American supply convoys far to the rear of the swift advance. On the US television networks, retired generals worried that the situation had become bogged down and vulnerable lines of provision were overexposed.

As the storm raged, it hugged the ground but continued to give a clear sky to the Coalition's JSTAR surveillance aircraft flying high above. [26] Using Synthetic Aperture Radar, they could watch through the swirling dust and rain as the Iraqi tanks and troop columns moved silently, unsuspecting of their vulnerability, in the poor visibility thousands of feet below. Their ground-situation information was relayed to waiting bombers, and the unsuspecting defenders became helpless as devastating airstrikes suddenly came at them through the howling storm and sand. [27] Before the three-day storm moved on, thousands of Iraqi soldiers had lost their lives. Baghdad and Medina divisions melted into flaming wreckage any remaining capacity of the Republican Guards to counterattack.

Although US strategy was to head straight to Baghdad, bypassing whenever possible the urban centers in route, the Fedayeen fighters that remained in the cities to the rear were proving to be a problem. Facing guerilla-style strikes using AK-47s, rocket-propelled grenades, machine guns, and deception tactics on the more vulnerable supply convoys, the invading troops found it necessary to delay their advance about a week in order to protect their supply lines and root out these asymmetric irregulars.

If Iraq was going to use biological or chemical WMDs, the Americans believed that it would happen once their forces crossed an imaginary *'Red Line'* stretching from about 60 miles south of Baghdad into eastern Iraq. [28] Although concern for these weapons was one of the main justifications for the war, nothing of the sort ever happened. No biological or chemical materials, not a single Scud rocket was used or found throughout the entire war, even as the Ba'athist Regime faced its collapse. [29] Three months before, Saddam had told his top commanders they had no biological, chemical or nuclear weapons. The disclosure that the nation no longer had the poison gas and germ weapons, used in the 1980s against the Iranian attacks, sent morale plummeting amongst the general staff as they considered the overwhelming technological advantages of the threatening western powers. [30]

Now, as a dozen years before, the road to Baghdad once again became littered with the charred remains of Iraqi tanks and wrecked personnel carriers twisted about the dead bodies of the hapless Republican defenders. Unlike before, the vanquished thousands grew inversely to the distance to Baghdad – the ancient commercial and cultural center, a thousand years ago the greatest city in the world. Communications intercepts from the regime suggested it was unraveling, becoming increasingly isolated from what was left of its military. The Iraqi Army's collapse was accelerated by the work of CIA Special Activities Division officers who contacted and convinced several key officers to surrender their units to the invasion rather than try to resist. As the

CHARLES EDMUND COYOTE

268

American forces approached Saddam's capital, most of its organized resistance crumbled beneath the certainty that continuing the war symmetrically would be suicide. Later, CENTCOM Commander General Tommy Franks confirmed that the Coalition was paying Iraqi military leaders to defect.

> *The skillful leader subdues the enemy's troops without any fighting; he captures their cities without laying siege to them; he overthrows their kingdom without lengthy operations in the field.*
>
> Sun Tzu, The Art of War [31]

1991 Persian Gulf War, Highway of Death

As the US closed in on Baghdad, Iraqi troops faded away into the civilian population, leaving mostly Fedayeen and foreign fighters to continue to battle the invaders. [32] The outskirts of Baghdad were reached on April 5, and a week of fierce and close combat ensued when troops of the 1st Marine Division, the

IRAQ WAR 2003

Army's 3rd Infantry, and the 101st Airborne Division reached the Iraqi and Syrian defenders of Saddam International Airport, about 10 miles west of downtown. [33] As the fighting continued at Saddam International, other units from the 3rd Infantry Division entered downtown Baghdad where they seized Saddam's Republican and Sijood presidential palaces on April 7. Additional elements from the 1st Marine Division pressed into the eastern suburbs. The seizure of Saddam's presidential palaces shocked the remaining Iraqi military inside Baghdad and their resistance disintegrated.

There was one notable exception to this disintegration. On the 8th of April, as American troops and tanks rolled through the neighborhoods of Baghdad, Mohammed Saeed al-Sahaf, Iraq's Minister of Information, a.k.a. Baghdad Bob, informed the world that the Ba'athist Regime was continuing an indomitable resistance:

> *We are in control. They are in a state of hysteria.*
>
> *Iraqi Information Minister Mohammed Saeed al-Sahaf (Baghdad Bob), April 8, 2003* [34]

The following morning, in a staged PSYOPs production, US Marines helped crowds of celebrating Iraqis pull down the oversized statue of Saddam Hussein outside the Palestine Hotel in Baghdad's Firdos Square. The government of Saddam Hussein Abd al-Majid al-Tikriti was no more.

CHARLES EDMUND COYOTE

ALL DONNE, GO HOME [35]

CHAPTER 17 REFERENCES

[1] Coalition of the billing - or unwilling? by Laura McClure, salon.com, 12 March 2003;
http://dir.salon.com/story/news/feature/2003/03/12/foreig n_aid/
(SHORTENED URL: http://tinyurl.com/hisare)

[2] Iraq war unjustified says human rights group, by Ewen MacAskill, diplomatic editor, The Guardian, 27 January 2004;
http://www.guardian.co.uk/politics/2004/jan/27/uk.humanr ights
(SHORTENED URL: http://tinyurl.com/gumari)

[3] OPERATION IRAQI FREEDOM, ©2003 National Broadcasting Company Inc., Andrews McMeel Publishing; CD - Chapter 2, The Ultimatum.

[4] Excerpts: Annan interview, BBC World Service, 16

September 2004;
http://news.bbc.co.uk/2/hi/middle_east/3661640.stm
(SHORTENED URL: http://tinyurl.com/xevise)

[5] US Congress opts for "freedom fries", BBC NEWS, 12 March 2003;
http://news.bbc.co.uk/2/hi/americas/2842493.stm
(SHORTENED URL: http://tinyurl.com/reneco)

[6] French fries protester regrets war jibe, by Jamie Wilson, The Guardian, 25 May 2005;
http://www.guardian.co.uk/world/2005/may/25/usa.jamiewilson1
(SHORTENED URL: http://tinyurl.com/jijawi)

[7] MISPERCEPTIONS, THE MEDIA AND THE IRAQ WAR, PIPA/Knowledge Networks, 2 October 2003;
http://www.worldpublicopinion.org/pipa/pdf/oct03/IraqMedia_Oct03_rpt.pdf
(SHORTENED URL: http://tinyurl.com/qipapu)

[8] Surrogate Warfare: The Role of US Army Special Forces, MAJ Isaac J. Peltier; US Army School of Advanced Military Studies, United States Army Command and General Staff College, Fort Leavenworth, Kansas; 05/26/05;
http://cgsc.cdmhost.com/cdm/singleitem/collection/p4013coll3/id/363/rec/68
(SHORTENED URL: http://tinyurl.com/peroma)

[9] Contemporary Security Challenges: Irregular Warfare and Indirect Approaches; JSOU Report 09-3 - Surrogate Warfare: The Role of US Army Special Forces, by Isaac J. Peltier, Joint Special Operations University 2009, Scribd.com pp 55-80;
http://www.scribd.com/doc/90140575/Irregular-Warfare-Indirect-Approaches-Contemporary-Security-Challenges
(SHORTENED URL: http://tinyurl.com/hafadi)

[10] Operation IRAQI FREEDOM - By The Numbers, United States Central Command Air Forces (USAFCENT) Assessment and Analysis Division, T. Michael Moseley, Lt Gen, USAF, Commander, 30 April 2003;
http://www.globalsecurity.org/military/library/report/2003/

CHARLES EDMUND COYOTE

uscentaf_oif_report_30apr2003.pdf
(SHORTENED URL: http://tinyurl.com/setoli)

[11] Iraq: Special report, Global Message - March 17, 2003;
http://georgewbush-whitehouse.archives.gov/infocus/iraq/news/20030317-10.html
(SHORTENED URL: http://tinyurl.com/posama)

[12] "Why We Know Iraq is Lying" A Column by Dr. Condoleezza Rice, Originally appeared in the New York Times on 23 January 2003;
http://georgewbush-whitehouse.archives.gov/news/releases/2003/01/20030123-1.html
(SHORTENED URL: http://tinyurl.com/jelehi)

[13] Paveway™ Laser and GPS/Laser Precision Guided Bombs, Raytheon Company;
http://www.businesswireindia.com/attachments/1(20).pdf
(SHORTENED URL: http://tinyurl.com/busuri)

[14] Iraqi Leader, in Frantic Flight, Eluded US Strikes, by Michael R. Gordon and Bernard E. Trainor, The New York Times, 12 March 2006;
http://travel.nytimes.com/2006/03/12/international/middleeast/12escape.html
(SHORTENED URL: http://tinyurl.com/rulubi)

[15] Errors Are Seen in Early Attacks on Iraqi Leaders, by Douglas Jehl and Eric Schmitt, The New York Times, 13 June 2004;
http://www.nytimes.com/2004/06/13/international/middleeast/13SADD.html?ex=1402459200&en=8dd94fca60901354&ei=5007
(SHORTENED URL: http://tinyurl.com/tadesa)

[16] Bush speech in full, BBC News Americas, 20 March 2003; http://news.bbc.co.uk/2/hi/americas/2866715.stm
(SHORTENED URL: http://tinyurl.com/fofufe)

[17] Shock & Awe: Achieving Rapid Dominance, by Harlan

K. Ullman and James P. Wade, National Defense University, 1996; http://www.dodccrp.org/files/Ullman_Shock.pdf (SHORTENED URL: http://tinyurl.com/pimina)

[18] Iraq Faces Massive US Missile Barrage, by Sue Chan, CBS Evening News, 24 January 2003; http://www.cbsnews.com/8301-18563_162-537928.html (SHORTENED URL: http://tinyurl.com/tetosa)

[19] Baghdad SHOCK and AWE 21.03.2003 21h Lokal, You Tube; http://www.youtube.com/watch?v=83Smjn9wou8 (SHORTENED URL: http://tinyurl.com/molopa)

[20] Sky News - Shock & Awe Iraq, You Tube; http://www.youtube.com/watch?v=neDgVb9YHcA&feature=related (SHORTENED URL: http://tinyurl.com/wature)

[21] Gains in south spur thrust to Baghdad , by Luke Harding, Oliver Burkeman, Nicholas Watt and Richard Norton-Taylor, The Guardian, 22 March 2003; http://www.guardian.co.uk/world/2003/mar/22/iraq.richardnortontaylor1 (SHORTENED URL: http://tinyurl.com/gurate)

[22] 3rd Brigade Combat Team, 3rd Infantry Division (Mechanized), "Sledgehammer", GlobalSecurity.org; http://www.globalsecurity.org/military/agency/army/3id-3bde.htm (SHORTENED URL: http://tinyurl.com/semita)

[23] Operation Iraqi Freedom, by Marc Kusnetz: William M. Arkin; General Montgomery Meigs, retired, and Neal Shapiro, NBC News; Andrews McMeel Publishing, Kansas City, © 2003 by National Broadcasting Company, Inc., pp 37-38.

[24] Agent April Fool tricked Saddam, by Tony Allen-Mills, The Sunday Times, 1 August 2004, (Free Republic.com Posting); http://www.freerepublic.com/focus/f-news/1182619/posts (SHORTENED URL: http://tinyurl.com/feripo)

[25] Operation Iraqi Freedom, by Marc Kusnetz: William M.

274

Arkin; General Montgomery Meigs, retired, and Neal
Shapiro, NBC News: Chapter 4, STORM AND PAUSE, pages
55-75; Andrews McMeel Publishing, Kansas City, © 2003 by
National Broadcasting Company, Inc.

[26] JSTARS, United States of America, airforce-
technology.com;
http://www.airforce-technology.com/projects/jstars/
(SHORTENED URL: http://tinyurl.com/syneti)

[27] Synthetic Aperture Radar, Sandia National
Laboratories; http://www.sandia.gov/radar/sar.html
(SHORTENED URL: http://tinyurl.com/sanedi)

[28] Chemical Warfare and the Defense of Baghdad, Iraq's
Chemical Warfare Program, Central Intelligence Agency, 30
September 2004;
https://www.cia.gov/library/reports/general-reports-
1/iraq_wmd_2004/chap5_annxG.html
(SHORTENED URL: http://tinyurl.com/hefaro)

[29] Operation Iraqi Freedom, by Marc Kusnetz: William M.
Arkin; General Montgomery Meigs, retired, and Neal
Shapiro, NBC News, p 155; Andrews McMeel Publishing,
Kansas City, © 2003 by National Broadcasting Company,
Inc.

[30] Even as US Invaded, Hussein Saw Iraqi Unrest as Top
Threat, by Michael R. Gordon and Bernard E. Trainor, The
New York Times, 12 March 2006;
http://www.nytimes.com/2006/03/12/international/middlee
ast/12saddam.html?_r=1
(SHORTENED URL: http://tinyurl.com/nytena)

[31] The Art of War, Sun Tzu, Edited by James Clavell, p
16, Dell Publishing a division of Bantam Doubleday Dell
Publishing Group, Inc, 1540 Broadway New York, New York,
Copyright © 1983 by James Clavell.

[32] Operation Iraqi Freedom, by Marc Kusnetz: William M.
Arkin; General Montgomery Meigs, retired, and Neal
Shapiro, NBC News; Andrews McMeel Publishing, Kansas
City, © 2003 by National Broadcasting Company, Inc., pp

95-98.

[33] The Thunder Run, US 3rd Infantry Division's Drive to Baghdad, 5th April 2003;
http://www.youtube.com/watch?v=a9oQpBH9Zcw&feature=related
(SHORTENED URL: http://tinyurl.com/watetu)

[34] Actual Quotes From the Iraqi Information Minister (aka 'Baghdad Bob'), About.com: Political Humor;
http://politicalhumor.about.com/library/jokes/bljoke-iraqinfominister.htm
(SHORTENED URL: http://tinyurl.com/hutetu)

[35] ALL 'DONNE' GO HOME - Rx, IRAQ: BRING OUR SOLDIERS HOME - FRIENDS FOR RESPONSIBLE GOVERNMENT;
http://www.freewebs.com/alldonne/

CHAPTER 18

IT WAS NOT A PEACEFUL WELCOME

I think we are welcomed. But it was not a peaceful wel-come.

George W. Bush, Philadelphia, December 12, 2005, on the reception of American forces in Iraq

Iraqi Air and Naval resistance had been virtually non-existent during the three week assault, and the invasion force had used its ownership of the skies to pulverize what remained of the already demoralized Iraqi army. The militaries of the four countries that participated in the three-week opening phase of the Iraq War – the US, the UK, Australia, and Poland (Spain and Denmark deployed their contingents from Kuwait in April) – had good officers and good personnel who did what good officers and good personnel do: they obeyed orders. Instructed to plan an attack designed to destroy the government of Saddam, they used the considerable resources at their disposal to take down the government of Saddam Hussein with prompt efficiency. But as the sun set on the exuberance of apparent quick success, more temperate voices slowly began to be heard:

In 1971, the rock group The Who released the antiwar anthem Won't Get Fooled Again. To most in my generation, the song conveyed a sense of betrayal by the nation's leaders, who had led our country into a costly and unnecessary war in Vietnam. To those of us who were truly counterculture – who became career members of the military during those rough times – the song conveyed a very different message. To us, its lyrics evoked a feeling that we must never again stand by quietly while those ignorant of and casual about war lead us into another one and then mismanage the con-

duct of it. Never again, we thought, would our military's senior leaders remain silent as American troops were marched off to an ill-considered engagement. It's 35 years later, and the judgment is in: the Who had it wrong. We have been fooled again.

Marine Lieutenant General Greg Newbold (Retired), 9 April 2006 [1], [2]

The invading armies of the four countries brought down Saddam Hussein's government in 21 days. Baghdad was occupied on 9 April; the northern city of Kirkuk on the 10th; and by the 15th, Tikrit, the birthplace of Saddam Hussein Abd al-Majid al-Tikriti, had fallen. As the billboards and statues that had plastered Saddam's cult of personality all over Iraq came down, so did the Iraqi civil society. Throughout the country, widespread looting broke out and, within days, a suicide bomber in Baghdad blew himself up in an attack on US Marines. Much of the country was unsecured, yet US Secretary of Defense Donald Rumsfeld was untroubled:

Stuff Happens. And it's untidy. Freedom's untidy and free people are free to make mistakes and commit crimes and do bad things.

Defense Secretary Donald Rumsfeld [3], [4]

And so, bad things began to happen. Rumsfeld did not notice, perhaps would not understand, that most of the looters were Shi'ite Muslims that had long been repressed by Saddam Hussein's Sunni regime. Now they wanted what had always been withheld. It was an early sign of things to come. [5]

Sufficient US and Coalition forces had been sent to the Persian Gulf to guarantee a successful invasion. With that stage coming to a swift conclusion, large portions of those forces were sent back home without ever

CHARLES EDMUND COYOTE

having seen duty in Iraq. Until the troop surge of 2007, there would never be nearly enough troops to maintain order, protect the people and stabilize the country. The Office of Reconstruction and Humanitarian Assistance (ORHA) had been established by the President before the invasion to help CENTCOM meet its responsibilities in post-invasion Iraq. However, out of the 16 important cultural, governmental, and historic sites in Baghdad alone that ORHA had asked the military to secure, only the Headquarters of the Ministry of Oil – the last Building on the list – was protected. [6]

US Marines Guard Iraq's Ministry of Oil April 16 2003 [7]

The world-famous National Museum of Iraq, home to artifacts of the Mesopotamian peoples that had given birth to the very first cities of western civilization, was extensively looted. [8] Thousands of items were lost, some dating back as far as 5,000 years to ancient Sumer. [9] L. Paul Bremer, the Administrator of the Coalition Provisional Authority of Iraq from May 2003 to June 2004, has testified that the Bush administration's initial failure to control the looting and violence had cost Iraq some $12 billion, a significant portion of its nominal 60-70 billion dollar GDP. [10] Anarchy *'in the land where law was first devised'* sent the message that the Coalition was unconcerned about its obligation to provide basic security in the nation it had conquered. [11] Iraqis began to question America's intent.

> *The looting, of course, you know, went from the spontaneous looting of ministries – it pretty soon got into the homes, the neighborhoods, the shops. It then became carjackings and kidnappings and unstructured crime and organized crime. And you could even probably do a DNA chain to the insurgency. That was the spark.*
>
> *Ambassador Barbara Bodine, Coordinator for Central Iraq in charge of Baghdad for the Office of Reconstruction and Humanitarian Assistance* [12]

With President Saddam Hussein and his Ba'athist leadership scattered and hiding, President George W. Bush donned a flight suit and jetted out to the USS Abraham Lincoln, a Nimitz-class Supercarrier. There, in front of a soon-to-be infamous red, white and blue *'MISSION ACCOMPLISHED'* banner, he formally announced the end of major combat operations in Iraq. [13] Bush later referred to the PR stunt as *'Mission Impossible'*. [14]

CHARLES EDMUND COYOTE

The evidence is now overwhelming that the Pentagon conducted no planning for 'postwar' stabilization operations. Other government departments did, but their plans were ignored. George W. Bush, Dick Cheney, Donald Rumsfeld & Co. persuaded themselves that their favored Iraqi exiles would quickly form a new government and that most American troops would be home by late summer 2003 – hence no need for long-term planning. It's appalling enough to be wrong (everybody is sometimes); it's disgraceful and irresponsible to dismiss the notion that you might be and that you should devise a backup plan accordingly.

Fred Kaplan, Slate, 4 October 2005 [15]

With the Administration's scant planning for the war's aftermath, its expected quick and easy victory began to transform itself into something else. In February 2003, the Chief of Staff of the Army, General Eric Shinseki, had testified to the Senate Armed Services Committee that *'several hundred thousand soldiers'* would probably be needed to keep order in post-invasion Iraq. [16] His bosses, Secretary of Defense Donald Rumsfeld and Rumsfeld's deputy, Paul Wolfowitz, ridiculed the General's analysis and forced him into retirement. [17] A year later, Secretary Rumsfeld turned down a similar request from L. Paul Bremer – the highest authority in Iraq – asking for an additional 500,000 troops to stabilize the dis-integrating nation. [18] The year before, Bremer had significantly contributed to the incipient loss of control and culture of violence by banning the Ba'ath party and prohibiting the Iraqi Army from helping out with keeping order in Iraq. Consequently, he lost the support of Iraq's experienced administrative staff and security forces, which now had idle time and reason to turn against the Coalition Provisional Authority.

> *Our own flags should be substituted for those of the
> enemy, and the chariots mingled and used in con-
> junction with ours. The captured soldiers should be kindly
> treated and kept. This is called using the conquered foe
> to augment one's own strength.*
>
> *The Art of War, Sun Tzu* [19]

Once the Coalition had removed Iraqi's secular
Ba'athists from power, the sectarian conflicts, which
had smoldered since the time of the Abbasid Caliphate
more than a thousand years ago, began to burn again.
The fire became a conflagration when al-Qaeda in Iraq
succeeded in touching off civil war by bombing the
golden domed Al 'Askarī Mosque in the city of
Sāmarrā. The inability of the United States to maintain order brought about the brutal deaths of scores of
thousands as Iraq's sects and tribes tortured, mur-
dered and annihilated one another.

> *One Iraqi colonel told me, You know, our planning
> before the war was that we assumed that you guys
> couldn't take casualties, and that was obviously wrong.
> I looked at him and said, What makes you think that
> was wrong? He goes, Well, if you didn't want to take
> casualties, you would have never made that decision
> about the army.*
>
> *Charles Duelfer, Iraq weapons inspector* [20]

The Muslim world had largely understood the American
attack on Afghanistan in response to 9/11, but it had
considerably less tolerance for America's unprovoked
attack on Iraq. When US troops were closing in on
Baghdad, about half of the paramilitary groups
standing in opposition were foreign fighters from
nearby Arab countries. [21]

As the insurgency grew, Defense Secretary Rumsfeld

ordered the rounding up and detention of thousands of civilian suspects in Abu Ghraib, the same prison Saddam Hussein had used for his own chambers of horror. As it became known that Iraq's new interrogators were also using torture to break down innocent civilians, the enraged Muslim world was spurred into action. For a brief period, al-Qaeda reveled in the role of defender of the Muslim homelands. Experts, such as the Senior US Air Force Interrogator writing under the name *Matthew Alexander*, have estimated that half of the US causalities and deaths in Iraq came about as a direct response to the Bush Administration's use of torture. Instead of reducing the terrorist threat, Bush and Cheney were feeding its winds.

> *I learned in Iraq that the No. 1 reason foreign fighters flocked there to fight were the abuses carried out at Abu Ghraib and Guantanamo. Our policy of torture was directly and swiftly recruiting fighters for al-Qaeda in Iraq. The large majority of suicide bombings in Iraq are still carried out by these foreigners. They are also involved in most of the attacks on US and coalition forces in Iraq. It's no exaggeration to say that at least half of our losses and casualties in that country have come at the hands of foreigners who joined the fray because of our program of detainee abuse. The number of US soldiers who have died because of our torture policy will never be definitively known, but it is fair to say that it is close to the number of lives lost on Sept. 11, 2001. How anyone can say that torture keeps Americans safe is beyond me -- unless you don't count American soldiers as Americans.*
>
> *Matthew Alexander (pseudonym), writing 30 November 2008, Senior US Air Force Interrogator and leader of the team of interrogators that successfully eliminated Abu Musab al-Zarqawi, the leader of al-Qaeda in Iraq* [22]

Philosophers of War from Sun Tzu to America's own John

Boyd have emphasized particular factors that, when taken into proper account, prepare the way to victory. The most important of these is the Moral Law, which leads the people into agreement with their ruler. Ignorance of this law leads to the failure in leadership. [23] The average person cares little about who governs them or the direction in which they are being led so long as they feel they are being treated fairly and their leaders exhibit the virtues of wisdom, sincerity, and benevolence. This is as it should be. Humans are so constituted that they function poorly without justice. They will dream, glimpse the imprisoned lightning, and reach for the stars if allowed to build upon its foundation. The Moral Law is the central basis of a good government, without which all its other functions have little meaning.

As a result of the Bush administration's abandonment of moral leadership, the costs to the United States, the United Kingdom, and to the people of Iraq have proved to be horrific. As of 2012, there have been more than 4,804 Coalition Military fatalities in Iraq. [24] 4,486 US troops have died, and more than 32,200 US troops have been wounded. If the military fatalities in Afghanistan are also included, those numbers rise to more than 7,990 Coalition dead. [25] There have been more than 6,500 military fatalities and 47,500 seriously wounded Americans in both wars.

The number of civilian deaths in Iraq brought about as a consequence of the 2003 invasion and the subsequent breakdown of social order in the country has been difficult to determine. Death in this ancient land became so rampant at times that the morgues were unable to handle the load and had to turn the freshly killed and their grieving relatives away. A relatively conservative number of deaths have been recognized by the Iraq Body Count (IBC), which has established a range of 107,000 to 116,000 violent civilian deaths as of June 2012. [26] A much higher range of figures was published by *The Opinion Research Business*, which found that as many as 946,000-1,120,000 Iraqis had died from gunshot wounds, car bombs, aerial bombardment, and assorted other blast/ordnance from the March 2003 US invasion through August 2007. [27]

Earlier, in October 2006, *The Lancet*, one of the world's most authoritative medical journals, published the 2nd of two peer-reviewed studies on the impact of the 2003 invasion and its ensuing strife on mortality rates in Iraq. Both studies were attempts to approximate the excess number of civilian deaths brought about by military action, increased violence, fraying infrastructure, degrading healthcare, etc. A 2006 study titled *"Mortality after the 2003 invasion of Iraq: a cross-sectional cluster sample survey"* was carried out – in association with the Johns Hopkins Bloomberg School of Public Health in Baltimore, Maryland – by Gilbert Burnham, MD; Riyadh Lafta, MD; Shannon Doocy, PhD; and Les Roberts, PhD. It found that during the 40 months from March 2003 to July 2006, Iraq's mortality rates had risen to 13.3/1000 people/year, compared to 5.5/1000 people/year before the invasion. This translated into an estimated 654,965 excess deaths as a direct consequence of the war. Approximately 601,027 of those were violently killed, with the three leading causes being gunshot wounds, explosive ordnance (including car bombs) and air strikes. 31 percent of violent deaths were attributed to Coalition forces. [28]

The fear among the Iraqis began to increase more than it was during Saddam's regime. Now they have to fear going to work, sending their children to schools, providing decent life for themselves, or even being safe while in their own homes. The danger engulfed the lives of the Iraqis in every way, leaving them desperately worrying of what next steps they needed to take in order to stay alive. Amid all the chaos and bloodshed, people began to pine for the days under Saddam's brutal but orderly rule.

Huda Ahmed, MIT Center for International Studies, 2007 [29]

Since the 2003 invasion, more than 4.5 million Iraqis, one out of every six people, lost their homes and became refugees. 2.5 million Iraqis fled to safer locations inside the country, while more than 2 million sought refuge in other countries, including 1.4 million in Syria. The numbers have remained quite high as of January 2011. [30] Because of already existing job shortages in Jordan and Syria, governments in those nations did not allow the refuges to find employment, leaving them to depend largely on their own resources, savings, and the sale of personal possessions, informal child labor, and even prostitution in order to meet their needs for food, rent and healthcare. [31]

The consequences of George W. Bush's invasion of Iraq include between 1 and 2 million new widows. More than one third of the nation's children no longer have fathers, making them – in the Arabic culture – 'orphans'. [32], [33], [34] There have been multiple reports, including those from sources such as the International Red Cross, Amnesty International, the Pentagon, former President Jimmy Carter, and Human Rights Watch, that Coalition incarceration and abuse of Iraq's

CHARLES EDMUND COYOTE

civilians has extended to children even as young as 10 years of age. [35], [36]

The backbone of any nation is its middle class. During Iraq's lawless years, militants and criminal gangs singled out the nation's highly trained professionals. Following 2003, Iraq lost 40 percent of its civil servants, middle managers, and professionals. This created significant shortages of the expertise needed to rebuild and maintain the country's economy. En-rollment in Iraqi schools dropped about 45 percent from 2005 to 2007, with missing teachers being a leading factor. [37] More than 2,200 doctors and nurses have been killed or kidnapped since the 2003 invasion. Of the 34,000 registered physicians in 1990, at least 20,000 left the country. Only 2,000 had returned by 2009. [38]

Once free to worship as they pleased under Saddam, at least half of the 1.5 million Iraqi Christians, inclu-ding the ancient Chaldean Church, have either left the country or been killed. 500 years ago, Christians com-posed about 50 percent of the Mesopotamian popu-lation. Those numbers are now down to 2-3 percent, with the most dramatic shift coming after the 2003 invasion. [39]

Since 2003, the US has spent more than $53 billion for infrastructure reconstruction in Iraq. This sum exceeds the total amount of what our country spent (in present day dollars) to rebuild both Germany and Japan fol-lowing the Second World War. [40] The monumental attempt to rebuild Iraq's infrastructure was conducted within the context of almost insurmountable security challenges and a culture of corruption and no-bid contracts that pervaded both the US and the additional

$91 billion Iraqi effort. [41], [42] By 2010, Iraq had been able to return or exceed pre-2003 levels (low relative to 1990) for electrical production, potable water, sewerage and telephone availability. It continued to lag behind pre-war levels in oil production.

> *America has entered one of its periods of historical madness, but this is the worst I can remember: worse than McCarthyism, worse than the Bay of Pigs and in the long term potentially more disastrous than the Vietnam War.*

> *John le Carré, 13 January 2010* [43]

The face America presented to the Middle East under the Bush administration was not that of the country its citizens know and love. The achievements of any US Presidential administration must be judged by its ability to uphold the best this country has to offer in its hopes and traditions. Before entering office an oath is taken by all government officials to uphold and defend the constitution. The importance of that oath, and the meaning of the document it is intended to uphold, seem to have been forgotten in the self-destructive stampede the Bush Administration orchestrated in its haste to attack the relatively small and defenseless nation of Iraq. The consequences of taking America into *'one of its periods of historical madness'* (John le Carré) were horrifying for the people of Iraq, and a dimming of the Reaganite vision of America as *'the Shining City on a Hill'* leading the way, by example, for the people of the world. [44] A great nation seemed to be losing its way; its character had become something ordinary and unrecognizable. Will we come back to our senses before it is too late?

> *One of our doctrines is: Live your values. And there are two arguments for living your values. One is you have*

CHARLES EDMUND COYOTE

the moral obligation to do it. It is the right thing to do. If you don't buy that, you have a practical reason to do it, because every time you violate it, you pay for it.

General David Petraeus [45]

CHAPTER 18 REFERENCES

[1] Why Iraq Was a Mistake, by Lieutenant General Greg Newbold (Retired), Time Magazine, 9 April 2006;
http://www.time.com/time/magazine/article/0,9171,11816 29,00.html
(SHORTENED URL: http://tinyurl.com/katage)

[2] Won't Get Fooled Again, The Who, YouTube;
http://www.youtube.com/watch?v=SHhrZgojY1Q&feature=r elated
(SHORTENED URL: http://tinyurl.com/wofuge)

[3] "Stuff Happens!" - Rumsfeld on looting after fall of Baghdad, YouTube;
http://www.youtube.com/watch?v=RY9l73Yo9Pw&feature=r elated
(SHORTENED URL: http://tinyurl.com/rusaha)

[4] Stuff Happens; YouTube;
http://www.youtube.com/watch?v=1bsrmwaHHIA&feature= related
(SHORTENED URL: http://tinyurl.com/yorehe)

[5] Oil ministry an untouched building in ravaged Baghdad, The Sydney Morning Herald, 16 April 2003;
http://www.smh.com.au/articles/2003/04/16/10501726438 95.html
(SHORTENED URL: http://tinyurl.com/pimiti)

[6] President Barack Obama's Obligation To Iraq Regarding the National Museum of Antiquities, p 6, Zaylore Sapphos Stout, University of St. Thomas School of Law, 12 February 2009; American Bar Association # 01556193;
http://www.docstoc.com/docs/51040709/President-Barack-Obama%E2%80%99s-Obligation-To-Iraq-Regarding-the-

National
(SHORTENED URL: http://tinyurl.com/rokama)

[7] Iraq under US Occupation - Post-Invasion Looting,
History Commons;
http://www.historycommons.org/timeline.jsp?timeline=us
_occupation_of_iraq_tmln&us_occupation_of_iraq_tmln_gene_
_ral_topics=us_occupation_of_iraq_tmln_post_invasion_looti_
_ng_
(SHORTENED URL: http://tinyurl.com/bokuti)

[8] Priceless manuscripts, books go up in smoke, The
Sydney Morning Herald, 16 April 2003;
http://www.smh.com.au/articles/2003/04/15/10501726004
04.html
(SHORTENED URL: http://tinyurl.com/manubo)

[9] IRAQ: The Cradle of Civilization;
http://www.amazon.com/gp/product/B003L7LCOM/ref=atv
_feed_catalog?tag=imdb-amazonvideo-20_
(SHORTENED URL: http://tinyurl.com/zamilo)

[10] Iraq war badly planned, poorly resourced: Bremer, by
Michael Holden, Reuters/Reuters.com, 28 May 2010;
http://www.reuters.com/article/idUSTRE64R2P620100528?t
ype=politicsNews

[11] IRAQ: The Cradle of Civilization;
http://www.amazon.com/gp/product/B003L7LCOM/ref=atv
_feed_catalog?tag=imdb-amazonvideo-20_
(SHORTENED URL: http://tinyurl.com/zamilo)

_[12]_

(a) Ambassador Bodine's quote found at the Frontline
Transcript ~p 4 of 28, Bush's War, NIGHT TWO, Frontline,
PBS.org;
http://www.pbs.org/wgbh/pages/frontline/bushswar/etc/scr
ipt2.html
(SHORTENED URL: http://tinyurl.com/bofoba)

(b) The Lost Year In Iraq, October 17, 2006, Frontline,
PBS.org;
http://www.pbs.org/wgbh/pages/frontline/yeariniraq/etc/sy

CHARLES EDMUND COYOTE

290

nopsis.html
(SHORTENED URL: http://tinyurl.com/zohera)

[13] Commander in chief's visit sets aircraft carrier's crew abuzz, M.L. Lyke, 2 May 2003, SEATTLE POST-INTELLIGENCER;
http://www.seattlepi.com/local/120279_lincolnsub.html
(SHORTENED URL: http://tinyurl.com/selige)

[14] Bush: I regret standing in front of the 'Mission Impossible' banner, by Amanda Terkel, Think Progress, 23 October 2009;
http://thinkprogress.org/politics/2009/10/23/65934/bush-soul/?mobile=nc
(SHORTENED URL: http://tinyurl.com/taromi)

[15] The Dumbing-Down of the US Army, by Fred Kaplan, Slate, 4 October2005;
http://www.slate.com/id/2127487/
(SHORTENED URL: http://tinyurl.com/dudoni)

[16] THREATS AND RESPONSES: MILITARY SPENDING; Pentagon Contradicts General On Iraq Occupation Force's Size, by Eric Schmitt, The New York Times, 28 February 2003;
http://www.nytimes.com/2003/02/28/us/threats-responses-military-spending-pentagon-contradicts-general-iraq-occupation.html?pagewanted=all&src=pm
(SHORTENED URL: http://tinyurl.com/dureti)

[17] New Strategy Vindicates Ex-Army Chief Shinseki, Thom Shanker, The New York Times, 12 January 2007;
http://www.nytimes.com/2007/01/12/washington/12shinseki.html?_r=1
(SHORTENED URL: http://tinyurl.com/vehija)

[18] Iraq war badly planned, poorly resourced: Bremer, by Michael Holden, Reuters/Reuters.com, 28 May 2010;
http://www.reuters.com/article/idUSTRE64R2P620100528?type=politicsNews
(SHORTENED URL: http://tinyurl.com/banera)

[19] Sun Tzu, The Art of War, p 14, Edited by James

Clavell, Copyright © 1983 by James Clavell.

[20] Farewell to All That: An Oral History of the Bush White House, by Cullen Murphy and Todd S. Purdum, Vanity Fair, February 2009; http://www.vanityfair.com/politics/features/2009/02/bush-oral-history200902?printable=true&currentPage=all (SHORTENED URL: http://tinyurl.com/faheri)

[21] Operation Iraqi Freedom, by Marc Kusnetz, pp 94-95 & 171-172: William M. Arkin; General Montgomery Meigs, retired, and Neal Shapiro, NBC News; Andrews McMeel Publishing, Kansas City, © 2003 by National Broadcasting Company, Inc.

[22] I'm Still Tortured by What I Saw in Iraq, by Matthew Alexander, The Washington Post, November 30, 2008; http://articles.washingtonpost.com/2008-11-30/opinions/36832875_1_interrogations-zarqawi-suicide-bombings (SHORTENED URL: http://tinyurl.com/tosami)

[23] SUN TZU ON THE ART OF WAR, THE OLDEST MILITARY TREATISE IN THE WORLD; Translated from the Chinese By LIONEL GILES, M.A. (1910); Main Text of: Sun Tzu on the Art of War (Lionel Giles, translat.); May, 1994, This text is in the PUBLIC DOMAIN; http://www.au.af.mil/au/awc/awcgate/artofwar.htm: http://www.au.af.mil/au/awc/awcgate/artofwar.htm#1 (Laying Plans)

[24] Operation Iraqi Freedom, icasualties.org; http://icasualties.org/Iraq/Index.aspx

[25] Operation Enduring Freedom, iCasualities.org; http://icasualties.org/OEF/index.aspx

[26] Iraq Body Count; http://www.iraqbodycount.org/

[27] New analysis 'confirms' 1 million + Iraq casualties, The Opinion Research Business, 28 January 2008, Global Research; http://www.globalresearch.ca/index.php?context=va&aid=7

CHARLES EDMUND COYOTE

950
(SHORTENED URL: http://tinyurl.com/balyma)

[28] Mortality after the 2003 invasion of Iraq: a cross-sectional cluster sample survey, by Gilbert Burnham, MD; Riyadh Lafta, MD; Shannon Doocy, PhD; and Les Roberts, PhD; www.thelancet.com, Published online 11 October 2006; http://brusselstribunal.org/pdf/lancet111006.pdf
(SHORTENED URL: http://tinyurl.com/movasi)

[29] An Iraqi Woman Regards the Human Cost of the War in Iraq, Huda Ahmed, Elizabeth Neuffer Fellow at the MIT Center for International Studies, 2006-07, Iraq: the Human Cost;
http://web.mit.edu/humancostiraq/reports/huda-ahmed-report.html
(SHORTENED URL: http://tinyurl.com/remako)

[30] 2012 UNHCR country operations profile - Iraq, United Nations High Commissioner for Refugees (UNHCR);
http://www.unhcr.org/cgi-bin/texis/vtx/page?page=49e486426
(SHORTENED URL: http://tinyurl.com/filehi)

[31] Iraq: Rhetoric and reality: the Iraqi refugee crisis, Amnesty International June 2008;
http://www.amnesty.org/en/library/asset/MDE14/011/2008/en/2e602733-42da-11dd-9452-091b75948109/mde140112008eng.pdf
(SHORTENED URL: http://tinyurl.com/remali)

[32] 5 Million Orphans, by Khalil Ibn Hussein, Gorilla's Guides, 15 December 2007;
http://gorillasguides.com/2007/12/15/5-million-orphans/
(SHORTENED URL: http://tinyurl.com/hagori)

[33] Iraq's Shocking Human Toll: About 1 Million Killed, 4.5 Million Displaced, 1-2 Million Widows, 5 Million Orphans, by John Tirman, The Nation, 2 February 2009;
http://www.alternet.org/world/123818/

[34] Iraq's Dispensable Children, by Dahr Jamail, Anti-War.com, 24 May 2006;

http://www.antiwar.com/jamail/?articleid=9028
(SHORTENED URL: http://tinyurl.com/depeka)

[35] Brussells Tribunal Dossier Children of Iraq - Living with War - PART 3;
http://www.brusselstribunal.org/pdf/Children3.pdf
(SHORTENED URL: http://tinyurl.com/busele)

[36] Child Soldiers Global Report 2008 - Iraq;
http://www.refworld.org/docid/486cb10937.html
(SHORTENED URL: http://tinyurl.com/sosema)

[37] Economic Doldrums in Iraq - Council on Foreign Relations, 2007;
http://www.cfr.org/publication/13629/economic_doldrums_i
n_iraq.html
(SHORTENED URL: http://tinyurl.com/doruni)

[38] Iraq: The Age of Darkness, by Dirk Adriaensens, truthout, 2 October 2010;
http://archive.truthout.org/iraq-the-age-darkness63770
(SHORTENED URL: http://tinyurl.com/genari)

[39] Christianity in Iraq, Wikipedia encyclopedia;
http://en.wikipedia.org/wiki/Iraqi_Christians
(SHORTENED URL: http://tinyurl.com/jirapo)

[40] The Iraq War Ledger A Tabulation of the Human, Financial, and Strategic Costs, by Matthew Duss, Peter Juul, and Brian Katulis, Center for American Progress, 6 May, 2010, p 5;
http://www.americanprogress.org/issues/2010/05/pdf/cost
ofiraq_memo.pdf
(SHORTENED URL: http://tinyurl.com/buhuna)

[41] The New American Century, Top Documentary Films;
http://topdocumentaryfilms.com/new-american-century/
(SHORTENED URL: http://tinyurl.com/bemeri)

[42] How KBR Killed My Career, by Bunnatine Greenhouse, Counterpunch, Weekend Edition, 24-25 September 2011;
http://www.counterpunch.org/2011/09/23/how-kbr-killed-my-career/
(SHORTENED URL: http://tinyurl.com/bunare)

294

[43] *The United States of America Has Gone Mad*, by John le Carré, originally published in *The Times/UK*, 16 January 2003, CommonDreams.org;
http://www.commondreams.org/views03/0115-01.htm
(SHORTENED URL: http://tinyurl.com/nimema)

[44] *5 Million Iraqis Killed, Maimed, Tortured, Displaced -- Think That Bothers War Boosters Like Christopher Hitchens?* by Fred Branfman, AlterNet, 21 June 2012;
http://www.alternet.org/story/147281/5_million_iraqis_killed,_maimed,_tortured,_displaced_--_think_that_bothers_war_boosters_like_christopher_hitchens/
(SHORTENED URL: http://tinyurl.com/vimato)

[45] *The Professor of War*, by Mark Bowden, Vanity Fair, May 2010;
http://www.vanityfair.com/politics/features/2010/05/petraeus-201005
(SHORTENED URL: http://tinyurl.com/rofeso)

CHAPTER 19

NEW WAYS TO HARM

Our enemies are innovative and resourceful, and so are we. They never stop thinking about new ways to harm our country and our people, and neither do we.

George W. Bush, Washington D.C., August 2004

After the 9/11 attacks, the nation pulled itself together and stood, not *'shocked and terrorized'* as some had said, but *'shocked and angry'* as did the children of the Pearl Harbor generation. But unlike the triumphant emergence from World War II, the costliest conflict in American history, the children and grandchildren of its *'Greatest Generation'* now struggle to move on from the impacts of the Iraq War, the second costliest conflict in all of American history. Decades of free trade policies and neo-liberal economics had hallowed out the middle class and industrial base of what was once *'the Arsenal of Democracy'*, drowning the nation and its various levels of government in oceans of debt and strained budgets. A broad middle class is the backbone and strength of any nation, and Americans not long ago were able to raise and educate their families in prosperity sufficient to rocket to the moon. Now they wonder if they will be able to keep their homes. A nation that once fought to advance the rule of law and roll back aggressive tyranny now flirts with designs for torturing those not bending to their aggressive fabrications. It was not the American people that had changed. It was the direction they were being taken by their leaders.

In transforming Iraq from the stable, defanged position it was in as a result of the 1991 Persian Gulf

War, the Bush Administration created a crucible for terrorism. The Iraq War became a rallying point for violent Islamists and an environment in which they were able to develop, test, and perfect the tactics of extremism and export them back to those fighting the neglected war in Afghanistan. As the US left the Iraq conflict behind, Iraq's new leaders were building ties with Iran, a state of affairs impossible under Saddam. [1] George W. Bush's investment of American blood and treasure worked to create the previously non-existent 'Axis of Evil' presently involving Iran, Shiite Iraq, Hezbollah and Alawite Syria.

Positioned for victory in the 'War on Terror' only three months after it had begun, the Bush administration repurposed America's resolve to take down bin Laden and al-Qaeda into the long-haul misadventures of Middle Eastern nation building. By the time generals, such as David Petraeus, were politely pointing out how Bush Administration activities such as Abu Ghraib were undermining the stated purposes and values of America, the damage had been done to the moral power of the United States. [2]

> There is no surer way to make a man your enemy than to tell him you are going to remake him in your image for his own good.
>
> Russell Kirk

By the end of November 2001, the Bush administration's inattentiveness to the Afghan war transformed it from one quick and stunning resolution into the longest war in US history. It has now cost the lives of more than 3,191 US and Coalition personnel and more than $571 billion, most of it borrowed, by the US alone. [3], [4] Losses for the Afghan Security Forces have exceeded more than 10,100 through the end of 2011. [5]

The Bush administration's inattentiveness to the many warnings given before September 11, 2001 about impending catastrophic terrorist attacks transformed those attacks from possibility to reality. The remedy to 9/11 would have been as simple as locking the cockpit doors and arming the pilots – something Israeli airlines had been doing for 30 years – and listening to the concerns of the FBI's field agents and the CIA's directors.

The Bush administration's inattentiveness to the importance of Moral Law – from its duty to protect a conquered population to its use of torture against them – cost it the Iraq War and the accord of the Iraqi people. If the unspoken goal of the Bush administration's Middle Eastern Wars was to secure access to the vast reserves of oil in the Persian Gulf and Central Asia, nothing would have promoted this end nearly as well as demonstrating competence in the arts of war and governance.

There is no surer way to induce a man to follow your plan than to demonstrate an ability to get the job done. This does not mean destroying his home, his family and his life. The misunderstanding of these factors demonstrated by Washington's neoconservatives demonstrates the words of James Clavel in his Forward to Sun Tzu's treatise on The Art of War:

> *I truly believe that if our military and political leaders in recent times had studied this work of genius, Vietnam could not have happened as it happened; we would not have lost the war in Korea (we lost because we did not achieve victory); the Bay of Pigs could not have occur-*

CHARLES EDMUND COYOTE

red; the hostage fiasco in Iran would not have come to pass; the British Empire would not have been dismembered; and, in all probability, World Wars I and II would have been avoided – certainly they would not have been waged as they were waged, and the millions of youths obliterated unnecessarily and stupidly by monsters calling themselves generals would have lived out their lives.

James Clavel, Forward to Sun Tzu's The Art of War, 1983 [6]

One of the roots of this lack of understanding amongst the political elites lies in the fact that almost without exception, the signatories to the Project for the New American Century, though quick to send other people's children off to war, had avoided military experience both for themselves and for their own children. When, in 1989, *The Washington Post* had asked former Secretary of Defense Dick Cheney about his multiple deferments from military service, he responded:

I had other priorities in the '60s than military service.
Dick Cheney, 5 April 1989 [7], [8]

The abstinence from military service of the children of America's political elites was virtually non-existent throughout most of its history and development as a great power. It has become, however, the *'rule of thumb'* for the conflicts of choice which have frequently characterized American foreign policy since the Second World War, and is likely a significant factor in the rise of that self-destructive phenomenon. The fact that George H.W. Bush, Sr. was a genuine war hero, personally familiar with the brutality of armed combat, contributed to the measured application of diplomatic and military power he successfully demonstrated during his term as the nation's Commander-in-

Chief.

> *The art of war is of vital importance to the State.*
>   *Sun Tzu* [9]

The 2003 invasion of Iraq had few advocates in high office with actual military experience. Those in power ridiculed the seasoned advice offered by the few military leaders who actually did speak out. This led to Iraq's struggle to prevent collapsing into a failed state hospitable to the very terrorist organizations that had previously been denied access to the country. So consuming did that struggle become that it was necessary to divert resources badly needed for the real *'War on Terror'*. In 2005, the Bush administration found it necessary to close Alec Station, the CIA Unit that had been created for the purpose of finding and eliminating Osama bin Laden. [10], [11] The 2010 Rand Corporation study, commissioned by the United States Air Force and entitled the *'Iraq Effect'*, found that Iraq's instability after the 2003 invasion demonstrated that democratization can bring undesirable consequences. This became an excuse for other Middle Eastern governments to delay reform:

> *The net effect has been a deferral of any 'domestic experiments' that might weaken regime authority. In this, local governments have been aided by an apparent decrease in US pressure for political liberalization since 2003. Reformists and democracy activists in a number of states told us that their governments had been effectively granted a reprieve on reform because of Washington's preoccupation with Iraq and, more recently, building a regional coalition against Iran. In other cases, democratization appears to have lost its luster among certain population segments because it is seen as a 'U.S. project' and as the catalyst for the ongoing strife in Iraq.*

CHARLES EDMUND COYOTE

THE IRAQ EFFECT, RAND Corporation monograph, 2010 [12]

The invasion of Iraq enabled al-Qaeda to rise again from the bleak season of bin Laden's narrow Tora Bora escape to the realization of its broadly stated intent to draw America into an economically draining Middle Eastern conflict. [13] Although the most effective means for dealing with terrorist organizations lies in the judicious use of police, intelligence, and Special Forces, the Bush administration unwittingly nurtured al-Qaeda's goals, giving them, not one, but two major economically draining Middle Eastern conflicts for the price of one! [14] Terrorist organizations have hardly ever been defeated by military force. The sledge hammer of the military is best reserved for situations such as Tora Bora, where al-Qaeda gathered itself together in mass – the very place the Bush administration chose not to focus military power.

The power, size, and consequent imprecision of military force tend to make it too blunt an instrument to use effectively against small, non-state, terrorist-oriented organizations. The almost inevitable blunders a large invading military will make favors terrorist recruitment, particularly when disproportionate power is used. An occupying authority inspires resistance. It enrages locals by bombing and shooting up their country, destroying the things its people hold dear. This makes the occupier, in turn, less safe and requires the incremental commitment of more resources to a progressively downward spiral. [15]

Yet, even if a person sympathizes with the resistance, he will likely refrain from active participation in their cause so long as he has a home, a family and a life he loves dearly to look after. If that home or family is lost to a bombing gone awry, a battle, or campaign, then he will be driven by the pain of that loss to join the struggle against the occupiers of his country.

> *The general who wins a battle makes many calculations in his temple before the battle is fought. The general who loses a battle makes but few calculations beforehand. Thus do many calculations lead to victory, and few calculations to defeat; how much more no calculation at all! It is by attention to this point that I can foresee who is likely to win or lose.*
>
> *Sun Tzu, The Art of War, p 11* [16]

The cost of deploying the high-tech military of the United States is enormous. Al-Qaeda's recognition of this fact lies at the heart of the strategy the organization developed and sought to use to its advantage. The average cost for every US soldier that fought in Iraq was about $775,000 per year. That amounts more than $2,000 per soldier per day. [17] The costs of insurgency are less well known, but, at the height of the Iraqi uprising in 2006, the US Government estimated the resistance in that country was probably being financed by something in the range of $70 to $200 million a year, i.e., about $2 per insurgent per day. [18] Fighting that insurgency cost US taxpayers about $2 billion per week, a spending disadvantage in the range of 500-1,500 to 1. [19]

Al-Qaeda attacked America in order to incite a massive and expensive US response. The Bush administration gave them what they wanted, and even added a second gratuitous war. This forced the US economy to bear an immense cost relative to the low-cost of the localized insurgencies in opposition. The war in Iraq put our armed forces in the position of having to

CHARLES EDMUND COYOTE

spend scores of billions of dollars trying to protect against IEDs (Improvised Explosive Devices) made of fertilizer and a few dollars' worth of batteries, wire, and casing. Roadside bombs that cost $30 to $300 to make were used to disable Bradley Fighting Vehicles that cost more than $3 million. The US became trapped in an expensive quagmire, and the wars in Afghanistan and Iraq became, respectively, the war of longest duration and the second most expensive war in all of American history.

While the insurgent forces walk or travel in pickups, the field generators, M1A1 Abrams tanks, Mine Resistant Ambush Protected (MRAP) vehicles, and the aircraft for the US troops deployed to Afghanistan require about 22 gallons of fuel per person per day. There were 90,000 troops in addition to the 41,000 International Security Assistance Force (ISAF) and the hugely expensive and profitable private military contractors. [20] For the West, the Afghan War became a struggle to maintain the long and difficult supply line – the NATO led mission established by United Nations Security Council Resolution 1386. This supply line runs more than 1,200 miles from the refineries of Karachi, Pakistan, through the easily assaulted mountain passes of the north, where highway barons skim an average of $5,000 off each vehicle, and the Taliban pretty much operates at will. [21]

An M1 Abrams Main Battle Tank requires 10 gallons of fuel merely to start its engine. Its 1,500 horsepower Honeywell AGT1500 engine uses up another 10 gallons to go 6 miles and normally burns about 60 gallons per hour of self-propelled travel. [22] With transpiration and significant outlays for protection, the average cost of fuel for the troops in Afghanistan becomes $48 per gallon. At 22 gallons per soldier per day, the Afghan War is being conducted on fuel expenditure that runs an average of $7,390 a week for each soldier deployed, i.e., $384,000 per year per soldier. The White House calculates the total cost per year of the War in Afghanistan comes to about $1.0-$1.2 million for each member of the Armed Forces deployed there, making it not only the longest war in US history, but also the most expensive war in the history of the world per deployed Western combatant. [23]

In 2005, the Government Accounting Office (GAO) reported that US forces (including training) use about 1.8 billion rounds of small-arms ammunition per year. Based on the GAO figures, America's armed forces expended a total of about six billion bullets in the 'wars on terror', between 2002 and 2005. John Pike, the Director of GlobalSecurity.org, points out that with an estimated 20,000 insurgents killed in Afghanistan and Iraq during that same period, an average of about 300,000 bullets was fired per each dead insurgent. This number would actually be much higher if the high percentage of insurgents actually taken out by aircraft, bombs, and tanks were factored into the ratio. [24] The US Air Force spends $22,500 an hour to send an F-16 fighter jet chasing after a handful of insurgents in a pickup truck. [25] The cost of mujahedeen operating in pick-up trucks and sandals is known to be considerably less.

> *Being on the wrong side of cost imposition is not a characteristic of strategic competence.*
>
> *Dr. Andrew Krepinevich, President of the Center for Strategic and Budgetary Assessments, 1 September 2009* [26]

CHARLES EDMUND COYOTE

We spend considerably more during one day of fighting the insurgents on their own turf than those insurgents spend during an entire year. Almost entirely forgotten in this very costly process of waging war is the fact that on multiple occasions, during both the late Clinton and the early Bush administrations, particular factions within the Taliban regime indicated their willingness to turn bin Laden over to the United States or to a third party, especially if evidence of his guilt were to be given. [27], [28]

Kabir Mohabbat, an Afghan-American who had worked for the US Department of Defense and the National Security Agency as a go-between to the Taliban, testified to the 9/11 Commission that at least 3 times after the 9/11 attacks (November 2000, February 2001, and September 2001) the Taliban offered to deliver up Osama bin Laden to the US government. During the Clinton years, officials within the Taliban government had even put the al-Qaeda leader under house arrest at his Daronta training camp. They also supplied the coordinates of the location to the US government, encouraging it to send a couple of Cruise Missiles to that location. When nothing happened, the Taliban began joking that if Washington could not afford the fuel for its rockets, they would even be willing to provide that.

> The Taliban, who had confined bin Laden and his key aides to his compound at Daronta, 30 miles from Kabul, invited the US to send one or two Cruise missiles as the easiest way to solve the problem but the Clinton administration delayed in taking action. The Bush administration also dispatched Mohabbat repeatedly to Kabul -- three times in 2001 -- to discuss bin Laden. In other words, at minimum, one can say that the State Department knew, and we should know, and Obama should

know, the Taliban and al-Qaeda are two very different things.

Gary Leupp, Tufts University Professor of History and Religion, 30 November 2009 [29]

Bin Laden had the support of the Taliban's leader, Mullah Omar, who was grateful for his efforts against the Soviets and indebted to him for his support of the Taliban regime. But, as with most governments, the Taliban appears to have been multifaceted. Many within its leadership were not happy with Osama bin Laden, and were concerned that he was going to attract unwanted foreign attention. [30] Even Mullah Omar was upset over the al-Qaeda leader's widely broadcast threats against the US, concerned that these could be a danger to his own regime.

When the US counterattacked following 9/11, bin Laden and Ayman al-Zawahiri escaped to the White Mountains of Tora Bora near the Pakistan border. [31] Although the US government believed that bin Laden was at that location, CENTCOM would not allow either the 800 Army Rangers requested by Gary Berntsen or the brigade of 1,200 US Marines, freshly arrived in Kandahar with helicopter transport, to go to Tora Bora. [32], [33], [34]

But even at that point, some people were saying, 'Oh, the United States was diverting resources.' We didn't need that much more in resources to finish it -- 600 to 800 guys at that point, had we done it at the right time. It was the failure to make the adjustment. As I've stated in other places, it was a flawed masterpiece... that we were able to have an equation where US forces and CIA officers working in tandem with insurgent forces could defeat a much larger group. But at that final moment when we closed with bin Laden, at that point they failed to recognize that we needed our own men to do that final bit of fighting...

Gary Berntsen, 20 January 2006 [35]

CENTCOM claimed the 9,000 foot elevation of the al-Qaeda encampments and 150F late fall weather was too cold for the Army Rangers, and the small team of CIA, UK and US Special Forces could depend on the Afghan mercenaries to do the job. And so, the 50 or 60 American and British personnel present at the battle soon found themselves outnumbered by the journalists and cameramen assembling about them to video the bombing, conduct interviews, and occasionally listen in as our Afghan mercenaries arranged to take payoffs from both sides. [36] On the night of December 12, 2001, the hired Afghans held the US Delta Force at gunpoint for 12 hours when they tried to prevent al-Qaeda from using an unauthorized truce to prepare their escape to Pakistan. [37]

> *There appears to be a real disconnect between what the US military was engaged in trying to do during the battle for Tora Bora – which was to destroy Al Qaeda and the Taliban – and the earlier rhetoric of President Bush, which had focused on getting bin Laden. There are citizens all over the Middle East now saying that the US military couldn't do it – couldn't catch Osama – while ignoring the fact that the US military campaign, apart from not capturing Mr. bin Laden was, up the that point, staggeringly effective.*

> *Charles Heyman, editor of Jane's World Armies* [38]

The war in Afghanistan had opened with stunning success and the opportunity to finish it off in 2001. Once al-Qaeda and the Taliban had been allowed to escape to safety in Pakistan's remote Tribal Areas, the conflict in *'the Land where Empires go to die'* was fated to be long, difficult, and expensive at best. George Bush then followed that anti-climax by handing al-Qaeda not just the one dissipating war they had hoped for but a second one as well.

The Taliban, by themselves, never were a danger to the US, and if the Washington had taken them up on their multiple offers to turn over bin Laden, it is likely al-Qaeda would have been a spent force long ago. In 2010, the CIA estimated that the number of al-Qaeda remaining in Afghanistan was about 50 to 100 individuals, which means the $110 billion the US spent to fight the War in Afghanistan during FY 2010 worked out to about $1.5 billion per member of al-Qaeda. The math indicates Washington surely could have found a better way to pursue its stated objectives rather than falling in line with al-Qaeda's clearly stated purpose of bankrupting the USA. [39]

The American strategist, Colonel John Boyd, often and emphatically pointed out that victorious fighter pilots, armies, and organizations are successful because they are able to react faster than their adversaries. In what Colonel Boyd called the OODA Loop, (Observe, Orient, Decide, and Act), those who have the best situational awareness are positioned to orient most effectively to an ever-changing environment and determine the actions most likely to bring success. Successful organizations can maximize the effectiveness of their teams by using decentralized chains of command that allow them to quickly move through these decision cycles. [40] The foundation of a winning organization depends on the high degree of mutual trust built from common perspective. It will be oriented more toward the pursuit of clear and specific objectives than toward the implementation of particular methods. [41] The role of a command center is to formulate the organization's objectives. It must insure that those in charge are capable and competent in applying the methods appropriate to achieve the desired end. The field personnel, the troops, must have confidence the command center will not assign objectives without good reason and without providing the support necessary to reach success. [42]

Mutual trust is undermined if an administration is actually pursuing hidden objectives which are different than what it is telling those it sent to pursue them. By announcing to the world the objective of bringing bin Laden, *'dead or alive'*, to justice, then denying its field personnel the means to do so, the Bush administration failed to understand the moral dimension of war. This was understood by the Roosevelt administration during World War II. It was put into play when, four months after Pearl Harbor, Lieutenant Colonel Jimmy Doolittle and sixteen B-25B Mitchell bombers were sent on a raid to the Japanese Home Islands. In doing so, America's leaders demonstrated during that war what was possible, rather than stalling at what was risky. Therein they began to sow confusion and doubt amongst the Japanese while giving the American people the boost that began the road to victory.

CIA agent Gary Berntsen made it clear in his reports on Tora Bora that Washington would not be able to rely on its Afghan mercenaries in the fight against bin Laden. Although refusing to disparage CENTCOM's commander, General Tommy Franks, for his decisions during the Battle, Berntsen has painted a picture – not dissimilar to what has frustrated the philosophers of war from Sun Tzu to Colonel John Boyd – of a military leadership more oriented toward bureaucracy and doctrine than flexible approaches to important objectives. [43]

Al-Qaeda escaped through the snow covered mountains of Parachinar, Pakistan, by following the same strategy insurgents have always used: in the face of overwhelming odds, withdraw and return to the fight another day. For insurgents, *'victory'* means being able to escape. When military power claims, *'we have got them on the run'*, that usually means the insurgent resistance is successfully using hit and run tactics. The opportunity to prevent al-Qaeda from doing that was thrown away in December 2001, when the warnings of those present at Tora Bora was disregarded.

The consequences of that fact for America have been immense. It transformed what began as a brilliant 3-month, $4 billion dollar decapitation of America's enemies into the lengthy 3 or 4 trillion dollar grinding war. The Bush administration had little to show for their cost, apart from facilitating bin Laden's becoming the most expensive public enemy in American history, and causing the deaths of hundreds of thousands of people, most of them innocent. [44], [45], [46]

From the Bush administration's ignoring the abundant warnings that proceeded the September 11 attacks, to permitting Osama bin Laden to escape shortly thereafter; from trying to repress a public and conscientious review of the circumstances surrounding the preventable tragedy of 9/11, to pulling resources away from the war on terror in order to attack Saddam Hussein; from misleading Congress and the American people to gain support for the attack on Iraq, to mismanaging the Occupations of both Afghanistan and

Iraq; from the death, injury, and displacement of hundreds of thousands of American military personnel in a war of choice, to the death, deprivation, and displacement of millions of innocent civilians in that war; from frittering away the Cold War peace dividend used by the Clinton administration to bring about the most prosperous decade ever experienced by the American people, to inciting what has become the most expensive war in American History; from reinstituting the crushing burden of Federal Debt, to the onset of the Great Recession that continues to demote the general Welfare of the People of the United States. The neocons' record of harm to the American people stands unequaled by any foreign enemy, past or present. [47]

Iraq is not America, and the time and resources that the Bush administration threw away in its effort to rearrange the government of a people on the other side of the world had little to do with its constitutional responsibility to provide for the common defense of the American people, and much to do, albeit unwittingly, with its undermining. [48]

One person, in particular, greatly benefitted from the Bush administration's decisions. Evidence suggests that Osama bin Laden did what he could to help George W. Bush win re-election in 2004 by releasing a threatening video tape mocking Bush just 4 days before the November 2 general elections. [49] Rightwing pundits and talk-show hosts immediately portrayed it as an effort to hurt the President and, with headlines such as *'Bin Laden Threatens US Not to Vote for Bush'*, American voters were prompted to do just the opposite thinking that Bush would keep them safe.

At CIA headquarters in Langley, Virginia, intelligence

experts concluded bin Laden was fully aware that his videotape would encourage US citizens to vote contrary to what he recommended. By offering Americans terms of surrender, bin Laden knew they would instinctively want to fight. The 6-point bounce in the polls that President Bush gained immediately following the tape's release helped propel him into a second term and the continuation of his clumsy *'War on Terror'* with its consequent impelling of thousands of new recruits into al-Qaeda. [50]

Bin Laden's *'jihad'* against America had been undertaken with loud intent to draw the United States into a major Middle Eastern conflict designed to push America towards bankruptcy and diminish its ability to remain in the Middle East. America, the Islamists knew, could not be defeated on the battlefield. But the technological sophistication that gave the US military such power also meant that it was hugely expensive for the United States to wage a major, extended asymmetric war. Therein lay its Achilles heel. The Bush administration's empowerment of the self-deluding neoconservatives proved to be a gift to the Islamists, a mindset very much to their benefit.

> *If you know the enemy and know yourself, you need not fear the result of a hundred battles. If you know yourself but not the enemy, for every victory gained you will also suffer a defeat. If you know neither the enemy nor yourself, you will succumb in every battle.*
>
> Sun Tzu, The Art of War [51]

By striking and hiding undercover, insurgencies can cheaply and effectively fight for decades an expensive occupying military force that outnumbers them almost 100 to 1. The Bush administration's use of a massive war-fighting machine to fight al-Qaeda, an essentially criminal organization, facilitated the accomplishment of al-Qaeda's objectives. [52]

Spending $775,000 per soldier per year in Iraq (all of it borrowed), then handing the Obama administration the $1,000,000-$1,200,000 per soldier per year Afghan War, (40 percent of it borrowed), did little more than illustrate Sun Tzu's teaching that the failure to know neither the enemy nor yourself brings dire consequences. [53], [54], [55]

> So we are continuing this policy in bleeding America to the point of bankruptcy. Allah willing, and nothing is too great for Allah.
>
> That being said, those who say that al-Qaida has won against the administration in the White House or that the administration has lost in this war have not been precise, because when one scrutinizes the results, one cannot say that al-Qaida is the sole factor in achieving those spectacular gains.
>
> Rather, the policy of the White House that demands the opening of war fronts to keep busy their various corporations – whether they be working in the field of arms or oil or reconstruction – has helped al-Qaida to achieve these enormous results.
>
> And so it has appeared to some analysts and diplomats that the White House and us are playing as one team towards the economic goals of the United States, even if the intentions differ.
>
> And it was to these sorts of notions and their like that the the British diplomat and others were referring in their lectures at the Royal Institute of International Affairs. [When they pointed out that] for example, al-Qaida spent $500,000 on the event, while America, in the incident and its aftermath, lost – according to the lowest estimate – more than $500 billion.

Meaning that every dollar of al-Qaida defeated a million dollars by the permission of Allah, besides the loss of a huge number of jobs.

As for the size of the economic deficit, it has reached record astronomical numbers estimated to total more than a trillion dollars.

    Osama bin Laden, 30 October 2004 [56]

Osama bin Laden had been broadcasting to the world his intent to draw the United States into a major Middle Eastern conflict since 1996. Al-Qaeda intended to use a low cost, long term insurgency to drive the cost of operations to America's disadvantage, and toward that end it undertook the training of thousands of insurgents. Such a conflict was intended to destabilize the Middle East and drive up oil prices which would further strain the US economy in addition to military expenses. [57]

In realizing those ends, Osama bin Laden had no one more useful than George W. Bush. Osama was determined to get his war. W was determined to provide it. And so, the Bush administration became good at finding terrorists, its policies manufacturing a large portion of them.

CHAPTER 19 REFERENCES

[1] Maplecroft's latest country risk briefings provide high level analysis of the key risk issues for investors in Iraq and Syria, 7 September 2011;
http://maplecroft.com/about/news/country-briefings-september8.html
(SHORTENED URL: http://tinyurl.com/kalate)

[2] COUNTERINSURGENCY, Field Manual No. 3-24,
Headquarters Department of the Army, Marine Corps

CHARLES EDMUND COYOTE

314

Warfighting Publication No. 3-33.5, Headquarters Marine
Corps Combat Development Command, 15 December 2006;
Lead authors David Petraeus (Lieutenant General, US
Army), Dr. Conrad Crane (Colonel, US Army retired), James
Mattis (Lieutenant General, US Marine Corps);
http://www.fas.org/irp/doddir/army/fm3-24.pdf
(SHORTENED URL: http://tinyurl.com/karasa)

[3] Operation Enduring Freedom, Fatalities by Country,
iCasualities.org; http://www.icasualties.org/oef/

[4] COSTOFWAR.COM, NATIONAL PRIORITIES PROJECT;
http://costofwar.com/

[5] List of Afghan security forces fatality reports in
Afghanistan, Wikipedia encyclopedia;
http://en.wikipedia.org/wiki/List_of_Afghan_security_forces
_fatality_reports_in_Afghanistan#cite_note-1
(SHORTENED URL: http://tinyurl.com/kofoto)

[6] Sun Tzu, The Art of War, Edited by James Clavell, pp 1-
2, Dell Publishing a division of Bantam Doubleday Dell
Publishing Group, Inc, 1540 Broadway New York, New York,
Copyright © 1983 by James Clavell.

[7] Cheney's Five Draft Deferments During the Vietnam Era
Emerge as a Campaign Issue, by Katharine Q. Seelye, The
New York Times, 1 May 2004;
http://www.nytimes.com/2004/05/01/politics/campaign/01
CHEN.html?ex=1398830400&en=1c0259e620183dd6&ei=5
007&partner=USERLAND
(SHORTENED URL: http://tinyurl.com/hevita)

[8] Profile: Vice President Dick Cheney, abc News, 6
January 2006;
http://abcnews.go.com/Politics/Inauguration/story?id=4216
66&page=1
(SHORTENED URL: http://tinyurl.com/vedine)

[9] SUN TZU ON THE ART OF WAR, THE OLDEST MILITARY
TREATISE IN THE WORLD, Translated from the Chinese by
LIONEL GILES, M.A. (1910), Laying Plans:
http://www.au.af.mil/au/awc/awcgate/artofwar.htm#1

(SHORTENED URL: http://tinyurl.com/zuwami)

[10] C.I.A. Closes Unit Focused on Capture of bin Laden, by Mark Mazzetti, The New York Times, 4 July 2006;
http://www.nytimes.com/2006/07/04/washington/04intel.ht ml?_r=1
(SHORTENED URL: http://tinyurl.com/pofoku)

[11] Context of 'Late 2005: CIA Closes Unit Hunting Bin Laden', History Commons;
http://www.historycommons.org/context.jsp?item=alate05a lecclosed
(SHORTENED URL: http://tinyurl.com/cohimo)

[12] THE IRAQ EFFECT, The Middle East After the Iraq War, by Frederic Wehrey, Dalia Dassa Kaye, Jessica Watkins, Jeffrey Martini, Robert A. Guffey, The RAND Corporation, RAND Project AIR FORCE, © Copyright 2010 RAND Corporation;
http://www.rand.org/pubs/monographs/2010/RAND_MG892 .pdf
(SHORTENED URL: http://tinyurl.com/farase)

[13] The Osama bin Laden I Know, An Oral History of al Qaeda's Leader, by Peter L. Bergen; © 2006, Free Press, a Division of Simon & Schuster, Inc., pp 350-368.

[14] HOW TERRORIST GROUPS END Lessons for Countering al Qa'ida, SETH G. JONES and MARTIN C. LIBICKI, RAND Corporation, © Copyright 2008 RAND Corporation;
http://www.rand.org/pubs/monographs/2008/RAND_MG741 -1.pdf
(SHORTENED URL: http://tinyurl.com/tepema)

[15] Campaign in Iraq has increased terrorism threat, says American intelligence report, Dan Glaister, The Guardian, 25 September 2006;
http://www.guardian.co.uk/world/2006/sep/25/usa.iraq/pri nt
(SHORTENED URL: http://tinyurl.com/veresa)

[16] The Art of War, Sun Tzu, Edited by James Clavell, p

316

11, Dell Publishing a division of Bantam Doubleday Dell
Publishing Group, Inc, 1540 Broadway New York, New York,
Copyright © 1983 by James Clavell.

[17] Cost of the Wars in Iraq and Afghanistan, and Other
Military Operations Through 2008 and Beyond, Steven M.
Kosiak, Center for Strategic and Budgetary Assessments,
2008, p 38;
http://www.csbaonline.org/4Publications/PubLibrary/R.2008
1215.Cost_of_the_Wars_i/R.20081215.Cost_of_the_Wars_i.
pdf
(SHORTENED URL: http://tinyurl.com/kosipe)

[18] US Finds Iraq Insurgency Has Funds to Sustain Itself,
by John F. Burns and Kirk Semple, The New York Times,
November 26, 2006;
http://www.nytimes.com/2006/11/26/world/middleeast/26i
nsurgency.html?ei=5088&en=1bd1f805c30e2ae2&ex=1322
197200&partner=rssnyt&emc=rss&pagewanted=print
(SHORTENED URL: http://tinyurl.com/fihasu)

[19] Cost of Iraq war nearly $2b a week, by Bryan Bender,
The Boston Globe, 28 September 2006;
http://www.boston.com/news/world/middleeast/articles/20
06/09/28/cost_of_iraq_war_nearly_2b_a_week/
(SHORTENED URL: http://tinyurl.com/rabade)

[20] Burning borrowed money in America's wars, Bernd
Debusmann, 17 December 2009, Reuters;
http://blogs.reuters.com/great-
debate/2009/12/17/burning-borrowed-money-in-americas-
wars/
(SHORTENED URL: http://tinyurl.com/bumoda)

[21] Supply route may decide outcome of Afghan war –
thestar.com, Minstrel Boy, 5 October 2010;
http://minstrelboy.blogspot.com/2010/10/supply-route-
may-decide-outcome-of.html
(SHORTENED URL: http://tinyurl.com/sumadi)

[22] M1 Abrams Main Battle Tank, GlobalSecurity.org;
http://www.globalsecurity.org/military/systems/ground/m1-
specs.htm

(SHORTENED URL: http://tinyurl.com/rataki)

[23] Burning borrowed money in America's wars, Bernd Debusmann, 17 December 2009, Reuters; http://blogs.reuters.com/great-debate/2009/12/17/burning-borrowed-money-in-americas-wars/
(SHORTENED URL: http://tinyurl.com/bumoda)

[24] US forced to import bullets from Israel as troops use 250,000 for every rebel killed, by Andrew Buncombe, The Independent, 25 September 2005; Global Security.org; http://www.globalsecurity.org/org/news/2005/050925-israel-bullets.htm
(SHORTENED URL: http://tinyurl.com/burali)

[25] How the F-35 Doubled in Price, by Winslow T. Wheeler, Counterpunch, 10 July 2012; http://www.counterpunch.org/2012/07/10/how-the-f-35-doubled-in-price/
SHORTENED URL: http://tinyurl.com/dokupa)

[26] Regaining Strategic Competence, by Dr. Andrew Krepinevich, Center for Strategic and Budgetary Assessments, 1 September 2009, p 17; http://www.csbaonline.org/4Publications/PubLibrary/R.2009 0901.Regaining_Strategi/R.20090901.Regaining_Strategi.pdf
(SHORTENED URL: http://tinyurl.com/vegano)

[27] Bush Rejects Osama Surrender - 02.21.2001, YouTube; http://www.youtube.com/watch?v=HDvVZ2Gn-9g
(SHORTENED URL: http://tinyurl.com/bureda)

[28] How Bush Was Offered Bin Laden and Blew It, by Alexander Cockburn and Jeffrey St. Clair, Counterpunch, 1 November 2004, Information Clearing House; http://www.informationclearinghouse.info/article9332.htm
(SHORTENED URL: http://tinyurl.com/zelaxa)

[29] It's Obama's War Now, by Gary Leupp, Counterpunch, 30 November 2009;

CHARLES EDMUND COYOTE

http://counterpunch.org/leupp11302009.html
(SHORTENED URL: http://tinyurl.com/supona)

*[30] Taliban disarm Arabs, Pakistanis in Afghanistan,
Afghanistan News October 1999;
http://www.afghanistannewscenter.com/news/1999/october
/oct31b1999.htm*
(SHORTENED URL: http://tinyurl.com/tasara)

*[31] How Bin Laden Got Away, TOPDOG08.COM, 25
October 2004; http://www.topdog04.com/000781.html*
(SHORTENED URL: http://tinyurl.com/vigoto)

*[32] Bush's Tora Bora Bull, by Paul Sperry, ANTIWAR.COM,
May 18, 2007;
http://www.antiwar.com/sperry/?articleid=10981*
(SHORTENED URL: http://tinyurl.com/topaka)

*[33] War in Afghanistan: Battle of Tora Bora, by Kennedy
Hickman, About.com: Military History;
http://militaryhistory.about.com/od/afghanistan/p/torabora.
htm*
(SHORTENED URL: http://tinyurl.com/gapati)

*[34] Context of 'December 5, 2001: Head of US Marines
Not Allowed to Send His Troops to Tora Bora' History
Commons;
http://www.historycommons.org/context.jsp?item=a120501
mattis*
(SHORTENED URL: http://tinyurl.com/sehela)

*[35] The Dark Side, PBS Frontline Interviews Gary
Berntsen;
http://www.pbs.org/wgbh/pages/frontline/darkside/intervie
ws/berntsen.html*
(SHORTENED URL: http://tinyurl.com/fabera)

*[36] The Osama bin Laden I Know, An Oral History of al
Qaeda's Leader, by Peter L. Bergen; © 2006, Free Press, a
Division of Simon & Schuster, Inc., p 336.*

*[37] Battle of Tora Bora, Fury's account, Wikipedia
encyclopedia;*

IRAQ WAR 2003

http://en.wikipedia.org/wiki/Battle_of_Tora_Bora
(SHORTENED URL: http://tinyurl.com/tofudi)

[38] How bin Laden got away, by Philip Smucker, The
Christian Science Monitor, March 4, 2002;
http://www.csmonitor.com/2002/0304/p01s03-wosc.html
(SHORTENED URL: http://tinyurl.com/himuri)

[39] Fewer than 100 Al Qaeda in Afghanistan: CIA chief,
ABC NEWS, 28 June 2010;
http://www.abc.net.au/news/stories/2010/06/28/2938358.
htm?section=world
(SHORTENED URL: http://tinyurl.com/fecani)

[40] OODA Loop, Bad Martial Arts, © 2010;
http://www.badmartialarts.com/SelfDefense/ooda.php
(SHORTENED URL: http://tinyurl.com/sodalo)

[41] War, Chaos, and Business, Belisarius.com;
http://hbswk.hbs.edu/archive/2675.html

[42] John R. Boyd, Colonel, United States Air Force,
Arlington National Cemetery Website;
http://www.arlingtoncemetery.net/jrboyd.htm
(SHORTENED URL: http://tinyurl.com/zorapa)

[43] Ex-CIA agent says US missed bin Laden in
Afghanistan, by Peter Spiegel, Defense Correspondent,
Financial Times, 3 January 2006;
http://www.ft.com/intl/cms/s/0/33df64d0-7c7d-11da-936a-
0000779e2340.html#axzz2cdgEQaNj
(SHORTENED URL: http://tinyurl.com/xibele)

[44] TORA BORA REVISITED: HOW WE FAILED TO GET BIN
LADEN AND WHY IT MATTERS TODAY, A Report To Members
Of The Committee On Foreign Relations United States
Senate, John F. Kerry, Chairman, 30 November 2009, p 31;
www.foreign.senate.gov/imo/media/doc/Tora_Bora_Report.
pdf
(SHORTENED URL: http://tinyurl.com/xirela)

[45] Cost of War in Afghanistan, Cost of War to the United
States, National Priorities Project;
http://costofwar.com/en/

CHARLES EDMUND COYOTE

320

[46] The cost of bin Laden: $3 trillion over 15 years, by
Tim Fernholz and Jim Tankersley, National Journal, 6 May
2011; http://www.nationaljournal.com/magazine/the-cost-
of-bin-laden-3-trillion-over-15-years-20110505
(SHORTENED URL: http://tinyurl.com/vaxati)

[47] New NSA docs contradict 9/11 claims, by Jordan
Michael Smith, Salon, 19 June 2012;
http://www.salon.com/2012/06/19/new_nsa_docs_reveal_9
11_truths/singleton/
(SHORTENED URL: http://tinyurl.com/jorese)

[48] Defense Spending: $700 Billion a Year and We're Still
Not Safe, by David Wood, POLITICS DAILY, 01/13/10;
http://www.politicsdaily.com/2010/01/13/defense-
spending-700-billion-a-year-and-were-still-not-safe/
(SHORTENED URL: http://tinyurl.com/wesafa)

[49] CIA: Osama Helped Bush in '04, by Robert Perry,
Consortiumnews.com, 4 July 2012;
http://www.consortiumnews.com/2006/070306.html
(SHORTENED URL: http://tinyurl.com/botine)

[50] Bush takes a six-point lead after new bin Laden tape,
by Philip Sherwell, The Telegraph, 31 October 2004;
http://www.telegraph.co.uk/news/worldnews/northamerica/
usa/1475515/Bush-takes-a-six-point-lead-after-new-bin-
Laden-tape.html
(SHORTENED URL: http://tinyurl.com/tasala)

[51] The Art of War, Sun Tzu, Edited by James Clavell, p
18, Dell Publishing a division of Bantam Doubleday, 1540
Broadway New York, New York, Copyright © 1983 by James
Clavell.

[52] Cost of the Wars in Iraq and Afghanistan, and Other
Military Operations Through 2008 and Beyond, by Steven M.
Kosiak, Center for Strategic and Budgetary Assessments,
2008, p 38;
http://www.csbaonline.org/4Publications/PubLibrary/R.2008
1215.Cost_of_the_Wars_i/R.20081215.Cost_of_the_Wars_i.
pdf
(SHORTENED URL: http://tinyurl.com/waraco)

[53] HOW TERRORIST GROUPS END Lessons for Countering al Qa'ida, by Seth G. Jones and Martin C. Libicki, RAND Corporation, © Copyright 2008 RAND Corporation; http://www.rand.org/pubs/monographs/2008/RAND_MG741-1.pdf
(SHORTENED URL: http://tinyurl.com/berake)

[54] Burning borrowed money in America's wars, by Bernd Debusmann, 17 December 2009, Reuters; http://blogs.reuters.com/great-debate/2009/12/17/burning-borrowed-money-in-americas-wars/
(SHORTENED URL: http://tinyurl.com/batebu)

[55] SUN TZU ON THE ART OF WAR, THE OLDEST MILITARY TREATISE IN THE WORLD, Translated from the Chinese by Lionel Giles, M.A. (1910), Attack by Stratagem; http://www.au.af.mil/au/awc/awcgate/artofwar.htm#3
(SHORTENED URL: http://tinyurl.com/seliza)

[56] Transcript of Osama bin Laden's Speech, Aljazeera.net (online publication), Doha, Qatar, 30 October 2004; http://worldpress.org/Americas/1964.cfm
(SHORTENED URL: http://tinyurl.com/takama)

[57] FLASHBACK: Ten Years Ago, Bin Laden Demanded Barrel Of Oil Should Cost $144, by Faiz Shakir, Think Progress, 5 July 2008; http://thinkprogress.org/2008/07/05/bin-laden-144-oil/
(SHORTENED URL: http://tinyurl.com/beteba)

CHARLES EDMUND COYOTE

Chapter 20

Plenty of Money

We got plenty of money in Washington. What we need is more priority.

George W. Bush, Washington D.C., June 2, 2008

Since October 7, 2001, the government of the United States has spent an average of $3,990 per second, $14,400,000 per hour, $2,410,000,000 per week, $125,000,000,000 per year for the twelve years, to date, of war in Afghanistan and Iraq. [1]

That totals about $4,390 for every man, woman, and child in the US or about $17,600 for a family of four. Because this spending has been largely financed by *'supplemental appropriations'* (7 years) and deficits (4 years), and because veterans benefits, disability, and compensation derived from these wars will not peak until 50 or more years past their conclusion, it is likely that eventual costs for these military misadventures will be in the same league, for the US government, as was World War II.

Put another way, that amounts to about $149,000,000 per year for a US city of about a half million people. That is a staggering amount to be removed from local economies at a time when debt has soared to catastrophic proportions and the nation's economy continues to barely move forward. [2] It would have been enough money to provide a comfortable middle class income to more than 3 million Americans, and enough to end the severity of the *'Great Recession'*.

How have we, the American People, benefited from our government's channeling vast sums of money to the whirlpools of endless war? Would we have bene-fited more by tackling the problems of global terrorism by means of the proven, effective and considerably less expensive methods of good police, intelligence work and appropriate applications of Special Forces? Shouldn't the government have considered the advice of the Founding Fathers: *'Observing good faith and justice towards all nations; cultivating peace and harmony with all'*? [3] The Bush administration's disre-gard of the opportunity to corner al-Qaeda's leaders three months after 9/11 diminished the consequences of attacking a superpower. Afraid to upset the locals in Afghanistan and focused on the irrelevant issue of Saddam Hussein, George W. Bush made a significant contribution to the *'Muslim cult of the insurgent'*, awarding the aura of success to the small band of ra-dicals that had managed to wound a great nation on the cheap.

Although allegedly fought to promote democracy and American values, the Iraq War was marketed and funded by hiding its real reasons and costs from the taxpaying public. Transparency is fundamental to de-mocracy, and means contrary to that end invariably undermine that end. The Bush administration financed its wars almost entirely off-budget, with supplemental appropriations, which kept people uninformed about the extent to which the nation was being placed into debt. The term *'Supplemental appropriations'* refers to additional funds applied to appropriations already divided into the fiscal budget of the United States gov-ernment. They are added while the fiscal year is in progress, i.e., after the budget has already been approved.

CHARLES EDMUND COYOTE

The Bush administration was also responsible for the last two Budget Years: Fiscal Year (FY) 2008 and Fiscal Year (FY) 2009 which – including Social Security – ran actual deficits of $1.0 Trillion and $1.89 Trillion, respectively, despite the officially projected total deficits of $239 billion and $407 billion. [4], [5], [6] The Bush administration's actual FY 2009 deficit was $233 billion higher than the Obama administration's first budgetary deficit of $1.65 Trillion for FY 2010. [7]

In October 2007, the Congressional Budget Office (CBO) estimated that the wars in Iraq and Afghanistan could cost US taxpayers a total of $2.4 Trillion dollars by 2017, with interest costs for those wars totaling an additional $700 billion. [8] Joseph Stiglitz, a Noble Prize winning economist, and Linda Blimes, a Harvard University public finance expert, have published estimates of the long-term costs for these conflicts that also factor in the increased oil prices they produced, as well as reduced economic output, foregone investment opportunities, wealth transfer to foreign interests, and valuations of injury and death to veterans. For the reasons above, they argued in 2008 that the Iraq and Afghanistan Wars would ultimately cost US taxpayers $3 Trillion. [9] By 2011, with War-fighting costs continuing to push $200 billion/year and veterans costs projected to reach $1 Trillion, Blimes and Stiglitz increased their estimate of costs eventually reaching $4-$6 Trillion. [10], [11]

As pointed out by the conservative political philosopher Edmund Burke, a nation's scheme of government is a natural outcome of the social forces shaping and reflecting that country's history and circumstances. The effort required to change this natural order means there will inevitably arise unforeseen and costly expenditures attending to any attempt by one nation to impose its political will on the internal affairs of another nation. Had they been genuine conservatives, the neo-conservatives would have had little problem understanding that the impositions they so lightly proposed risked the ruin of complex social structures built over centuries and were more likely to accrue to disadvantage, rather than success.

John Gray, author of the best-selling book, *Men Are from Mars, Women Are from Venus*, suggests that learning to understand the innate differences between the sexes is the key to happy and successful long-term personal relationships between men and women. Not surprisingly, so it is also with nations. Genuine conservatism is an approach that recommends mending your own fences is the most appropriate course of action, rather than *'Regime Change'* for the other guy.

> *In history a great volume is unrolled for our instruction, drawing the materials of future wisdom from the past errors and infirmities of mankind. It may, in the perversion, serve for a magazine furnishing offensive and defensive weapons for parties in church and state, and supplying the means of keeping alive or reviving dissensions and animosities, and adding fuel to civil fury. History consists for the greater part of the miseries brought upon the world by pride, ambition, avarice, revenge, lust, sedition, hypocrisy, ungoverned zeal, and all the train of disorderly appetites which shake the public with the same troublous storms that toss the private state, and render life unsweet.*
>
> *Edmund Burke, 1790* [12]

The straightest path toward these *'miseries that toss the private state and render life unsweet'* is tread when institutions and governments forsake due process, the rule of law, and the obligations of justice to indulge in these *'disorderly appetites'*, seeking to impose their consequently degraded will upon the affairs of a people – their own or another.

The Bush administration neglected its responsibility to bring bin Laden to quick justice, apparently choosing instead to use him as an excuse to undertake nation building in the Middle East, the part of the world vital to American interests because it is rich in oil and because Israel is there. Emerging triumphant from the global conflicts of World War II and the Cold War that followed, Washington assumed the mantle of the once great British Empire and began to define the United States as *'the indispensable nation'*, able to reshape the affairs of the world to its own advantage. Delusions of exceptionalism (excessive pride) go before the fall of an individual or a nation.

> *In an essay at the beginning of the year, a few days before Obama took office, the Harvard historian Paul Kennedy, author of The Rise and Fall of the Great Powers, commented that no country on earth had 'anywhere like the staggering array of overseas military commitments and deployments' as the U.S.*
>
> *That is more true today than it was at the beginning of the year. Along with more troops, there is more reason to wonder how right Kennedy was in saying in his essay that US dependency on foreign investors resembled 'more and more that state of international indebtedness we historians associate with the reigns of Philip II of Spain and Louis XIV of France...'*
>
> *If Obama read that, he should have been worried. Under the reign of Philip II from 1556 to 1598, Spain reached the peak of its power, a global empire controlling territories from Europe and the Americas to Asia. It sank to second-rate status through a combination of factors that included wars and massive foreign debt. Louis XIV*

was involved in four big wars and on his death in 1715, left France deep in debt.

Bernd Debusmann, 17 DECEMBER 2009, Reuters [13]

In his *'Axis of Evil'* Speech that launched the broad *'War on Terror'*, President Bush declared:

Once we have funded our national security and our homeland security, the final great priority of my budget is economic security for the American people. To achieve these great national objectives -- to win the war, protect the homeland and revitalize our economy -- our budget will run a deficit that will be small and short term so long as Congress restrains spending and acts in a fiscally responsible way.

George W. Bush, State of the Union Address, 29 January 2002 [14]

That speech launched an era of deficit spending previously exceeded only by World War II, with Bush himself pushing Congress to abandon fiscal responsibility and pass his tax cuts, war supplementals, Medicare Part D spending, and financial sector bailouts. Unlike the shared sacrifice of *'the greatest generation's'* successful resolution of economic challenge and war, Bush's trillion dollar increases in federal spending were accompanied by an undermining of the tax base with an average of 250,000 middle class jobs being sent out of the country every month of George W. Bush's Presidency.

In 2002, George W. Bush's Secretary of the Treasury, Paul O'Neill, commissioned a study which found that if the Bush administration was going to increase the size of government as much as they were planning to do, undertake as many wars as they were considering, and cut taxes without linking those cuts to spending re-

CHARLES EDMUND COYOTE

straint, the US would quickly find itself back into the huge federal deficits that had preceded the Clinton years. If that deficit spending were to continue, the study found, future decades would face heavy tax increases and entitlement cuts. [15] The Bush administration dropped the forewarnings from the 2004 budget proposed a few months later and rewarded O'Neill's diligence by forcing him to resign. [16]

You know, Paul, Reagan proved that deficits don't matter. We won the midterm elections, this is our due.

Richard 'Dick' Cheney, November 2002 [17]

Supplemental spending appropriations – money supplemental to and appropriated outside of the budget – were designed to make the Bush administration's deficits appear smaller than they actually were. Nearly all the budget initiatives undertaken by the Bush administration, such as Medicare Part D's $400 billion Prescription Drug benefits and the wars in Afghanistan and Iraq, were carried out by means of these off-budget schemes. This increased the Federal deficit from $555 billion during the first year of the Iraq War, FY 2003 (October 2002 - September 2003), to $1.02 trillion dollars for FY 2008 (October 2007 - September 2008) and $1.89 trillion during the Bush administration's final budget year, FY 2009 (October 1, 2008 - September 30, 2009).

According to the US Treasury, the Federal Debt increased from $10.0 Trillion on September 30, 2008 to $11.9 Trillion on September 30, 2009, the end of the Bush Budgets. [18] $108 billion of FY 2009 spending included the American recovery and Reinvestment Act passed in February 2009 under President Obama. When that is separated out, the Bush administration was responsible for about $3.41 Trillion of FY 2009 spending, which included additional outlays for the financial bailouts enacted supplemental to the 2009 budget in late 2008 ($154 billion for TARP and $91 billion for Fannie Mae and Freddie Mac).

Effective application of the martial arts principle of the *'soft method'* involves sufficient environmental awareness to facilitate the ability to adapt quickly. For example, if an assailant uses a powerful attack to overwhelm resistance, the defending opponent can be thrust off balance by fading to the side and redirecting the blunt force. In the case of an insurgency, if the blunt force is sufficiently redirected toward civilian injury and the loss of innocent life, the invaders intent to win over the indigenous population is foiled and its campaigns begin to spiral towards defeat. Therefore, superior size and strength is negated. It will win the battle but lose the war.

> *...Our own flags should be substituted for those of the enemy, and the chariots mingled and used in conjunction with ours. The captured soldiers should be kindly treated and kept... This is called, using the conquered foe to augment one's own strength... In war, then, let your great object be victory, not lengthy campaigns.*
>
> *Sun Tzu, The Art of War* [19]

The skill set of the United States military lies in its ability to deliver massive frontal attacks that powerfully dominate the battle space. Rather than using the precise, subtle and relatively inexpensive tools of intelligence, as was demonstrated so effectively during the first few months of the Afghan War, the militarized response to 911 instituted a policy designed to impose American hegemony over the foreign cultures of the

Middle East. Consequently, the neoconservatives fulfilled bin Laden's hopes. Al-Qaeda's leadership was
very nearly done in by the combination of Special
Forces and air power that the US and Britain inserted
into Afghanistan early in the war. However, once Donald Rumsfeld's Pentagon assumed control, bin Laden
was able to survive, recover, and be handed the
opportunity he sought in the Bush Administration's
extension of war into Iraq.

It often takes time for an established military power to
understand an unconventional opponent, even when
that opponent has been openly broadcasting his strategy for years. [20] The metrics that brought victory in
the previous war may not be those that bring success in
the next.

In his treatise on military leadership, Sun Tzu emphasized the necessity to *know the enemy'*. Throughout
most of its *'War on Terror'* the Bush administration
demonstrated an almost complete lack of concern for
knowing the enemy, and little interest even in knowing
themselves. [21]

Tossing away a quick and meaningful victory in
Afghanistan, the White House let it be known they
were interested in the self-defeating *'Long War'* and
handed the absurd notion over to the US military to
get it done. After making the usual historical blunder
of predicting a cheap and easy victory, the administration followed up with a lack of post-invasion planning that enabled the development of a murderous
insurgency in Iraq that guaranteed the Bush administration was going to get its *'Long War'*. The Bush
administration followed its illegal invasion with a
widespread incarceration and torture of innocents,

adding additional fuel to the conflagration as knowledge of these violations of fundamental American principles spread throughout the Muslim world. The popular insurgency, long sought by al-Qaeda, had been ignited. Carried out by multitudes of offended foreign and indigenous groups, the insurgencies struck and killed thousands of American troops and gravely wounded additional tens of thousands. Many of those slaughtered represented the best of America's youth. Many of our young people, like Pat Tillman who was first deployed in Iraq, had responded to the duty they felt to defend their country once it had been attacked. When instead they were sent to Iraq, their investment of blood and toil would accrue to the making of something that had previously existed only in the Bush administration's fantasies, the new 'Axis of Evil' that would form through Iran, Iraq, and Alawite Syria.

By 2004, as the Middle East destabilized, oil prices began their climb from $30 per barrel. Three years later, by the 3rd Quarter of 2007, the financial lubricants of America's deregulated economy were beginning to run dry and oil had reached $80 per barrel. By the 1st Quarter of 2008, the world's largest economy had dipped into the Great Recession with a GDP contraction of 1.8 percent. [22]

By the 2nd Quarter of 2008, oil prices had reached $147 per barrel. As the economy, supported by the Bush Administration's Economic Stimulus Act of February 2008, struggled to regain its footing, large numbers of US consumers, particularly in the subprime market, now had to choose between paying the high price of fuel or the advancing rates of their resetting home mortgages. By the 3rd Quarter of 2008, Wall

CHARLES EDMUND COYOTE

Street's poorly constructed Mortgage Backed Securities, excessively loaded with subprime products, were causing the credit markets to seize up. By the time the Bush Administration reached its end, the economic decline had accelerated to 8.9 percent. Industries were brought to their knees, and millions of people were thrown out of work. [23], [24] The hollowed-out US economy – once the manufacturing power-house of the world – was now dominated by finance and military spending, staring into the yawning chasm of the Great Recession.

Under the Clinton administration, the growth of Big Government had been halted. The federal payroll was reduced by more than 370,000, and deficit spending was reversed. The federal government was put on track to being free of its public debt by the year 2010. [25], [26], [27] Given a strong and prosperous America, with government reduced in size and paying its debts, the Bush Administration, fully supported by the Republican Party, managed in eight years' time to plunge the nation deeply into debt, tie the working class to economic stagnation, and bog down the nation's military in multiple fruitless wars. The Republican Party's handling of the country under George W. Bush grew the Federal bureaucracy by 40 percent and annual Federal spending by more than 80 percent. [28]

Though continuing to market itself as the party of limited government, over the decades, the Republican Party had become the party of Borrow-and-Spend Big Government, a fact its voting base choose to ignore. [29]

CHAPTER 20 REFERENCES

[1] Cost of War, National Priorities Project;
http://costofwar.com/

[2] US & World Population Clocks, US Census Bureau;
http://www.census.gov/main/www/popclock.html
(SHORTENED URL: http://tinyurl.com/sinapa)

[3] Washington's Farewell Address 1796, The Avalon
Project at Yale Law School;
http://avalon.law.yale.edu/18th_century/washing.asp
(SHORTENED URL: http://tinyurl.com/wafeta)

[4] THE BUDGET OF THE UNITED STATES GOVERNMENT
FOR FISCAL YEAR 2008, HISTORICAL TABLE 1.4 -
RECEIPTS, OUTLAYS, AND SURPLUSES AND DEFICITS,
whitehouse.gov;
http://www.whitehouse.gov/sites/default/files/omb/budget/
fy2008/pdf/hist.pdf
(SHORTENED URL: http://tinyurl.com/vunita)

[5] THE BUDGET OF THE UNITED STATES GOVERNMENT
FOR FISCAL YEAR 2009, HISTORICAL TABLE 1.4 -
RECEIPTS, OUTLAYS, AND SURPLUSES AND DEFICITS,
whitehouse.gov;
http://www.whitehouse.gov/sites/default/files/omb/budget/
fy2009/pdf/hist.pdf
(SHORTENED URL: http://tinyurl.com/vonita)

[6]   Don't Blame Obama for Bush's 2009 Deficit, Posted by
Daniel J. Mitchell, CATO@LIBERTY, 19 November 2009;
http://www.cato-at-liberty.org/dont-blame-obama-for-
bushs-2009-deficit/
(SHORTENED URL: http://tinyurl.com/sepomi)

[7] Historical Debt Outstanding - Annual 2000-2010,
TreasuryDirect;
http://www.treasurydirect.gov/govt/reports/pd/histdebt/his
tdebt_histo5.htm
(SHORTENED URL: http://tinyurl.com/hitora)

[8] US CBO estimates $2.4 trillion long-term war costs,

334

REUTERS, 24 October 2007;
http://www.reuters.com/article/idUSN2450753720071024
(SHORTENED URL: http://tinyurl.com/retese)

[9] Three Trillion Dollar War, Joseph Stiglitz and Linda
Blimes Blog; http://threetrilliondollarwar.org/

10] Book authors claim U.S Iraq. war to cost over 4
trillions, by northsunm32, ALLVOICES, 30 September 2010;
http://www.allvoices.com/contributed-news/6897698-book-
authors-claim-us-wars-to-cost-3-trillion-to-4-trillions
(SHORTENED URL: http://tinyurl.com/vokone)

[11] Five Painful Lessons from the Iraq War, Joseph Stiglitz
and Linda Blimes, 25 November 2011;
http://threetrilliondollarwar.org/2011/11/25/five-painful-
lessons-from-the-iraq-war/
(SHORTENED URL: http://tinyurl.com/filesa)

[12] Reflections on the Revolution in France, by Edmund
Burke, 1790;
http://www.constitution.org/eb/rev_fran.htm
(SHORTENED URL: http://tinyurl.com/rerebu)

[13] Burning borrowed money in America's wars, by Bernd
Debusmann, Reuters, 17 December 2009;
http://blogs.reuters.com/great-
debate/2009/12/17/burning-borrowed-money-in-americas-
wars/
(SHORTENED URL: http://tinyurl.com/zumote)

[14] George W. Bush, State of the Union Address, 29
January 2002, CNN.com, inside politics;
http://archives.cnn.com/2002/ALLPOLITICS/01/29/bush.sp
eech.txt/
(SHORTENED URL: http://tinyurl.com/getare)

[15] Paul O'Neill (Secretary of the Treasury), Section 4,
Wikipedia encyclopedia;
http://en.wikipedia.org/wiki/Paul_O%27Neill_(cabinet_mem
ber)
(SHORTENED URL: http://tinyurl.com/panesa)

[16] Confessions of a White House Insider, by JOHN F.

DICKERSON, TIME Magazine World, 10 January 2004;
http://www.time.com/time/magazine/article/0,9171,57480
9,00.html
(SHORTENED URL: http://tinyurl.com/cohera)

[17] Bush Sought 'Way' To Invade Iraq? CBS News 60
Minutes, by Rebecca Leung, 11 January. 2004;
http://www.cbsnews.com/stories/2004/01/09/60minutes/m
ain592330.shtml
(SHORTENED URL: http://tinyurl.com/tovami)

[18] TreasuryDirect, Historical Debt Outstanding;
http://www.treasurydirect.gov/govt/reports/pd/histdebt/his
tdebt_histo5.htm
(SHORTENED URL: http://tinyurl.com/tedari)

[19] SUN TZU ON THE ART OF WAR, THE OLDEST
MILITARY TREATISE IN THE WORLD, Translated from the
Chinese By LIONEL GILES, M.A. (1910), Waging War;
http://www.au.af.mil/au/awc/awcgate/artofwar.htm#2
(SHORTENED URL: http://tinyurl.com/suwami)

[20] Countering evolved insurgent networks, by Thomas X.
Hammes, Military Review, July-August 2006;
http://www.questia.com/library/1P3-
1125210431/countering-evolved-insurgent-networks
(SHORTENED URL: http://tinyurl.com/sunepa)

[21] Confessions of a White House Insider, by John F.
Dickerson, TIME Magazine World, 10 January 2004;
http://www.time.com/time/magazine/article/0,9171,57480
9,00.html
(SHORTENED URL: http://tinyurl.com/maxora)

[22] United States GDP Growth Rate, Trading Economics;
http://www.tradingeconomics.com/united-states/gdp-
growth
(SHORTENED URL: http://tinyurl.com/gorasi)

[23] United States GDP Growth Rate, Trading Economics;
http://www.tradingeconomics.com/united-states/gdp-
growth
(SHORTENED URL: http://tinyurl.com/gorasi)

[24] Chart Book: The Legacy of the Great Recession,
Center on Budget and Policy Priorities, 28 June 2012;
http://www.cbpp.org/cms/index.cfm?fa=view&id=3252
(SHORTENED URL: http://tinyurl.com/zupoli)

[25] The Budget and Deficit Under Clinton, FactCheck.org;
http://www.factcheck.org/2008/02/the-budget-and-deficit-
under-clinton/
(SHORTENED URL: http://tinyurl.com/zimara)

[26] Bill Clinton touts fiscal record as president during
campaign stop in New Jersey, PolitiFact;
http://www.politifact.com/new-
jersey/statements/2012/jun/08/bill-clinton/bill-clinton-
touts-fiscal-record-president-during-/
(SHORTENED URL: http://tinyurl.com/torezi)

[27] The Budget and Economic Outlook: Fiscal Years 2000-
2009, Congressional Budget Office, January 1999;
http://cbo.gov/sites/default/files/cbofiles/ftpdocs/10xx/doc1
059/eb0199.pdf
(SHORTENED URL: http://tinyurl.com/fazola)

[28] George W. Bush: Biggest Spender Since LBJ, CATO
INSTITUTE;
http://www.cato-at-liberty.org/2009/12/19/george-w-bush-
biggest-spender-since-lbj/
(SHORTENED URL: http://tinyurl.com/gepeda)

[29] Obama: A Little League Socialist, by Duane Graham,
The Erstwhile Conservative, 24 May 2012;
http://duanegraham.wordpress.com/tag/federal-spending/
(SHORTENED URL: http://tinyurl.com/govada)

CHAPTER 21

MAKE THE PIE HIGHER

What we Republicans should stand for is growth in the economy. We ought to make the pie higher.

George W. Bush, Republican Debate, February 15, 2000

They had forgotten to be Republicans. The party that liked to promote itself as the defender of Main Street, Small Business, Limited Government and Fiscal Responsibility had become the Party of Wall Street, Big Government, War, and Massive Public Debt – the very stances most antithetical to genuine republican government.

It had been a long time since a Republican head-of-state had actually governed according to the values his party claimed to champion. The last Republican President to produce a balanced budget was Dwight D. Eisenhower in 1957. [1] Even Ronald Reagan, influenced by a combination of Donald Rumsfeld's *'Team B'* paranoia and a desire to negotiate an end to the Cold War by means of a massive military bargaining chip, had plunged the United States deeply into debt during the time when the Soviet Union was doing a pretty good job of collapsing on its own. [2], [3]

The United States had emerged from the Second World War relatively unscathed, richer and stronger by far. It was the only major war participant to do so. It had been taken to its new position on the world stage by millions of unassuming country boys and citizen soldiers, who, along with its great financial, industrial, political and scientific elite, had assembled the greatest economic and military power the world had ever seen.

CHARLES EDMUND COYOTE

America had become that Great Power not because it was quick to join the entanglements of war, but because of its relative isolation and undeveloped expanse that had allowed its people the opportunity to create a society which was intent on promoting its own general welfare. [4]

America came with a wide welcome by those who thought they were seeing something new. It appeared to be a Great Power of less arrogant character, disinclined toward the usual abuse of the tired and poor that huddled in teaming masses on so many tempest-tossed shores. [5] Rather than coming to stride and conquer like so many other brazen giants, America seemed to lift higher the common understanding that governments are justly instituted by the consent of the governed to establish Justice, insure domestic Tranquility, promote the general Welfare, and secure the Blessings of Liberty for the people and their descendants.

In distant Indochina, Ho Chi Minh, who had lived in the United States for a couple of years before the First World War, celebrated the ideals of America's 1776 Declaration of Independence and wrote hopeful letters to the American President and Secretary of State:

> Our Vietnamese people, after so many years of spoliation and devastation, are just beginning its building-up work. It needs security and freedom, first to achieve internal prosperity and welfare, and later to bring its small contribution to world-reconstruction.
>
> These security and freedom can only be guaranteed by our independence from any colonial power, and our free cooperation with all other powers. It is with this firm conviction that we request of the United Sates as guardians and champions of World Justice to take a decisive

step in support of our independence.

What we ask has been graciously granted to the Philippines. Like the Philippines our goal is full independence and full cooperation with the UNITED STATES. We will do our best to make this independence and cooperation profitable to the whole world.

> Ho Chi Minh, Letter to President Truman, 16 February 1945 [6]

It was a hopeful new world. The old world had destroyed itself in Great Wars and the longing of people everywhere, if they had any longings left, was that the flame of imprisoned lightning – now held high – could be theirs also. If our relations with other peoples represent the broad sentiments expressed in its founding documents, the Declaration of Independence, the Constitution and Washington's Farewell Address, then America would be that *'Shining City on a Hill'*. If we remain dedicated to Lincoln's unfinished work that government of the people, by the people, for the people, shall not perish from the earth, then America would remain a place and an idea indispensable on the stage of history. [7]

Let the colonies always keep the idea of their civil rights associated with your government – they will cling and grapple to you, and no force under heaven will be of power to tear them from their allegiance. But let it be once understood that your government may be one thing and their privileges another, that these two things may exist without any mutual relation – the cement is gone, the cohesion is loosened, and everything hastens to decay and dissolution. As long as you have the wisdom to keep the sovereign authority of this country as the sanctuary of liberty, the sacred temple consecrated to our common faith, wherever the chosen race and sons of England worship freedom, they will turn their faces towards you. The more they multiply, the more

CHARLES EDMUND COYOTE

*friends you will have, the more ardently they love li-
berty, the more perfect will be their obedience. Slavery
they can have anywhere. It is a weed that grows in
every soil. They may have it from Spain, they may have
it from Prussia. But until you become lost to all feeling of
your true interest and your natural dignity, freedom they
can have from none but you. This is the commodity of
price, of which you have the monopoly. This is the true
Act of Navigation, which binds to you the commerce of
the colonies, and through them secures to you the
wealth of the world. Deny them this participation of
freedom, and you break that sole bond which originally
made, and must still preserve, the unity of the empire.*

*Edmund Burke, Speech on Conciliation with America,
22 March 1775* [8]

Justice is the bond of all society, the unity of all
nations. It is the primary function of all governments.
If people have justice, they care not who or what form
their government takes. Their government has their
loyalty and rightfully so. If people do not have justice,
they care not who or what their rulers call themselves.
That government is not their own and justice will number its years. None is better now that America's new
'conservatives' have forgotten the wisdom of their
better counselor – Edmund Burke. None is better now
that Washington's namesake capital has forgotten his
example of striving to be 'The Indispensable Man'. It is
richness of soul alone that makes possible Liberty and
sustains the rule of law.

*Observe good faith and justice towards all nations;
cultivate peace and harmony with all. Religion and
morality enjoin this conduct; and can it be, that good
policy does not equally enjoin it – It will be worthy of a
free, enlightened, and at no distant period, a great
nation, to give to mankind the magnanimous and too
novel example of a people always guided by an exalted
justice and benevolence. Who can doubt that, in the*

course of time and things, the fruits of such a plan would richly repay any temporary advantages which might be lost by a steady adherence to it? Can it be that Providence has not connected the permanent felicity of a nation with its virtue? The experiment, at least, is recommended by every sentiment which ennobles human nature. Alas! is it rendered impossible by its vices?

Washington's Farewell Address 1796 [9]

The America the world wanted was not its bombs and generals, its CIA orchestrated regime-changes and tyrannical client states, the reoccurring nightmares that never answered, never satisfied, and never resolved... The America the world wanted was its Carnegies, Fords and Bill Gates; Marilyn Monroes and Elvis Presleys; Bo Diddleys, Muhammad Alis and Michael Jordans. These represented the lightning breaking loose its prison, the spark of creative vision breathing life into otherwise exhausting patterns of culture, the unseen hand enriching the lives of those it touched.

America's heritage was Britain's long struggle to make sovereign the Rule of Law. This is Lincoln's great remaining task: that government *'by the people, for the people, shall not perish from the earth'*. If America is to share this with the world, then let it first conquer itself. Life and Liberty are seldom carried from some distant seat of power. No one owns the imprisoned lightning and though many would try, all who did would become the dust of history:

I met a traveller from an antique land
Who said: "Two vast and trunkless legs of stone
Stand in the desert. Near them on the sand,
Half sunk, a shattered visage lies, whose frown
And wrinkled lip and sneer of cold command
Tell that its sculptor well those passions read

CHARLES EDMUND COYOTE

Which yet survive, stamped on these lifeless things,
The hand that mocked them and the heart that fed.
And on the pedestal these words appear:
`My name is Ozymandias, King of Kings:
Look on my works, ye mighty, and despair!'
Nothing beside remains. Round the decay
Of that colossal wreck, boundless and bare,
The lone and level sands stretch far away.

Percy Bysshe Shelley

The 'indispensable' America the world needed would never be understood by Washington's *Project for the New American Century* types. They could only be relied upon to advocate ever more strategic blunders leading to the depletion of the nation's strength and treasure. They are the ones who view government as a means of providing feeding troughs of plenty for themselves while they divert it from its responsibilities for the welfare of the people as a whole. Disinclined to take any job with a title shorter than a sentence, these masters of polysyllabic chatter talk of 'moral clarity', the 'revolution in military affairs', the 'unipolar moment', and 'spreading democracy' as they continue to pile mountains of public and intergenerational debt on troubled taxpayers unlikely to benefit from the political fashion of the moment.

> Those who seek absolute power, even though they seek it to do what they regard as good, are simply demanding the right to enforce their own version of heaven on earth. And let me remind you, they are the very ones who always create the most hellish tyrannies. Absolute power does corrupt, and those who seek it must be suspect and must be opposed. Their mistaken course stems from false notions of equality, ladies and gentlemen. Equality, rightly understood, as our founding fathers understood it, leads to liberty and to the emancipation of

creative differences. Wrongly understood, as it has been so tragically in our time, it leads first to conformity and then to despotism.

> *Barry Goldwater, Acceptance Speech for the Republican Presidential Nomination, 1964* [10]

The US military is very proficient at taking down a government, but it will only waste its strength and resources if it tries to impose an unsought government and way-of-life on disinterested people. Striving to rearrange the internal affairs of sovereign nations that are not a threat to us does not fall within the mission statement of the Constitution of the United States, or within the possibilities of fiscal prudence.

Most of those who call themselves *'conservatives'* claim they don't like Washington taking on an excessive role in people's lives. If that were really true, then it should not be too hard to understand that other people, in other parts of the world, have at least as much of a claim on not wanting Washington taking on an excessive role in their lives either. If one believes *'that government is best which governs least'*, then that assertion has to have a universal application in order to have meaning. If by freedom one only means *'free to be like me'*, then one doesn't mean freedom at all.

The post-World-War world wanted America, but only on its own terms, the terms that America stated for itself. Once upon a time Americans understood the balance in that equation. It was called *'Business'* and it was something that Americans got to be pretty good at. When Osama bin Laden taped his messages of hatred against the United States, he often did so while wearing a camouflage-style military jacket, speaking

CHARLES EDMUND COYOTE

into a microphone and being videotaped for broadcast and dissemination. All of these are fashions, instruments, and techniques of production which America had played a significant role in developing. American hegemony had been well advanced with considerably more success by Coca-Cola, Elvis, Hollywood and individual Americans giving people something they actually wanted than by all the Right/Left wing Think-Tanks, Generals and claims to being *the indispensable nation'* that Washington will ever come up with.

America remains America the Beautiful so long as it remembers the Beauty of Choice. The failure to remember that essential truth is the failure to remember the essential America. The character of the essential America is the recognition that government is instituted with the responsibility to protect the unalienable Rights of Life, Liberty and the pursuit of Happiness. The corruption of these individual rights by the moneyed pursuit of global hegemony reduces America to another chapter in the long history of Empire. *'Government of the elite, by the elite, and for the elite'*, is not a core American value.

> *Every ambitious would-be empire, clarions it abroad that she is conquering the world to bring it peace, security and freedom, and is sacrificing her sons only for the most noble and humanitarian purposes. That is a lie, and it is an ancient lie, yet generations still rise and believe it.*
>
> *Henry David Thoreau*

Lasting Dominion is always of the Heart, and Empires of the Heart are always Kingdoms of Choice. On March 17, 2003, George W. Bush took to the television waves to demand Saddam Hussein and his sons leave Iraq, giving them 48 hours to comply. The bombing

IRAQ WAR 2003

and cruise missile attacks that followed began an accumulation of civilian casualties that totaled more than 30,000 civilians before the fall of Baghdad three weeks later. [11] Then, the suffering and dying of innocents paused briefly before beginning another climb, reaching later more than 130,000 direct, and perhaps as many as 1,000,000 indirect civilian deaths, as Iraqi society shattered into pieces. [12] *'Democracy'* had been brought to Iraq, and the country now echoed with the emptiness of more than one million widows and five million orphans. In cities such as Fallujah, hospital wards were filled with young women *"...terrified of having children because of the increasing number of babies born grotesquely deformed, with no heads, two heads, a single eye in their foreheads, scaly bodies or missing limbs."* Their children and adult family members were succumbing to cancer, lymphoma and brain tumors as a result of the extensive use of Depleted Uranium and White Phosphorous Munitions during the heavy fighting between the US and Iraq's urban insurgencies, most particularly in 2004. [13], [14]

Coalition military deaths in Iraq, including those of the Iraqi Security Forces aligned with the Coalition, have amounted to more than 14,900 as of February 2012. [15] In attempting a hopeless stand against the vastly superior Coalition force, deaths of Iraqi military and paramilitary defenders during the first three weeks of the invasion were estimated at around 20,000. [16] The US military suffered more than 32,200 wounded during the period of more than 8 years that followed the 2003 invasion, and has experienced very high levels of suicide and mental health problems among returning veterans. [17], [18]

CHARLES EDMUND COYOTE

As a result of the invasion, the nation of Iraq opened up to al-Qaeda's operations and gave the organization a new lease on life. The war's chief beneficiary, however, was the Islamic Republic of Iran, which the Bush administration freed from the thorn of Saddam, thus inadvertently facilitating the creation of an *'axis of evil'* linking Iraq and Iran in ways that did not exist previous to the Bush invasion. For its efforts, the US government added to its massive debt burden, as a consequence of the Bush administration's choice to finance the unnecessary war almost entirely with borrowed money.

Few decisions by a Head of State carry more weight than that of committing a nation, its military, and its youth to war. Under the US Constitution, this is not even a decision that belongs to the President. To take such a step as lightly and as deceptively as the Bush presidency did betrays that high office. That wars go quickly out of control is a reality understood best by those who have lived them. Eager as they were to send others off to war, almost none of the noisy neo-conservatives who held high office under George W. Bush had an experienced understanding of its consequences.

> *My sincere view is that the commitment of our forces to this fight was done with a casualness and swagger that are the special province of those who have never had to execute these missions -- or bury the results.*
>
> *Why Iraq Was a Mistake, Marine Lieutenant General Greg Newbold (Retired), 9 April 2006* [19]

But these unknown knowns did not seem to trouble the President and his neo-conservative team much in March of 2003. For George W. Bush it was *'Mission accomplished'*.

IRAQ WAR 2003

W got his War.

The rest of us will have to make the pie higher.

The New Colossus

Not like the brazen giant of Greek fame,
With conquering limbs astride from land to land;
Here at our sea-washed, sunset gates shall stand
A mighty woman with a torch, whose flame
Is the imprisoned lightning, and her name
Mother of Exiles. From her beacon-hand
Glows world-wide welcome; her mild eyes command
The air-bridged harbor that twin cities frame.
"Keep ancient lands, your storied pomp!" cries she
With silent lips. "Give me your tired, your poor,
Your huddled masses yearning to breathe free,
The wretched refuse of your teeming shore.
Send these, the homeless, tempest-tost to me,
I lift my lamp beside the golden door!"

Emma Lazarus

CHAPTER 21 REFERENCES

[1] TreasuryDirect, U.S.Government;
http://www.treasurydirect.gov/govt/reports/pd/histdebt/histdebt.htm
(SHORTENED URL: http://tinyurl.com/tedire)

[2] United States: inventing demons, by Philip S Golub, Le Monde diplomatique, March 2003;
http://mondediplo.com/2003/03/03radicalright
(SHORTENED URL: http://tinyurl.com/vepilu)

[3] Can the World Survive Washington's Hubris? by Paul Craig Roberts, PaulCraigRoberts.org - Institute for Political Economy, 28 June 2012;
http://www.paulcraigroberts.org/2012/06/28/can-the-

348

world-survive-washingtons-hubris/
(SHORTENED URL: http://tinyurl.com/suroza)

*[4] Washington's Farewell Address 1796, The Avalon Project at Yale Law School;
http://avalon.law.yale.edu/18th century/washing.asp
(SHORTENED URL: http://tinyurl.com/wafela)*

*[5] The Yalta Agreement; 11 February 1945, The Avalon Project, Yale Law School, Lillian Goldman Law Library;
http://avalon.law.yale.edu/wwii/yalta.asp
(SHORTENED URL: http://tinyurl.com/gagefa)*

*[6] Collection of Letters by Ho Chi Minh, RationalRevolution.net;
http://rationalrevolution.net/war/collection of letters by h o chi .htm
(SHORTENED URL: http://tinyurl.com/zolera)*

*[7] Farewell Address, Ronald Wilson Reagan, 11 January 1989, The Miller Center - University of Virginia;
http://millercenter.org/president/speeches/detail/3418
(SHORTENED URL: http://tinyurl.com/rorega)*

*[8] Speech on conciliation with America, Edmund Burke, 22 March 1775;
http://www.let.rug.nl/usa/documents/1751-1775/edmund-burke-speech-on-conciliation-with-america-march-22-1775.php
(SHORTENED URL: http://tinyurl.com/zoleme)*

*[9] Washington's Farewell Address 1796, The Avalon Project at Yale Law School;
http://avalon.law.yale.edu/18th century/washing.asp
(SHORTENED URL: http://tinyurl.com/walare)*

*[10] Berry Goldwater A True Conservative, YouTube;
http://www.youtube.com/watch?v=k7kdLEjb9gM
(SHORTENED URL: http://tinyurl.com/tucova)*

[11] Cancer, Infant Mortality and Birth Sex-Ratio in Fallujah, Iraq 2005-2009; Chris Busby, Malak Hamdan and Entesar Ariabi; International Journal of Environmental Research and Public Health;

http://www.mdpi.com/1660-4601/7/7/2828/pdf
(SHORTENED URL: http://tinyurl.com/zabila)

[12] Iraq War Logs: What the numbers reveal, IRAQ BODY COUNT, 23 October 2010;
http://www.iraqbodycount.org/analysis/numbers/warlogs/
(SHORTENED URL: http://tinyurl.com/wolona)

[13] The Suffering of Fallujah, by Robert Koehler, 29 July 2010;
http://original.antiwar.com/robert-koehler/2010/07/29/the-suffering-of-fallujah/
(SHORTENED URL: http://tinyurl.com/faluje)

[14] The curse of Fallujah: Women warned not to have babies because of rise in birth defects since US assault, Mail Online, 5 March 2010;
http://www.dailymail.co.uk/news/article-1255312/Birth-defects-Fallujah-rise-U-S-operation.html#ixzz1zv3yICSx
(SHORTENED URL: http://tinyurl.com/faluja)

[15] IRAQ COALITION CASUALITY COUNT, icasualties.org;
http://icasualties.org/Iraq/Index.aspx
(SHORTENED URL: http://tinyurl.com/colisu)

[16] 2003 Invasion of Iraq, Wikipedia Encyclopedia;
https://en.wikipedia.org/wiki/2003_invasion_of_Iraq
(SHORTENED URL: http://tinyurl.com/vakipe)

[17] Operation Iraqi Freedom, US Wounded, icasualties.org;
http://icasualties.org/Iraq/USCasualtiesByState.aspx
(SHORTENED URL: http://tinyurl.com/valape)

[18] Losing the Battle - The Challenge of Military Suicide, by Dr. Margaret C. Harrell and Nancy Berglass, Center for a New American Security, October 2011;
http://www.cnas.org/files/documents/publications/CNAS_LosingTheBattle_HarrellBerglass.pdf
(SHORTENED URL: http://tinyurl.com/bamira)

[19] Why Iraq Was a Mistake, by Lieutenant General Greg Newbold (Retired), Time Magazine, 9 April 2006;

CHARLES EDMUND COYOTE

http://www.time.com/time/magazine/article/0,9171,11816
29,00.html
(SHORTENED URL: http://tinyurl.com/womile)

UPDATES

I wanted to get this edition out, as it outlines a great deal of information the American people ought to be aware of if we are to have much chance of preventing similar disasters in the future. I intend to continue its development, however, along the lines of perspectives drawn from the philosophers of War (from Sun Tzu and Clausewitz, to America's own Colonel John Boyd) in order to provide a sharper understanding to the critical lessons that need to be drawn from the Bush administration's unfortunate choices.

To receive notification of new books, updates or articles, please visit:

www.TheCoyoteReport.com/Charles-Edmund-Coyote

(We never abuse or share your email with anyone.)

YOUR FEEDBACK IS IMPORTANT!
YOU CAN POST A BOOK REVIEW ON:

AMAZON: http://tinyurl.com/CharlesCoyote

GOODREADS: http://tinyurl.com/GoodreadsIraq

LIBRARY THING: http://tinyurl.com/LibraryThingIraq

IF YOU LIKED THE BOOK, PLEASE VOTE FOR IT:
http://tinyurl.com/IraqWarBooks

FACEBOOK: http://www.facebook.com/IraqWar
(Pictures and more)

CHARLES EDMUND COYOTE

IRAQ WAR 2003

NOTES

Made in the USA
Middletown, DE
19 February 2015